C000016475

International Praise for *The War is in the Mountains*

'Impressive and necessary… Matloff approaches her topic with a magic combination of wisdom and empathy, and it is impossible to not be moved'

Booklist, starred review

'This trip to some very different corners of the globe is recounted in clear, visceral language… Matloff's investigation is a worthy read for foreign affairs and anthropology buffs alike'

Publishers Weekly, starred review

'A sobering account of why mountainous regions often engender violence… a tightly focused study'

Kirkus Reviews

'Matloff's book is an indefatigable journalistic exploration of how mountains shape, sustain, and even determine war and culture around the world. Her argument, which her reporting makes undeniable, is at once obvious and original'

Robert D. Kaplan, bestselling author of *The Revenge of Geography*

'A vital, deeply revealing book of political travelogue and intrepid correspondence. Matloff is the ideal witness – learned, dogged, skeptical, but always listening out for new and credible voices. This is classical international journalism of the highest order'

Steve Coll, Pulitzer Prize-winning author of *Ghost Wars*

'Through thoughtful vignettes, [Matloff] weaves personal narratives alongside relevant historical and present-day circumstances to relate regional stories that consistently refer to and affirm the global tale she seeks to tell'

Library Journal

'Judith Matloff's book is a political geography of mountains, once the haunt of witches, now – in many parts of the world – strongholds of outlaws and rebels, told with a sense of drama by someone who has clearly done her fieldwork'
Yi-Fu Tuan, author of *Romantic Geography*

'Matloff – a brave, engaging, keenly observant guide – rides shuddering buses, boards decrepit helicopters, and hikes through mud and checkpoints in pursuit of answers and solutions... reveals the rich, surprising and perplexing life of places too often diminished by the flat imagery of war'
Sheri Fink, Pulitzer Prize-winning journalist
and author of *Five Days at Memorial* and *War Hospital*

'Vistas, vainglory, vengeance and violence mark Judith Matloff's engaging voyage across mountainous terrains. She reports with empathy on religious charities, anthropologists, guerrillas, and state armies all attempting to pacify some of the world's least governed spaces'
David D. Laitin, Professor of Political Science at Stanford
University and author of *Nations, States and Violence*

'A globe-hopping, more-often-than-not crushing investigation into mountain mayhem... chromatic stories, which can't help but be chromatic as they are smeared blood red, from the Sierra Madre, the Caucasus, Jammu and Kashmir, the Himalayas, and the Andes'
Christian Science Monitor

The War is in the Mountains

THE WAR
IS IN THE
MOUNTAINS

VIOLENCE IN THE WORLD'S HIGH PLACES

JUDITH MATLOFF

Duckworth Overlook

First published in the United Kingdom
by Duckworth Overlook in 2017

LONDON
30 Calvin Street, London E1 6NW
T: 020 7490 7300
E: info@duckworth-publishers.co.uk
www.ducknet.co.uk
For bulk and special sales please contact sales@duckworth-publishers.co.uk

Copyright © 2017 by Judith Matloff

All rights reserved. No part of this publication may be reproduced, stored in a retrieval system, or transmitted, in any form or by any means electronic, mechanical, photocopying, recording or otherwise, without the prior permission of the publisher.

The right of Judith Matloff to be identified as the Author of the Work has been asserted by her in accordance with the Copyright, Designs and Patents Act 1988.

First published in the United States by Basic Books, an imprint of Perseus Books, LLC, a subsidiary of Hachette Book Group, Inc

A catalogue record for this book is available from the British Library

Printed and bound in Great Britain by TJ International Ltd, Padstow

9780715651896

MIX
Paper from
responsible sources
FSC
www.fsc.org   FSC® C013056

To Anton and John
And to every mountain person who goes unheard

Contents

List of Maps

Here place and people seem to be
A world apart, alone;
Cut off from men by spate and scree

—Henrik Ibsen, "Mountain Life" (1859)

Introduction

A Towering Problem

◇

Everywhere: 200 to 20,000 feet

> The mountain seems no more a soulless thing,
> But rather as a shape of ancient fear,
> In darkness and the winds of Chaos born—
>
> —George Sterling, "Night on the Mountain" (1914)

I met Jean Lassalle and Mario Conejo in a ballroom in the Pyrenees, at a concert of Andean pipe music in the baroque town hall of Pau, a city with a fairy-tale castle surrounded by majestic peaks. They were an incongruous pair, so I was surprised when they called each other "brother." Lassalle wore a suit over a cuffed shirt, the uniform of the politician; a French parliamentarian, he represents shepherds in the region. At six feet seven inches and with an impressively craggy nose, he looms like a human cliff in business attire. Conejo, also an elected official, is at least two feet shorter, with a waist-length braid. He wore a bowler hat, and his white tunic identified him as an Indian of the Ecuador highlands, where he serves as mayor of the town of Otovalo. *Pachamama*, he called the Andes. Mother Earth.

Despite the dramatic height difference—the indigenous man's face just barely reached his friend's chest—they professed to see eye to eye. "Mountain people instantly understand each other," explained Lassalle. "We don't view things like folks from the plains." Conejo gave a solemn nod, and they embraced fraternally. They addressed each other in labored Spanish, a second language for both.

Lassalle heads the World Mountain People Association (WMPA) a network of proud highlanders from seventy countries who meet on scenic ascents every year to discuss their commonalities and their grievances. The association was born out of a global forum organized by UNESCO

1

in June 2000. Some nine hundred mountain dwellers from around the planet gathered in the French Alpine town of Chambéry with a common mission: to pursue "equitable and sustainable development and the continuity of mountain identity." The association survives on financing from French and Swiss authorities, organizations of native mountain groups, foundations, and private partners. Larger fears underlie the highlanders' stated concerns—fears about identity, and survival. Many members, like the Berbers and the Basques, aspire to self-determination.

WMPA meetings rotate among the world's major mountain ranges, so that everyone can visit each other's ancient communities. The gatherings call to mind the pointed multiculturalism of a Benetton ad, except the diversity here is genuine and unself-conscious. Turbaned Tuaregs and Bolivian coca growers in sandals sit alongside Sherpas from Nepal, all eagerly chatting away while sampling local sheep-milk delicacies. Much of the conversation, facilitated by teams of translators, focuses on shared concerns: How to gain control over the metals and water embedded in their traditional burial grounds? How, also, to prevent tourists from spoiling ancient pastures?

Sitting in this peaceful place, witness to the brotherly love flowing between the world's mountain peoples, and mellowed by the ethereal yet earthy pipe music, it was easy to forget why I was there: to report on the prevalence of violence in mountainous regions. Mountains cover one-fourth of the earth's surface and account for only 10 percent of its population. Yet they host a strikingly disproportionate share of its clashes. A 1999 United Nations report revealed that twenty-three of the twenty-seven major armed conflicts in the world were being fought in mountain areas, and that ratio remains roughly true today. The Sierra Madre, Afghanistan, the Caucasus—these and many other regions are plagued by drug violence, uprisings, Islamist extremists, and other dangers nurtured at high altitude.

The WMPA, for its part, focuses not on violence but on addressing the many challenges of life in the highlands. The organization is based in Oloron-Sainte-Marie, the picturesque stone town where Lassalle's family was, at the time that I met him, encouraging shepherds to mobilize against the importation of Slovenian bears to ancient grazing lands. In recent years the central government had relocated two of the creatures to this mountainous corner, and now it was rumored that more were coming. The shepherds were concerned that the bears would decimate their flocks. The protests included blocking roads and planting broken glass in honey pots to injure marauding bears.

The drama was trademark Lassalle, who stands out in French politics not just for his giant frame but also for his maverick tactics. There was his 2006 hunger strike, in which he lost forty-six pounds to save 150 local jobs at an aluminum-coating factory. (The government eventually caved in to his demands.) And the time, in 2003, when the WMPA was affronted that some of Lassalle's fellow politicians had deemed the Pyrenean village of Urdos too dull to accommodate gendarmes, reasoning that their urbanite wives would be bored there. In response, Lassalle protested the perceived slur against the village by interrupting parliamentary proceedings with loud singing.

Eventually the quarrel over the Slovenian bears reverberated all the way to Paris, where Carla Bruni, the former model and animal-friendly wife of then prime minister Nicolas Sarkozy, joined the fray in favor of biodiversity. "There should be no question, in our country, of choosing between bear and man," declared the First Lady; man and bear (and lamb) must live together. Lassalle disagreed—strongly.

In 2003, forty of the WMPA's member regions drafted the Charter of World Mountain Populations, three pages setting forth three primary objectives: to win respect for the unique cultures of mountain people, many of whom belong to indigenous minorities; convince sea-level governments to recognize territorial rights to land where mountain people have resided for millennia; and to improve the miserable living and educational conditions that plague most mountain communities. But so far, Lassalle told me, they hadn't had much luck with any of them.

Even Conejo's efforts to establish protections against land grabbers—a perennial problem for mountain people, who often lack official property titles for plots that have been passed down over generations—had yielded few changes. "Mountain people have a spiritual connection with the earth," Conejo explained ruefully.

"It's even sacred," agreed Lassalle.

I asked what other traits they shared.

"We're tough."

"Suspicious of outsiders."

"Stubborn." (This with a smile.)

The evening was drawing to an end, and the musicians began to pack up their instruments. Workers dimmed the massive crystal chandeliers suspended from the forty-foot ceilings. A steady stream of local towns-people, quite a few of them draped in furs, interrupted Conejo and Lassalle's conversation to express appreciation for the Ecuadorean's culture. "Entrancing music," said a woman with an impeccable bob, setting a glass down on the bar. "Enchanting." Then Lassalle's cell phone pinged. Some Basques had come across the border from Spain to discuss separatist matters. "Oui," he said. "I will join you momentarily." Enveloping Conejo in a farewell hug, the WMPA leader left, promising to pick up the various threads of their discussions the next day. As the waiters cleared ice buckets and dirty toothpicks from the tables, Conejo helped himself to one last sip of sweet Jurançon wine, the local delight, and leaned over to offer me some advice. "Don't mess with mountain folk."

◇◇◇◇◇◇◇

The word *mountain* is surprisingly loose and baggy. Because humanity lacks a common definition, a stubby three-hundred-foot protrusion is thrown into the same class as Mount Everest. The *Oxford English Dictionary* asserts that a mountain should be steep and measure over 1,000 feet high. Yet some hills are called mountains simply because they always have been called mountains. At 141 feet, Mount Wycheproof in Australia is a case in point; it falls way below the dictionary's yardstick. Acknowledging the "overwhelming" array of efforts to pinpoint what a mountain is, the pioneering geographer Roderick Peattie (1891–1955), author of *Mountain Geography: A Critique and a Field Study* (1936), left it for the observer to decide, stipulating only that a mountain is elevated and looms high in the imagination.

Peattie believed that individual mountains have distinct personalities, with the ability to provoke extreme emotions ranging from awe to dread. Mount Fuji, he wrote, is "sacred," with a serenity that explains its storied place in Japanese philosophy, whereas Italy's Etna, the highest active volcano in Europe, is "a devil, not a divinity." Some mountain chains are made of limestone or granite; others of schist or ice. Their colors range from purple to dun to hunter green. Peaks have strikingly different shapes: saws, pyramids, fangs. Mountain surfaces can consist of piedmonts, crests, or plateaus.

Yet despite the many topographical variations, all upland communities share cruel weather and harsh earth that together defeat most forms of agriculture and instill a deep sense of apartness. The WMPA affirms what behavioral geographers and anthropologists have been saying for many years: mountain topography not only yields common concerns, it breeds similar characteristics as well. There is ample evidence that the severe weather and physical barriers of mountain regions give rise to mental toughness, self-sufficiency, insularity, and a talent for improvisation, among other traits. From the Ozarks to the Pashtun tribal areas, "mountain people" acknowledge and often celebrate these commonalities.

The earth's elevated surfaces foster a distinctive lifestyle as well. From Tirol to Bolivia, herders make seasonal treks to upland communal pastures. Honor codes that disappeared from most of the world centuries ago still govern social relations in many mountainous regions. The distinguished French geo-historian Fernand Braudel (1902–1985), a founder of the Annales School, one of the most influential movements in twentieth-century historical thought, studied the societies of the Mediterranean basin. He likewise saw more continuity in the mountains than on the plains or coasts. Monarchies such as Andorra and Bhutan continue to thrive in highlands. Separatist movements, too, find havens on high. Kosovo, Corsica, Basques, Aceh, southern Thailand, Kachin, Nagorno-Karabakh, Chechnya: in each, ethnic minorities who live in the mountains have engaged in struggles against lowlanders. Chinese Communists even coined a term that translates to "mountaintop-ist," to describe an independent-minded soul who chafes at central party authority.

Up to the first part of the twentieth century, geographers were unabashed in their belief that environment determines human psychology and culture. Just before the outbreak of the First World War, the grand dame of American geography, Ellen Churchill Semple (1863–1932), conducted an exhaustive survey of the planet's elevated zones. A protégé of the first environmental anthropologist, the Berliner Friedrich Ratzel, Semple concluded that common personality traits could be found all the way from Kentucky to Kashmir. Harsh conditions produce closed and defensive communities that balk at being ruled by others. Mountain people are often so passionately attached to the earth they live on that they invest it with sacred properties. Religion imposed by colonial outsiders fails to take firm root, or is incorporated into indigenous beliefs.

Swamps and islands, Semple wrote, are like mountains insofar as they pose barriers to settlement and immigration, thus leaving archaic languages and customs intact. Coastal people are a different story entirely:

their exposure to other cultures through maritime trade made them more innovative and cosmopolitan than those in remote inland districts. Many elements of Semple's work, including her unexamined use of the word *civilized*, are likely to make twenty-first-century readers cringe. But few scholars today would quibble with her conclusion that the ocean, the original superhighway for goods and information, fosters openness to other cultures, as do rivers and plains. Quite unlike mountains, these other geographic features encourage mobility, invasion, immigration, and, as a consequence, diverse and often hybrid ways of life.

Semple relied heavily on geography to explain human behavior and cultural differences. Such environmental determinism fell out of academic favor over the decades, but it has recently made something of a comeback, especially among anthropologists. For all of Semple's simplistic reductions, many of her observations were astute. Jean Lassalle, the leader of the WMPA, would not quibble with her words: "Whether we consider [the mountain dweller] singly or in a group—family, clan, tribe or state—we must always consider him or his group in relation to a piece of land. The ancient Irish sept, Highland clan, Russian mir, Cherokee hill-town, Bedouin tribe, and the ancient Helvetian canton, like the political state of history, have meant always a group of people and a bit of land."

Of course, military strategists from Che Guevara to Carl von Clausewitz, the nineteenth-century Prussian general whose book *On War* remains a classic treatise for military planners, remarked on the unique qualities of mountains. "Do not linger in dangerously isolated positions," the ancient Chinese general Sun Tzu counseled would-be invaders. Mao Tse-tung dreamed up his theories of guerrilla warfare while sequestered in the snowy peaks of the Jinggang Mountains, the cradle of the Chinese Revolution. In their view, holding the high ground was key. But what is less understood is that mountains promote violence, both between mountain people and lowlanders and among mountain people themselves.

This seemingly faraway highland violence has global consequences, some of which has touched Americans and their allies in a direct way. Anger simmering in the mountains of Afghanistan and Yemen has brought lethal attacks to Manhattan and Paris. The elder of the Boston Marathon bombers became radicalized during a visit to Dagestan, whose jihadist movement sprang from the craggy peaks. Most of the cocaine and heroin that Americans consume is grown and smuggled by violent drug syndicates operating in the highlands of Latin America. The cartels' extending reach is feeding addiction and gangsterism in the American heartland. Ever since the Clinton administration, our country has funneled $10 billion into trying to stop a war in the Colombian Andes that has been sustained by mountainous terrain for half a century. Afghanistan's peaks and divided clans provide similar sanctuaries for the Taliban fighters.

Many of the world's most entrenched conflicts take place in mountains, and we neglect this fact at our peril. Far from being irrelevant, these remote, often archaic, and seemingly exotic exceptional communities are enormously important to the future safety and stability of the world at large. The mountain is friend to those who want to elude or destroy authority—the revolutionary, the poppy grower, and the jihadi, to name only a few. Mountains are the last place where roads are built and the first place people go to hide. Joaquín "El Chapo" Guzmán, the Houdini-esque cartel leader, built his opium and cocaine empire from a hideaway in Mexico's Sinaloa hills. His powerful operation continues to flourish there despite his capture.

We are bound to see even more threats in years to come, as extremist cells fan out from Central Asia to North Africa and violent drug traffickers extend their reach. Mountains not only harbor terrorists and other outlaws: they are where most of the world's water supply originates. Rivers rise in the hills, and wars have been threatened over control of high-altitude reservoirs. Rhetoric will only escalate as water grows ever scarcer in the Middle East, Africa, Asia, and the American West.

The impact of untamed landscape on the human psyche is striking in today's world of global terrorism and small, seemingly endless wars. We face enormous challenges as America withdraws from Afghanistan, having cost thousands of soldiers their lives, not to mention the billions of dollars spent, all for a myriad of unmet objectives; and as governments continue to be foiled by Islamic militants hiding in mountainous Pakistan and Dagestan. ISIS easily established footholds in the Qalamoun mountains between Lebanon and Syria, and heads to the northern slopes of Iraq when under pressure.

The precarious security of the United States and its allies urgently demands that we devote resources and time to resolving these remote conflicts. So far, the powers that be have responded to mountain violence either by ignoring it, or by invading—and sometimes both, when disenfranchisement has yielded anger and revolt. Meanwhile, governments and policy makers the world over have yet to accept the impossibility of conquering people for whom isolation is existential as well as physical. History brims with cases of indomitable mountain people; virtually no invader besides Alexander the Great has succeeded in subjugating a highland population. He only won them over, in Bactria, in what is today Afghanistan, by wedding a warlord's daughter and then encouraging his troops to follow suit. In contrast, every superpower to follow him there has failed.

The interplay of topography and geopolitics has an essential role in the violence that plagues modern life. Understanding these upland places and their concerns is crucial to devising solutions to the world's most stubborn and volatile situations—and to making life safer for all of us. How to engender lasting peace in the Colombian Andes? How to convince China to stop bullying Tibet? How to stop suicide bombers in Russia? How to dislodge heroin smugglers who feed American addictions? Again and again, the campaigns of nation-states have failed to subjugate mountain populations, or suffered dearly in the crossings. The world's largest expeditionary force, the mighty US Army, doesn't even have a specially trained mountain brigade, which held it back when pursuing Al Qaeda after 9/11. For half a century, India and Pakistan have been at a stalemate on a high Kashmiri glacier, losing more men to the elements than to each other. Islamic Nigeria, Kurdish Turkey, the North Caucasus: these are but a few of the elevated arenas that have resisted resolution. They speak to the immense difficulties that peacekeepers face in mountain conflict zones.

◇◇◇◇◇◇

My first brush with mountain warfare occurred before I ever climbed anything taller than a hill. A fifth-grade history book offered a mesmerizing illustration of Hannibal's quixotic crossing of the Alps. That gambit, in 218 BC, is often portrayed as a tour de force of strategy but all I could focus on were the elephants. The drawing showed the mighty, wretched beasts struggling against an alien habitat of deep snow, and tumbling off precipices like plastic toys. My ten-year-old mind was boggled by the hubris of herding hot-weather creatures across narrow icy paths as hostile tribes hurled boulders from above. The troops had it bad, too. Half of the forty-six thousand soldiers perished, many from the cold or falls. The twenty-five thousand survivors emerged from the mountains exhausted and spent; Polybius later wrote that they looked "more like animals than men." Their determination to conquer the environment, as well as the corresponding hostility of those defending it, captured my imagination. This, to me, was nuts.

I've maintained this view during a journalism career that has taken me to many of the world's most intractable conflicts. Reporting from five continents and thirty-nine countries, whenever I was sent to cover violence, I invariably found myself in rugged mountains, writing about all manner of hostilities, massacres, insurgencies, blood feuds, and putsches. These assignments required hiking boots and tablets for altitude sickness. In far-flung mountains the locals can be more threatening than avalanches and frostbite, and I bumped into gorillas as well as guerrillas. Mainly, though, I've met many angry hill people intent on independence. In these instances, topography was much more than a backdrop; it played a featured role right alongside its human inhabitants. The first tank I ever encountered rolled into the city of La Paz, for Bolivia's 147th coup. Nearly 12,000 feet above sea level, I spent the entire week confined to my hotel room, not out of fear of human violence but from altitude nausea, an affliction that often foils conventional soldiers.

Over three decades, mountains kept appearing in my work, or, more accurately, getting in the way. Because the highland paths were too hard to traverse, I spent an inordinate amount of time in aircraft, skimming tree canopies. And even helicopters couldn't always manage the altitude. The thin air of Kashmir became even harder to breathe when mixed with clouds of riot tear gas. I canceled a trip to Peru after Sendero Luminoso thugs from the mountains kidnapped a colleague. Mexico, Aceh, Chechnya: in all these highlands, it was difficult to make contact with the outlaws hiding on ridges.

When I was covering Angola's civil war, trouble resonated from the mesa highlands of Huambo, which the belligerent Jonas Savimbi used as a bunker. This leader of the Union for the Total Independence of Angola rebel group drew his greatest support from an upland tribe, the Ovimbundu, which harbored longstanding grievances against the lowland capital, Luanda. My most appalling memory is also of time spent in Africa, of a church in Rwanda that had been desecrated by dozens of skulls of genocide victims. Just beyond it lay emerald green hills, tightly terraced because there wasn't enough arable soil for all the farmers.

Still, it wasn't until I was immersed in a familiar domestic situation, far away from the world's zones of slaughter, that I made the connection between terrain and violence. I was in my house in flatland Manhattan, in the middle of a round of Risk with my son and husband. As aficionados know, the board game involves a tussle among superpowers for global domination. The men in my family play with unflagging vigor. That afternoon, as we battled over Afghanistan—who hasn't over the centuries?— our son, Anton, asked me to spread out a map of the world and show him where people were currently fighting. I marked about two dozen conflicts off the top of my head and threw in a few more spots that had seen strife over the past century. On a globe that showed elevations, Anton traced the uneven surface with his finger and made notes on a pad, so absorbed that he failed to notice his father rampaging through the Himalayas to take China. "Kosovo, Georgia, Nepal, Chiapas," Anton recited, among others, checking the altitude key for each. "Most occur in mountains. Why?"

Why, indeed.

People fight in mountains for every reason they do elsewhere: poverty, greed, discrimination, national security, suspicion, grudges, and natural resources. But what makes mountains more likely than lowlands to nurture conflict? Peaks contain uranium, watersheds, narcotic poppies, and many other natural resources that central governments and big business want to control and exploit. Rarely do the locals see a share of the profits. Natural resources can be found in lowlands, as well. What often distinguishes mountains is that, in Lassalle's words, they "constitute a natural frontier between countries and continents"—and the state on each side usually doesn't take the local populace into account. Residing at borders, says Lassalle, means that highlanders often find themselves at the "crossroads" of global conflicts. Moreover, mountain areas "constitute the refuge of the revolutionary or the hunted rebel" who go there to hide and to marshal their forces. Mountains are the planet's most intransigent feature, a natural wall that will always stand.

Besieged highlands—isolated from roads, the Internet, and sea-level capitals—harbor many of the world's most neglected people. Invisible to the dominant culture of the plains, as well as to the government, these unassimilated communities harbor deep grudges. It's little wonder that they resist being controlled more often and more tenaciously than flatlanders, who are generally more integrated into broader society.

In the last few years, my efforts to answer my son's question have taken me to many of the world's least hospitable environments. In all these places, the obdurate terrain is matched only by the obstinacy of its inhabitants. The areas visited in this book escalate in complexity. We'll start with the most intimate of disputes, the blood feuds that have been going on for centuries, if not millennia, in Albania's northern passes and crevasses. Then we'll move on to struggles for autonomy in Mexico's southern mountains, smothered by landslides and where the indigenous are enslaved by *narcotraficantes* and a callous government. The next chapter takes the reader to an isolated and forlorn army outpost on a summit in the Andes, the chain that has midwived half a century of civil war. Onward to a struggle over water, in Nepal's eastern highlands, and then to the North Caucasus range whose fragmented clan society nurtured Islamic jihad. The journey continues to the glacial borderland of Kashmir, which at 18,000 feet claims the distinction as the highest theater of war, and the most traumatized populace, anywhere in the world.

After examining the problems, the book explores possible solutions, starting with the tactical frustrations, if not futility, of trying to conquer mountain defenders, in Afghanistan and elsewhere. A better option comes into view in the form of Switzerland. While a model of peace today, Switzerland's main exports during the sixteenth and seventeenth centuries were mercenaries (not cuckoo clocks, as Orson Welles's Harry Lime had it), and as recently as 170 years ago the country was rent by internecine conflict. Yet it has become the world's most direct democracy, and one of the least violent places in the world. How that happened points the way toward achieving peace on remote mountaintops across the world.

I am a plains person who suffers from vertigo. I favor coasts with endless horizons and the predictability of pavement and elevators. Yet I've learned that it's critical to understand slope dwellers if we are to avoid further conflict in every range on earth. The Kurds have an expression: "No friends but the mountains." We flatlanders must learn how to be better friends with those who live at elevation. A great deal depends on it.

1

One for One

> I think no place where human beings live has given
> such an impression of majestic isolation from the
> world. It is a spot where centuries shrivel.
>
> —Edith Durham, *High Albania* (1909)

For thirty years, Marrash Kola had known that one day he would be summoned to his own murder. It finally happened one sparkling morning in April 2013, when he was fifty-six. The day started like most. Marrash stretched in bed and got up to light the wood stove without expecting anything unusual. Like most houses in rural Albania, his consisted of little more than a single stucco room containing the family's sleeping quarters and kitchen, its walls darkened over the years by smoke from the stove. His wife prepared sugary thick coffee as Marrash went to the toilet and dressed. They drank their coffee together at a rickety table, chatting about matters so inconsequential that later his wife couldn't recall what they were.

While his wife washed the espresso cups at the spigot outside, Marrash received a phone call. The man on the other end asked Marrash to meet him for coffee in Torrovice, the hamlet down the hill. For men in Albania's northern mountains, craggy impenetrable peaks with few roads and even less work, the *kafe* is the center of social life, a place to gossip and discuss soccer. An entire day could be spent lingering over a single espresso. "Going for coffee" doesn't necessarily mean actually drinking it; it can mean doing business, chatting, or, more likely, imbibing raki, a brandy distilled from fruit that sears the esophagus.

Marrash had a small field where he grew cucumbers and corn, and his cow and sheep grazed without requiring much attention beyond milking, which was largely a wifely chore. That left him free to meet the telephone caller in town. Marrash put on his rubber boots, told his wife he was going out, and began to walk down the 3,900 feet downhill to meet his killer.

The ground was soaked from a recent downpour. Marrash side-stepped puddles where the rain had collected, leaving shoe prints in the mud. He ran into a cousin, who walked halfway down the hill with him, until they reached a curve in the road. Someone called from a car parked on the road's shoulder, "Are you Marrash Kola?"

"If there is no other way, here I am," Marrash replied.

Marrash moved closer to the car and put his hands in the air as sixteen bullets ripped into him. The killer stared at him the whole time. Marrash was still standing as the car sped away.

Marrash's survivors included seven children, the oldest of whom was born in 1983, the same year the vendetta began. Like so many blood feuds in northern Albania, it started at a drunken wedding, this one near Brise, a community of a few hundred people where calling a man the wrong name is grounds for murder. At the party, Marrash's father quarreled with another villager, who attacked Marrash's father with a broken jar and scratched his forehead. A tiny drop of red trickled down. The Kanun, the ancient code of Albania's northern mountains, holds that a facial wound is one of the worst offenses to honor. A man must seek revenge, no matter how little blood was drawn. The villager knew the rules: he told Marrash's father, "One of you has to kill me." Within a year, Marrash's uncle shot the man dead at a village meeting. From that day on, Marrash and his two brothers knew that, in turn, one of them would be killed. Then the other family would wait for one of their men to be murdered, and so it would continue, back and forth for the foreseeable future. People here have been settling scores in this way for centuries.

This cycle of vengeance is called *gjak per gjak*, one for one, and a single thread can go on for generations, if not eternity. Technically, the *gjakmarrje*, or blood feuds, are illegal under national law, but in these isolated peaks the state wields little authority. The vendettas killed an estimated 10,470 Albanians in the two decades between 1991 and 2012. The nearest police precinct was hours away from Marrash's village. The only way to stop the gjakmarrje is if one party offers a *besa*, or truce, which then must be accepted by everyone in both clans. Often, consensus can't be reached in big extended families.

The clan that executed Marrash had behaved decently, all things considered. Not wanting to slay a man with young children, they put off the inevitable for years. When they eventually decided to kill Marrash rather than his brother, they did so because Marrash's children were older than his brother's and better able to support themselves.

By custom, the wronged family has one hundred years to exact revenge. (Sometimes the blood debt is exacted the day before the century limit is reached.) Marrash and his brothers had hoped to defy fate until 2083. After the feud started, they'd fled with their families to a town six hours south, where it would be more difficult to hunt them down. Still, their families, children included, rarely left their new houses, which they surrounded by walls tall as trees in an attempt to block snipers. Because an avenger cannot execute a victim in his home, it becomes his only sanctuary; many marked Albanian men never go outside. Marrash had dug a tunnel near his house for safe passage to his field. Eventually, though, he tired of the confinement and ventured outside.

And there he died, doomed to the same fate Albanian highlanders have suffered for ages.

◇◇◇◇◇◇◇

The history of blood feuds, also known as clan killings and honor feuds, spans huge swaths of time and territory, from the Norse sagas to contemporary Mafia vendettas, and has been studied endlessly. But what if that long history is even longer than most scholars have argued?

Indeed, what if Marrash's problems began long before the time of man? Was his fate sealed sixty-six million years ago, when huge tectonic plates crashed together under the earth's surface? The collision between Europe and Africa forced rock upward to six times the height of the Empire State Building to create the Dinaric Alps. I came to Albania because I thought the extreme environment might offer clues to this most intimate and enduring type of conflict. Why does nearly every modern clan killing on the planet occur in a mountain society? How could these ancient rites exist only an hour's flight from Rome? How was it possible that a parliamentary state seeking to join the European Union still harbored an archaic style of justice?

Wedged in the western Balkans, this mountainous country is one of the most undeveloped in Europe. In many rural parts folks thresh crops by hand and superstitiously predict the future from coffee grounds at the bottom of the cup. From the eighth century BC to the early twentieth century, easy access to the Adriatic lured a parade of occupiers, including Greeks, Romans, Venetians, Ottoman Turks, and the Italian and German Axis powers. After World War II, a vicious Stalinist regime paranoid about foreign influence banned travel into and out of the country for forty years. The Albanian dictatorship was so extreme that it even severed ties with the Soviet Union and China for their comparative softness. Since the collapse of Communism in 1991, Albania has been trying to emerge from this legacy of political isolation, allowing pluralist elections and restoring closer ties with the West. However, its rough and inaccessible nature poses barriers of another type.

Mountains cover three-fourths of Albania. The northernmost range where Marrash was killed is practically impenetrable, a limestone massif that has held back a series of would-be invaders for two thousand years, and continues to vex modern road builders. The grey rocks stab the air like fangs. The steep ranges are so uncultivated that you can drive for half a day without seeing another human being.

In the nineteenth century, the geologist Ami Boué described the mountain range as "unapproachable." That adjective still rings true.

The people who cling to the slopes get around on goat paths, and the dirt tracks that substitute for roads often wash away in the frequent torrential rains. Ice creates massive blockades in the winter, cutting off entire hamlets for months on end. And then, when the frost finally melts, boulders crash down to create fresh obstacles; those few who own vehicles know to pack dynamite in order to clear the way. Communication is a constant challenge. In the old days, villagers got in touch by shouting across gorges. The digital revolution hasn't made much of a difference today. There is practically no cell reception. There are few doctors. The seriously ill, and only the lucky ones, must be airlifted out on helicopters.

Only 39 percent of Albania's roads are paved. I traveled on the other 61 percent. En route from the capital to a village called Theth, in the heartland of the blood feuds, the jeep inched along passes 9,000 feet high and without guardrails. The moment the road turned from tar to pebbled mud, we lost the cell signal. "Damned mountains," the driver said, shaking his Samsung as though to coax reception. The winding path was worn away at many points, or blocked by huge rocks. Pines clung to the rock face as though they, too, feared falling off the precipice. Rain began to lash the crests and crevasses with ferocity. The jade-colored Shala River thundered thousands of feet below. The driver slugged raki every couple hours. The steering wheel was on the right, the wrong side for Albania. (Bought secondhand, the car would've been cheaper than those more appropriate for local driving.) Fortunately, we encountered no vehicles coming from the opposite direction. It took seven hours to cover forty-two miles. The only settlement we encountered along the treacherous route consisted of six stone houses. No police station, no school, no store. Just a kafe, where the entire male population, twenty-five shepherds in black leather jackets, was drinking raki. They stared sullenly when we entered, a saloon scene out of the Wild West. Women in these parts don't go to kafes, although the driver assured me that foreigners were not considered "real women."

The gray blocks of masonry were made from the bare mountain stone, making it hard to distinguish where the architecture ended and nature began. The feral landscape is unchanged from that described by British explorer Edith Durham back in 1909 when she traveled through the country by mule. In High Albania, she recorded her impressions of this area—deep gorges, crashing rivers, wolves that moved easily through it all—known as the Accursed Mountains. The Shala River, she wrote, "might be the world's wellspring, its banks the fit home of elemental instincts—passions that are red and rapid." The origin of the name Accursed, *Bjeshket e Namuna* in Albanian, is a source of debate. Some believe the Ottoman Turks coined the phrase when they finally gave up trying to cross the peaks. Others cite local lore: the forbidding crags embody the devil. To my mind, the name is justified by the more than ten thousand men who have been killed in blood feuds over the past two decades, and the untold numbers before that. The landscape helped generate this brutal custom; the topography, and the insularity it breeds, also make it virtually inescapable. Those who do try to leave the region, including Marrash's family, are pursued by whispers tipping off the aspiring executioners.

The French historian Fernand Braudel described how geography shaped worldviews. His main subject was the Mediterranean, including small mountain communities where each hill effectively formed a separate state. Blood feuds were part of everyday life, a fact that Braudel attributed to the high elevations. He published his findings in 1949, but I was struck by the continuing relevance of his insight, and not only for the Mediterranean region. The Kurds, the Maniot Greeks, and the clan cultures of highland Kenya and the North Caucasus all settle scores outside the law. Then there are the honor feuds that continue to plague the tribal hinterland of Afghanistan, where the degree of physical isolation is such that people in one valley don't speak the same language as those in the next. In the same vein, one can't ignore the infamous Sicilian rivalries that developed on high before manifesting in lower Manhattan's Mafia.

Yet of all the extant clan cultures, Albania's is particularly shocking. The gjakmarrje blood-taking has eliminated 20 percent of the male population in some small Albanian communities. In the parlance of anthropologists, this situation is one of "legal pluralism," whereby ancient codes exist in parallel with a modern parliamentary state. The reach of central government fades after a few valleys. For both the government in the lowlands and mountain feuders themselves, this is an urgent moral crisis: What is to be done about these archaic and brutal practices? Are they an inevitable feature of mountain life? Albania's authorities try to downplay the phenomenon by classifying most honor killings as ordinary homicides—a move no doubt meant to ingratiate itself to a European Union already skeptical about its Mafia racketeering, human trafficking, and corruption. Yet the Kanun predates Albania, and may well outlive it, and trying to stamp it out with jail terms rather than encouraging traditional besa truces only perpetuates the bloodletting more.

Indeed, the violence in these areas is indistinguishable from the clan fighting that prevailed in the flatlands before the rise of city-states. That primordial vendetta-fueled system of justice existed from biblical times through the Anglo-Saxon kingdoms of the sixth century to the Scottish highlanders of the seventeenth century, who then transported vendetta culture to the Appalachian mountains. The most infamous family feud in American history, the Hatfields versus the McCoys, was a hill country dispute about land and a pig, which lasted from 1863 to 1891 and killed thirteen people.

Some of the earliest accounts of clan hostilities, in *Beowulf* for instance, come from a time when the world was largely pastoral and retribution was considered a perfectly acceptable way to settle disputes. Before the eleventh century, towns that administered justice in an organized way barely existed in Europe. However, the rise of urban life, and later city-states, spawned more contemporary legal systems with common laws, courts, and juries. As large populations congregated, the new communities began to frame crimes as attacks against a centralized power, not just individuals.

However, this thinking has failed to overtake honor codes in more isolated communities. Many of these places thus lack institutions that embody and uphold the concept: functional and accountable courts, police forces, and prisons.

Cultural anthropologists agree that herding societies remain especially obsessed with honor codes outside organized legal systems. Such communities tend to be clan-organized and in mountains. Being patriarchal, overt displays of machismo are expected even over what we might consider a minor slight. Insult to pride justifies murder, it seems, when people are so socially isolated that the only reliable structure is the family. The rocky land is not productive, and possession of hoofed animals is a measure of a man's worth. The only assistance people are likely to receive is from male relatives with the same vested interests: protecting the purity of their sisters, who are considered a form of property, and the sheep that provide stew, cheese, and wool.

Albania's rugged northern corner is one of those places. Many historians speculate that the clans in the region descended from the bellicose Illyrian tribes thought to have moved to Albania during the Bronze Age, around 1000 BC. (The Illyrians garnered unfavorable mention by Polybius, who described them as "enemies of all humankind.") The country has had many clans over the centuries, each with their own codes of honor. The Kanuni i Lekë Dukagjinit, or the Canon of Leke Dukagjini, is the only code still followed today. The Kanun was first transmitted through oral tradition, and eventually written down in the fifteenth century. These days a printed form is sold in kiosks and bookstores, even in the capital, Tirana, although the codes are only observed in the north or by those who bring their feuds with them when they migrate—or flee— south. The volume's red cover sports a two-headed eagle, emblem of the people who call themselves *shqiptarë*, or sons of eagles. Legend has it that the eagles face outward to watch for attackers.

The Kanun delineates every facet of life, from what to do with a chained dog (give him his own kennel) to the exact weight of a wedding ox (282 pounds). Personal honor commands its own chapter, in which the reader is solemnly reminded that "there is no fine for an offense to honor." An offense to honor may include everything from reneging on a promise to removing the cover of a cooking pot on a hearth. But in each case the offense cannot be monetized or otherwise forgiven. The Kanun also enshrines an almost mystical reverence for blood. Take item 695: "For the Albanian of the mountains, the chain of relationships of blood and kinship are endless." And item 917: "Blood is never un-avenged."

◇◇◇◇◇◇

I visited Albania in May 2013—three weeks after Marrash died, though I didn't learn about him until already there. Rather, I'd timed my trip to dodge the annual spring deluge. The northern mountains get an average yearly rainfall of nearly eighty inches, making the area one of the most drenched in Europe. A heavy spring rain can drop as much as a foot of precipitation, knocking telephones out of order and forcing people out of their homes, which are sometimes rendered uninhabitable. Just three years earlier, floods had prompted the evacuation of thousands of Albanians and swamped pasturelands for weeks. Many people never returned.

Once there was a clear prognosis for the weather, I flew, as most foreigners do, into Tirana, a soulless place that boasts the country's only commercial airport. The city radiates from an overbearing square of fascist architecture that is gridlocked by traffic. Car imports were largely a fantasy under Communism, but now residents were making up for lost time; I saw Mercedes everywhere. The plaza is dominated by a large statue of Gjergj Kastriot Skanderbeg, who united noblemen to resist the Ottoman Turks in the fifteenth century. He is often depicted in art as a flaxen-haired superman resembling the comic book hero Thor.

The square is also home to the imposing National Historical Museum, whose echoing exhibition halls trace the history of the "nation" from the Bronze Age to the partisans who fought the Italian and German occupation in World War II. Nationalism was the primary theme, with geography following close behind. To my surprise, an entire room was dedicated to the English writer Edith Durham, nicknamed Mbretëresha e Malësoreve, or Queen of the Highlanders, who became a vociferous champion of Albanian independence, and by extension an adopted daughter. Taking advantage of the venerated position of guests, who must be protected under the Kanun, the intrepid Durham rode on horseback in petticoats and slept untroubled on goatskins next to tribal chiefs. She gained access to weddings and fights. Her physical stamina was matched by her romantic fascination with exotic ways. Many of the customs she documented are just as strong today, such as the blood feuds and Sworn Virgins—women who adopt the clothing of men and head the household after their fathers, husbands, and sons have been wiped out. They chop their hair short and take a vow of chastity in order to assume the masculine role of breadwinner.

Honor killings are still so prevalent in Albania that an industry of mediators has sprung into existence: private parties who offer their services for large sums, nongovernmental groups aiming to promote dialogue, and scholars who study the code's hold and try to loosen it. Many of the mediators jostle for influence and money, and several were facing accusations of extortion and perjury. Before heading into the heartland of the blood feud country, the Accursed Mountains, I met with a series of experts and scholars to ask why they thought the Kanun had such a lasting spell.

By far the most credible and eloquent interlocutor I encountered was Nedi Bardhoshi, a legal anthropologist from the north and one of the country's leading blood feud experts. He described the transition to Western values as a "public performance." If indeed this was a play, then he had assumed the part of the sophisticate, with his hipster black-frame eyewear and choice of meeting place: one of the capital's few bars where smoking was not allowed and it was not assumed that customers would drink Albania's traditional sweetened coffee. Bardhoshi was the only Albanian I met during my trip who spoke impeccable English—so quickly that my pen could barely keep up.

"The most bewildering part about the blood feuds for Westerners is the mind-set," he said, emptying three packets of sugar into his thick coffee as though to make a point about tradition. "A man's duty to ancestors is to uphold honor, and he will bring shame upon the clan if he does not accept retribution or exact revenge. His daughters will encounter trouble finding husbands. Ancestors will chastise him in the afterlife."

Bardhoshi went on to explain that the political-economic elite has traditionally resided in the southern plains and referred to the highlanders of the north as *malok*, or hillbillies. Popular culture reinforces this pejorative stereotype, as does the fact that northerners speak a dialect that southerners can't understand. One of the country's most watched television shows, roughly translated as *Orange*, features a brutish northerner who swings his fist aggressively at even the slightest provocation.

The closest anyone has come to stamping out the Kanun was during the forty-year rule of the Communist dictator Enver Hoxha, a southerner who abhorred blood feuds so intensely that his government publicly hung avengers in town squares. The codes persisted nonetheless, and after the collapse of Communism in 1991, they reappeared in public with even greater vigor, filling a vacuum in what is delicately described as an "emerging democracy." Just the day before, an official from the interior ministry had admitted to me that the government could not extend control throughout most of the north, which lacked sufficient police precincts.

Kanun adherents, who are invariably among the country's poorest citizens, find the codes easier to understand than the contemporary laws that are enforced—or abused—by the police. Bardhoshi believed the state's weakness drove mountain people to cling to old beliefs. In northern Albania, he said, the clan and Kanun offered the strongest sense of identity. Though there was no reliable census of Kanun followers, it was estimated that thousands of people were still affected directly or indirectly by feuds.

He paused and took a long sip of the sweet coffee. "There's little sense of a wider community, like in urban areas. The most important things are the sons and cousins and extended family. According to government law there's individual responsibility, but no one pays attention to that. They believe that they will have to explain themselves if they meet their ancestors in the afterlife. Honor is related to the social memory of the group. In order to weaken the blood feuds we would have to destroy their prestige. But the state has failed to provide an alternative."

The tragedy, he noted, was that the coexistence of two contradictory forms of justice, modern and prefeudal, made it impossible to let either run its course. If the traditional vengeance codes were allowed to follow their codified pattern, the antagonists would eventually resolve differences with a council of elders and a confession of guilt. But no resolution was possible while courts demanded that murderers be locked away.

Bardhoshi gestured for the bill, and waved dismissively when I pulled out my wallet. While we waited, he drew a rough map of Albania on a napkin, marking the pockets where the Kanun held deepest. "Talk to the families," he said.

◇◇◇◇◇◇◇

The next day, I hired a driver, a corpulent man with glistening slicked-back hair. He had a reputation for not driving drunk—unusual, perhaps, in a country notorious for breakfast shots of brandy. Since my knowledge of Albanian was confined to "yes" (*po*) and "no" (*jo*), our main form of communication was pantomime, which was in turn complicated by the fact that Albanians shake their heads for "yes" and nod for "no."

Our immediate destination was Shkodër, the city in the north that serves as the gateway to the blood feud heartland. I had arranged to meet a German nun, Sister Christina Färber, who first came to Albania from Donauworth, a city in Bavaria, in 1999, as a child therapist committed to working with young Kosovar refugees. But she was so shocked by the pervasive blood feuds that she stayed on and made it her mission to stop them. Everyone in the feud mediation circles recommended her as impartial; as a foreigner she could rise above the petty squabbles of local groups. However, the moral authority of the Catholic Church only went so far in a region where the Kanun took precedence. Since Sister Christina spoke fluent Albanian as well as English, she was my ideal intermediary to this otherwise impenetrable world.

To reach Shkodër, we drove for three hours on the two-lane highway through a landscape of gas stations, cedar trees, and roadside kafes filled with men in dark flat caps and oversized jackets. The driver conversed on his phone the entire time, pausing only when we stopped for gas. At one stop, I noticed a pistol when he opened the dashboard to get his wallet.

We were heading to a place where many people packed firearms, almost in the expectation of violence. "The Wild North" is how one mediator described Shkodër to me. Its eponymous lake serves as an unpoliced border with Montenegro, where it is relatively easy to smuggle cigarettes, marijuana, and trafficked women. The algae-slicked body of water attracts nesting herons and discarded beer bottles, thrown from the terrace restaurants that specialize in carp fished right from the lake.

At first glance, Shkodër was a slow-moving town of ninety-five thousand whose main form of transport was the bicycle and whose principal diversion was the *xhiro*, or promenade, where young lovers walked in the evenings. Kafes spilled onto the sidewalk alongside souvenir stands stocked with dolls in felt tunics and mugs with the wrinkled image of Mother Teresa, whose parents were of Albanian descent.

Albania is a largely secular country, where the nominal followers of the two main faiths, Catholicism and Islam, tend to define themselves more in terms of nation, kinship, and language than religion. Only a fraction of the population attends houses of worship regularly, perhaps as a hangover from the Communist era ban on all religious practices, and the Communists' destruction of mosques and churches. This lack of religious conviction means Shkodër's large Islamic population largely gets along with the Catholic majority.

Shkodër's distinguishing landmark is the crumbling Rozafa castle, a stone fortress with a commanding view of the distant mountains that was the site of a remarkable resistance against the Ottomans in 1478. The story goes that 1,600 defenders held out against 350,000 soldiers of the most powerful army of the time. The Ottoman chronicler Kemal Pashazade marveled: "In spite of our efforts, we could not uproot the people, who had sharp claws and bronze bodies. They stayed in the towers of their castles like tigers on the mountain tops."

The invaders ultimately conquered the town, but not the forested peaks north of it. To this day, those mountains harbor stone villages, each with at most a couple of dozen families, and all several hours apart by car. Some of the hamlets have lost three-quarters of their population since the fall of Communism. People leave their homesteads to seek work in Shkodër and to escape the blood feuds. Displaced families hope that the anonymity of the city will provide a haven. When it doesn't, the most desperate among them bang on the wooden door of Sister Christina's Community of the Holy Way, on a discreet lane fifteen minutes outside of town, where the nun with the alabaster skin and robes gives sanctuary without asking any questions.

Although there are signs of an economic revival, due in part to remittances sent home by relatives in cities including Munich and New York, much of Shkodër is decaying. The dubious plumbing and dirt-streaked facades that characterize so many post-Communist countries are ubiquitous here. My driver chose a hotel popular with truckers. It cost $10 a night. The toilet was filthy, and the pillowcase still bore the greasy outline of the previous occupant's head. I was relieved to move to Sister Christina's mission, which maintained the famously high standards of Teutonic cleanliness. The black metal gate opened to a clean L-shaped house, surrounded by a garden of lush strawberries and roses. A breeze wafted through the open windows of the sitting room, where nuns in white habits read quietly. I removed my shoes at the threshold as per local custom; the immaculate white floor tiles felt cool and fresh. Sister Christina rose to greet me.

"You have come," she said in lightly accented English.

Sister Christina was fifty-six years old but her skin was unlined, perhaps because it had rarely seen the sun. Hers was a weary face, though, and her back was noticeably curved, as though weighted down, or so I imagined, by Albania's many problems. Over the years, Sister Christina has driven her white Land Rover thousands of miles in the north, attempting to convince villagers to reconcile. Along the way she has taken in several families. Her mission provides the outcasts with jobs as housekeepers and handymen and her staff drives their kids to school, so that their parents won't be shot escorting them. Their thinking, or hope, was that no one would dare to attack a nun's vehicle.

Among Sister Christina's most beloved staff are Marrash's youngest brother, Sokol; his wife; and their three children. She found the family cowering in an abandoned stable, unwashed and hungry about ten years previously. They had initially fled from their village and rented a room in Shkodër, but were expelled when the landlady discovered they were escaping a blood feud. That's when they began living in the barn, stringing up a blanket found in the garbage to serve as a roof. Sister Christina coaxed them out with apples and the promise of hot showers, and eventually built the family a cinder block house, which they surrounded, naturally, with a high wall.

Sister Christina invited me along to pay a condolence call. On our way, we passed the usual kafes with men drinking and music booming, wires draped with grape vines, and mud as thick as Albanian coffee grounds at the bottom of a cup.

"The pressure on these isolated families is enormous," Sister Christina said as we ploughed through the sludge, bumping over tennis-ball-sized rocks. Before the Communist era, men seeking to evade killers sought shelter in defensive stone towers called *kulla* until reconciliation could be reached. Men could remain in these loaf-shaped sanctuaries for decades, sleeping on a thin mattress of goat skin, listening to the rush of the river outside, with nothing to do but look out of the narrow slats at the majestic mountains and hope someone would bring a bucket of milk and news of a truce. *Broken April*, a novel about blood feuds by Ismail Kadare, Albania's leading novelist, imagines a man on the run who seeks refuge in such a tower. Without explicitly passing judgment, Kadare conveys the tragedy of this ancient rite from which no one can escape: "It was not the blood of a single man, but the torrents of the blood of generations of human beings that streamed all over the High Plateau, the blood of young men and old men, for years and for centuries."

These days, men on the run often enjoy the creature comforts of modern homes, but the psychological stress remains constant. An estimated 6,000 Albanian males, including 650 children, were stuck at home. Boys are ordered to remain indoors and upon reaching puberty are sometimes handed rifles in case their turn comes to exact revenge. A confined family is shunned until the blood debt is paid. Friends don't visit, and the men can't go out to work. Because the Kanun decrees that only males can shoulder the blood curse, the women often end up supporting the family by working in factories or laundries.

For housebound husbands who nominally retain their role as head of the family, the inability to work and lack of social contact have a bitter, emasculating effect, and such men frequently turn to excessive drinking and wife beating. As for the younger generation, while the state provides teachers who pay house calls on isolated students, home schooling doesn't resolve the loneliness of teens who can't date or play soccer. Instead, they indulge in endless television watching and video games, or stare at grimy walls and torment siblings. The children grow lethargic or pace within their narrow boundaries like zoo animals. Some families have built walled courtyards where boys can kick balls around. The few who can afford cell phones can potentially communicate with former schoolmates, but often kids living under the blood curse are shunned on social media, too. In any event, they quickly run out of new things to say.

We drove past a bar with a shaded patio. The aroma of roasting lamb brochette drifted into the car window, as did the voices of men chattering loudly over traditional clarinet music: an ephemeral vision of al fresco relaxation. "There are so many who can't do this," the nun remarked grimly.

She personally knew of 134 youths, 47 of them in Shkodër alone, who lived in isolation. She counted the cases she was trying to mediate, softly, on her fingers. "1, 2, 3, 4, 5, 6, 7, 8, 9—no, that one is resolved—10, 11, 12, 13, 14. She continued quietly in German. "Maybe 20. No, more."

She wearily adjusted the bobby pin that secured her head covering. "It's not for me to judge. This obligation of honor is like a religion. We know a young man whose grandfather avenged his father's death after sixty-four years. He was such a Catholic believer, this old man; he wouldn't hurt a fly. I asked him, 'If you want, tell me please, why did you do this?' He said, 'All my life I fought against this. Sister, believe me, I could not leave my sons with this shame before I died. Before killing, I made the Sign of the Cross and said, 'God forgive me.'"

She fingered the cross hanging around her neck.

"The children are absorbing this mentality and they are psychologically broken. Some avengers starve the victims' families economically and socially. This is one reason people postpone the killings for many years, to torture them. Other families postpone because they don't want to do it."

I asked the obvious question, one that had been bothering me ever since I heard Marrash's story: Why did he leave the house after receiving the phone call? Did he understand that the person on the line was summoning him to his assassination?

"This question vexes his family, too. Some believe he wanted to protect his brother, Sokol, and died in his place." She sighed morosely.

Under the Kanun, Sokol or a male close to him now had to retaliate. The target could be the hit man himself, or a cousin or son or grandfather or uncle. Only men were supposed to die, although recently a young girl was shot by accident, presumably because she was wearing trousers and therefore mistaken for a boy. The other family could break the cycle by sending a representative to Sokol to seek reconciliation.

Herein lay a quandary that the legal anthropologist, Bardhoshi, had underlined. A besa requires a public acknowledgment of the murder, yet doing so would attract attention from the police. Because the state treats honor killings as homicides, Marrash's killer would be forgiven under the Kanun, and then taken to prison. The disconnect between the modern legal system and the customary one has aggravated the problem of honor killings. Albanian authorities did little or nothing to promote the reconciliation process, or consider a judicial amnesty for feuders who wanted to end the cyclical reprisals.

That left mediators, who are often self-appointed, to seek and achieve reconciliation without the state punishing anyone—an admittedly difficult task. Traditionally under the Kanun, the mediator is supposed to be male, but, as a foreigner, Sister Christina commanded a special status. She had approached a woman from the avenging family three years before Marrash's death, during a chance meeting at the cathedral. They whispered in a dark corner to avoid the gossips, Sister Christina said. "'Come to the mission and reconcile with my friends,' I told her. She said, 'I will come. But if my husband hears he will cut my throat.'" The woman met with Sokol and his wife, and she sounded committed to ending the violence. She spoke about it to her sons and grandsons, but they replied that they could not leave the world in such disgrace.

Sister Christina planned to speak to the woman again, but she had become less hopeful. "They fear Sokol's family will deliver the killer to the law."

Until Marrash's family exacted revenge, Sokol and the other males could return to normal life. The teenage boys could play in the street, the men could leave their houses to work and to fraternize in the kafes. But they were still locked into this ancient system. And so their lives, and that of thousands of others, remained in limbo, between the cherished customs of old and the official new laws of the twenty-first century.

◇◇◇◇◇◇◇

The house that Sister Christina had built for Sokol was a ten-minute walk down a muddy lane from her compound. The wall Sokol had erected was twelve feet, though the top remained uneven because construction had stopped when Marrash was killed. Sister Christina tapped the horn. There was no bell; when you're living under the blood curse, you don't get a lot of callers, and if someone knocks, you probably don't answer the door. A stooped man opened the heavy metal gate and peered out. He was about fifty and had intense amber eyes under caterpillar eyebrows. "Sokol," she said to me, her face tightening in anticipation. We drove up the graveled driveway as he shut the gate behind and, like a sleepwalker, led us to the backyard where a gardener was cutting grass with a hand scythe. A woman dressed in black with a broad face and hips stood waiting: Sokol's wife, Irena. The custom is to bring sweets to mourners, to lighten their pain, and Sister Christina handed her a plastic bag of white cherries, which had just come into season. "Modra"—Mother—the bereaved woman said, letting loose a sob. She sank into the nun's frail shoulder and they shuddered together for a few beats, before the nun gently let her go.

We took seats at a round table stacked with chipped china cups and a plate of chocolates. A somber boy who looked to be about thirteen tapped at a Samsung cell phone, his skin an unhealthy mushroom hue. This was Eduart, their middle child, who had never attended school without bodyguards.

As Irena poured us Coca-Cola, Sokol described his troubles falling asleep. Daytime tormented him as well; he felt guilty to be alive. He directed his speech to the cup, clasping it in his palms.

"When you live under the blood feud, you constantly fear that the avenger is coming. It's a tree that develops thorns instead of blossoms and wounds everyone walking by." Sokol stood and took a step. "When you take one step, you have to step backward and look behind. You can imagine how long it takes to move forward."

"You're free now," Sister Christina prompted gently.

Sokol made a noise like a deflating balloon. "My brother was killed. That's why I am free."

The nun offered to approach the other family about a besa. Under the Kanun, only the most recent avenger had the power to end the retaliation.

Irena moved her head in rejection. "You have to thank them first."

Sister Christina responded fiercely: "Thank them? How can I say, 'Thank you'? They killed the brother of my, my," her chin shook, "dear friends."

Sokol defended the assassin, urging the nun to understand the other family. "Destiny controls us. The avenger who killed Marrash restored honor to my family. My brother is honored by paying with his blood. My uncle killed someone. He took power from God and I feel guilty for that shame on the family."

For a few moments, we all watched the gardener with the scythe hack at the foot-high weeds. *Whoosh. Whoosh.*

Eduart spoke up, to no one in particular. "When I was little I thought I was like all the other kids. Then I turned nine and my mother told me." Irena choked on a sob and put her hands over her face. The boy wiped his eyes and pushed the cell phone toward me. It showed a Facebook page, on which there was a red stop sign and the words STOP GJAKMARRJES! (STOP THE BLOOD FEUDS!) "I started this group. We have thirty-five followers. Will you join? I don't want to die."

Doubt flickered on the adults' faces. They looked down and Irena pushed the chocolates toward the boy. He ignored this gesture of comfort, his eyes fixed on the screen.

◇◇◇◇◇◇◇

Sister Christina admitted that her mission could be seen as quixotic. Albanians in these remote communities had been living by blood feuds for eons, and they wouldn't stop because a German sister, or an Albanian policeman, wanted them to.

In order to show me the pernicious hold of the Kanun, Sister Christina invited me to observe a therapy group that she had organized for boys living in isolation, including Eduart. Through engaging the children in scenarios, she tried to give them the experience of having free choice. "They say, 'We have it in the blood, whether we want it or not.' We hear that all the time. It is taken for granted," she explained.

The first children to pass through the therapy group a decade before were now in their twenties, without much of a change to their lives. All but one had fled the country to escape assassination. The lone holdout was Victor, a gaunt twenty-three-year-old, who lived a protected life in the religious compound, doing odd jobs. When I visited Shkodër, Sister Christina had just started working with a new circle of boys, aged seven to fourteen, who met every Wednesday. She did so even though she had little hope that they might escape the blood feuds.

The group met across the road from Sister Christina's house, in another immaculate white structure that she had built. Barnlike in size and shape, it was encircled by ruby rose beds. The yard had a trampoline. The nun clipped a handful of blossoms as we went inside, into a space that smelled of freshly sawed pine, and which offered each child his own cubby. Before I met the boys, she told me, "In the group they are allowed to ask why." Each week she improvised a scene, responding to the latest threat or killing. When Marrash died, the boys talked about their feelings and cried along with Eduart as he mourned his uncle. They staged a ritual to honor the dead man. "After that, they never mentioned it."

The group met in a lofty rectangular space drenched in sunlight. It had a 360-degree view of the mountains, a reminder of what lay outside. Today's exercise was a tussle between good and evil, where evil meant blood revenge. Each boy decided whether to wear a white or a black cloak. The white group resembled angels and the black, Draculas. Eduart joined three other boys in white. They sat in a circle holding hands around a lit candle, a china dove, a glass angel, and four roses. Occasionally they picked up a Bible and lowered their heads in prayer.

There was no question that the four boys in black were having much more fun. They chased each other, tossed around a stuffed python, and shot a plastic AK-47 with gusto. Occasionally, the eldest of the group, a lanky thirteen-year-old named Leonart who wore a T-shirt that said "Chick Magnet," stood up and ferociously punched a life-size baby doll.

Sister Christina observed him thoughtfully. "Leonart comes of age in four months and knows he could be shot anytime after that."

The boys in black fought over the gun. Leonart's younger brother, Florian, a squirt in Spider-Man shorts, put the weapon against his head, and pretended to shoot himself. The others guffawed.

Sister Christina called proceedings to order. They reluctantly put down the gun.

She pretended to be a foreigner knocking on the door of a house, asking the Draculas for water. She offered the dove as a gift. Florian laughed cruelly. "What is this word 'pagje' (peace)?" He grabbed the dove. "Can we eat it? We have many ducks. Why do we need this stupid thing?"

Another boy aimed the gun at the nun. "Go, go, someone escort her out."

The black team then turned their scorn on the whites, who sat with downcast eyes on the other side of the room. "You are dressed like girls," mocked Rikardo, a little boy who slithered on his stomach under his cape. He looked like a satin snapping turtle.

Leonart pummeled the doll so hard that its head flew off.

Sister Christina gave the baddies the option of joining the peaceniks. Those who renounced evil received a dab of white paint on the back of the hand. All the devils acquiesced except Rikardo, who demurred: "I'm not sure."

The session ended with a final group chant: "NO TO BLOOD FEUDS! YES TO PEACE!" The boys rushed out of the room to play soccer, except for a trio who stayed back to talk to me.

Rikardo asked about New York. "My father fled there a year ago because his cousin killed someone. Sometimes we talk on the computer. My brother is twenty-five and he has to stay inside the house. I find it hard to focus on my studies. I fear I will be killed at eighteen."

Florian cut in. "My father is hiding, too. I don't know where he is." He got up and ran off.

Eduart remained behind with an agonized expression. He toyed with his sneaker laces, avoiding eye contact. "I always choose the white," he said, after a while.

◇◇◇◇◇◇◇

I'd reported on violence in mountains all over the world, and it usually appeared just as cyclical and inescapable as in Albania. Yet here, unlike in other regions, other forces—land grabs, exploitation by profit-seeking business or government ventures, ethnic strife—didn't come into play. The conflict here was fairly clear-cut. One might think that would make resolution easier. But that was not my sense. The blood feuds would remain intractable until the state figured out how to dilute, or accommodate, the mountains' own laws. Perhaps authorities could decriminalize it, by offering amnesties to those who were willing to end the reprisals. Perhaps incentives could be given to those who successfully negotiated a besa. Ignoring the Kanun, however, resolved nothing.

After returning to New York, I thought often of Eduart, Marrash's nephew, he of the stricken eyes and Facebook dreams. If he were a seventh-grader in the United States, he'd be worrying about acne and soccer meets. I thought about my own son, who was preparing for his Bar Mitzvah, choosing guest lists and memorizing Hebrew phrases. Eduart's rite of passage would likely involve a bullet.

I checked his Facebook page regularly. It got a few Likes, but not many. Sister Christina was pushing for a besa, and she wrote to me in the months after my return with periodic news about the negotiation process and Sokol's family's state of mind. They had come around to the idea of a besa, hoping at last to break the violent cycle. They couldn't meet the other family directly, so Sister Christina made the approach. For a while she hoped that she might arrange an armistice, after all. But the message I received after Christmas was grim. She had just met with the other family and, as it had done many times before, the modern court system was preventing traditional mountain justice from following its course.

"The meeting was more than bad. They are very angry and told me they didn't commit the revenge killing. They denied all, all. And they spoke very aggressively about Sokol. I know the name of the man who brought the message and I know that he denied to the police that he brought the message. He is protecting the killers. This is not supposed to happen with the Kanun. I am afraid now for Sokol and his son. It's terrible, Judith. But it's the reality here."

2

Our Land Is Our Land

SIERRA MADRE, 4,000 TO 8,500 FEET

Our cavalry soon discovered that it would not be able
to act at all among these rugged mountains.

> —Bernal Díaz del Castillo, *The True History of the*
> *Conquest of New Spain* (1568)

They said that they had never wanted to obey or
serve Monteczuma, who was the greatest lord of the
Indians, so why would they submit to the Christians?
The Yopes had always had wars in which they were
willing to die and prove themselves.

> —Diego Pardo, a Spanish colonial officer (1531)

The gateway to Zapatista rebel territory is San Cristóbal de las Casas, a misty highland town that attracts romantics seeking Mexico's indigenous heart. It is a *pueblo mágico*, so designated by the tourism board for its history and charm. The look here is quintessential colonial: cobbled lanes lining houses with red-tiled roofs and balconies with flower boxes. Walls are painted rich cobalt and rust. Life revolves around the mustard-colored cathedral, on whose pavement Indians from surrounding villages hawk textiles of eye-popping hues.

At 7,000 feet above sea level, San Cristóbal is enclosed by even higher mountains, which Graham Greene described in 1939 as "crouched all round like large and friendly dogs." The chilly climate requires one to

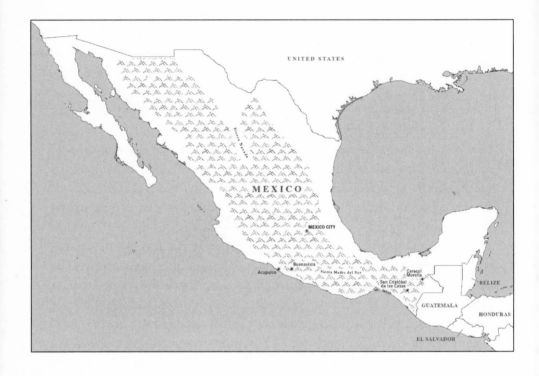

wear a sweater even in summer and nurtures coffee beans, whose cultivation sustains the myriad cafes in town. The mountains form part of the Sierra Madre de Chiapas chain, which run down from Chiapas, Mexico's southernmost state, into Central America. The tallest mountain in the region measures 10,000 feet. Locals call these highlands Los Altos. Large tracts of the area are blanketed by tangled cloud forests where endangered jaguars prowl and waterfalls cascade from several stories high. While densely wooded with 1,500 species of trees, the landscape is gentler and its trails easier to navigate than the jagged pinnacles of Albania.

This is the land of the ancient Maya, a learned civilization that built monumental cities and flourished between 250 and 900 AD. No one knows if the kingdom collapsed due to war or to environmental degradation; regardless, each possibility should be taken as a warning today. At its height this sophisticated society developed complex systems of hieroglyphics, astronomy, and mathematics. All that is left are ruined temples overgrown by vines and overrun by tourists.

The descendants of the Maya are the Tzotzil, Tzeltal, Tojolabal, and Chole ethnic groups, who live modestly in tiny communes. They grow their own corn, vegetables, beans, and bananas when not selling handicrafts. Together they constitute one of the poorest populations of Mexico; most of them lack the mathematical skills of the pre-Colombian kingdom but still subscribe to its cosmic beliefs. Like so many highlanders around the world, these groups have a profound spiritual connection with the land. They venerate trees, waterfalls, caves, trails, and rocks. Among these peoples, all living things are thought to have souls, and complex rituals surround the harvesting of corn and cutting of trees. The mountain is the most revered element of all. Gods dwell inside, as do ancestors and spirits. A peak is not just an exceptionally tall mound; it is where heaven and earth meet. Some anthropologists have speculated that pre-Colombian builders erected pyramids to replicate mountains' power. Priests sacrificed humans there to nourish the gods with blood.

Foreigners take excursions to the Mayan temples and the syncretic churches whose worshippers sacrifice hens and offer beer to Catholic saints on floors strewn with pine needles. Hikers trek the cloud forests to spot wild quetzal birds, whose resplendent emerald feathers adorned the headdresses of Mayan and Aztec kings. San Cristóbal has long attracted the vegan and yoga set, and today many New Age voyagers have a decidedly political bent thanks to the 1994 uprising of the Zapatista rebels,

descendants of the ancient Maya. The rebellion stirred tremendous sol-
idarity among internationalistas seeking a noble cause, and the town is
filled with European anarchists, as well as protestors who throw bricks at
Starbucks and well-meaning NGOs that raise money for the cause. Locals
call it Zapa-turismo. Bars have added Free Trade lattes to the menu and
protest songs to playlists. The souvenir ladies working the open-air markets sell felt dolls of guerrillas on horseback. Minibuses even make runs
to the nearest Zapatista command center so that radical foreigners can
glimpse the revolution across the well-fortified gates.

Crass commercialization aside, the fascination with these Mayan
rebels is understandable. Their sympathizers see a higher calling in the
indigenous people's attempt to take destiny into their own hands. Mexican history is studded with many extraordinary insults against the poor.
So is the present: across the country, drug cartels regularly perpetrate
massacres, taking ten thousand lives a year. There are epic floods and
earthquakes, and heinous abuses by the corrupt and authoritarian Revolutionary Institutional Party, the PRI, which has monopolized Mexican
governance for most of the past century.

Thus one of the single most astonishing days in Mexico's recent history was January 1, 1994. That morning, when most Mexicans were nursing hangovers from New Year's Eve, some three thousand Mayan Indians
wearing black ski masks occupied several towns in Chiapas. They freed
prisoners from a jail in San Cristóbal and set fire to police stations and
a military installation in the region. Their demand: equal treatment and
self-governance for indigenous Mexicans. For some reason no one in the
government had seen this coming, in part because the EZLN, or Zapatista Army of National Liberation, had been training for a decade in terrain so impenetrable that it escaped the notice of Mexican intelligence.
Embarrassed, the authoritarian state deployed twelve thousand heavily
armed troops to crush the insurgents. At least 145 people were killed over
twelve days before the rebels did what mountain warriors generally do
when under pressure: retreat to the highlands.

The Roman Catholic Church was a partner in the Spanish crown's
brutal colonization of Mexico, yet clerics in Chiapas have championed
Indian rights since the colonial times. Local church figures mediated a
truce, and in 1996 the two sides signed the San Andrés Accords, meant to
grant greater autonomy and rights to the rebels and the people they fought
for. It read like a manifesto for the World Mountain People Association,

calling for "basic respect" and autonomy for the indigenous population; preservation of natural resources within their lands; and greater participation in regional decisions over expenditures, development, and political and judicial policies.

To no one's surprise, the state never implemented this ambitious plan, and instead set up army camps outside Zapatista enclaves. It looked away when political bosses affiliated with the ruling PRI party harassed Zapatistas with abductions, arson, and worse. The party's modus operandi was to patrol the roads with high-caliber weapons and storm meetings of sympathizers. One of the worst incidents occurred on December 22, 1997, when paramilitary operatives going by the sinister name Mascara Roja, or Red Mask, slaughtered forty-five indigenous pacifists attending a prayer meeting in the pueblo of Acteal. Feeling betrayed, in August 2003 the Zapatistas decided to go it alone, sloughing off the slogan, "Never again a Mexico without us." They consolidated a patchwork of territory across 750,000 acres where they established their own schools, justice system, governance, clinics, and collectives.

Over the years, Mexico has seen hundreds of uprisings, but the Zapatistas' was remarkable. The country's 12.7 million indigenous people, or 13 percent of its population, are among its most destitute and disenfranchised. How did a tiny group manage to dislodge from the mainstream and get away with it? Without question, the mountains played a determining role.

I decided to go to Mexico to investigate. The conflict intrigued me in its own right, but also because it reverberated northward. Instability in Mexico has implications for the United States. The Mexican government could not control the huge illegal narcotics industry operating within its borders, nor could it stem the transport of drugs from other Latin American countries, through Mexico and into the United States. The waves of undocumented immigrants crossing into this country were also a result of violence and chaos in Mexico. Drugs, immigration, NAFTA, and more: Mexico was and is a major issue in American politics.

I was also curious to learn what the Zapatista movement implied for mountain arenas elsewhere. Was there a lesson to be taken away that applied to other restive highland communities? Albania made clear how mountains discourage cultural absorption and isolate their inhabitants socially, economically, and politically. Mexico, I found, illuminated another dimension to mountain life, one suggested by Mario Conejo, the

Ecuadoran representative in the World Mountain People Association. When we met at the concert of Quechua pipe music in the Pyrenees, the Andean Indian leader had stressed the sacred nature of the ground itself. The lonely countryside, he said, was both a refuge from enemies and a cherished homeland. Mountain people are often aboriginals, their attachment to the land dating back millennia. "The mountain makes a mark on people's identity and their attitude toward nature," Conejo said. "We in the indigenous communities see the mountain as a place that is spiritual and magical. We love the earth in a profound way. I know when I meet a mountain person, from all corners of the earth. There is something universal in the way of looking at the sky and walking on the earth."

Conejo noted that the Zapatistas differed from guerrillas in other Latin American countries—Colombia, Nicaragua, Peru, and El Salvador among them. The Zapatistas did not seek national political power, nor were they influenced by modern ideologies. They were struggling to preserve unique customs, and the territory where their ancestors were buried. A prominent political scientist, James Fearon, has a name for this dynamic: "sons of the soil."

I wanted to know if the Zapatistas' deep affection for their territory and detachment from wider society was as intractable as that of the followers of the Kanun in Albania. I knew that, to some extent, the Zapatistas lived off the grid as a function of geographic remoteness but also by choice. They were trying to live in a parallel society, according to their own rules. Yet in an age of Facebook and international trade deals, could this aloofness from mainstream society endure? How long would the physical barrier of the highlands serve to protect them from a hostile national government? Finding the answer to that inquiry became my quest.

◇◇◇◇◇◇◇

The Zapatista rebellion was the world's first by Internet. The EZLN's public face, a pipe-smoking former professor who went by the nom de guerre Subcomandante Marcos, deftly captivated international attention with a website regularly updated with communiqués. An urban intellectual who had joined the movement while it was forming in the jungles in the 1980s, Marcos understood the power of sound bites and photo ops, uttering enigmatic phrases through his balaclava as he sat atop his horse. He was witty, even poetic. "We are sorry for the inconvenience, but this is a revolution" was one of his many sardonic wisecracks. Another popular quote went, "In the cabaret of globalization, the state shows itself as a table dancer that strips off everything until it is left with only the minimum indispensable garments: the repressive force."

The Zapatistas were noble, and accessible to those who logged on to their website. That Marcos was not an Indian himself didn't deter leftist groupies who descended on Chiapas to catch a glimpse of this sexy phenomenon. Not since the Black Panthers, in their berets and leather jackets, had such a media-genic movement presented itself. It had all the ingredients necessary to enthrall a range of foreign comrades: lyricism, philosophy, and downtrodden minorities. Foreigners were attracted by the seeming purity and romanticism of Mexico's original people. They raised money for the cause and wore T-shirts bearing the EZLN star. Feminists were thrilled: the *numero uno* of the movement was not some burly guy but Comandanta Ramona, a petite woman. Marcos spoke for the group but he was a mere *subcomandante*, second in command, at least in name.

Much was made of Marcos's vitriol against globalization and neoliberal economic policies. He timed the dramatic 1994 uprising for the day the North American Free Trade Agreement went into effect. NAFTA's main thrust was to remove barriers to commerce by lifting tariffs on products traded among the United States, Mexico, and Canada. The initiative did not auger well for small-scale Mexican farmers, who feared the United States would cripple them by dumping in Mexico subsidized corn, their country's staple. They resented an amendment to Mexico's constitution that paved the way for NAFTA and allowed for the sale by Mexicans themselves of indigenous collective lands. Marcos's many essays—he published a whole book and more—prophesized a coming world war and the destruction of unique cultures.

Yet the average Tzotzil Indian doesn't know the word *neoliberal* or understand the nuances of international markets. Most subsistence farmers can barely read, let alone use computers. While the pretext for the rebellion was NAFTA, in fact land ownership and identity lay at the heart of the struggle. The movement took its name from Emiliano Zapata, the folk hero of the 1910 Mexican Revolution whose rallying call was "Tierra y Libertad"—Land and Freedom. These words motivated this particular struggle, too, as they had many others before. The Zapatistas believed they were waging a just fight for survival and ancient property.

The foreign media tended to focus on Marcos's antics rather than consider the historical and geographic context of the rebellion. Mexicans, according to various scholarly views, are a *pueblo levantisco*, or prone to rebellion. The country won its independence from Spain in 1821, and endured a 1910 revolution. There have been hundreds of peasant rebellions in Mexico over the centuries. The most tenacious struggles were waged against authorities by indigenous mountain populations, recurring over and over in the same crests and valleys where they have flared since the Spanish set their leather boots down in Mexico. Many mountain populations across the country, from the Yaquis and Tarahumara in the north to the Yopes and Oaxacans in the south, have risen up against those who held the political power.

Records of rebellion in Chiapas date back to 1523, when the first wave of conquistadores confronted the mountain-worshipping Tzotzils. The Spanish soldier of fortune, Bernal Díaz del Castillo, wrote a vivid, probably embellished, firsthand account of the terrifying defenders. Taking advantage of ravines and mist, the Tzotzils tormented the Europeans with bows and arrows, rocks, slingshots, spears, and boiling water. They added a petrifying din of screeching pipes, drums, and trumpets made from large conch shells. "They said we were all to be killed, for this had been promised by their gods," a shaken Díaz del Castillo recalled. Eventually this lot was subdued, but natives, from the Chiapa group, chose suicide over conquest. They leapt 3,333 feet into the deep waters of the Sumidero canyon, today a favored kayaking spot near San Cristóbal.

Abused and subjugated through taxes and forced labor, highlanders rose up again in 1712, and yet again in a rebellion known as the Caste War that lasted from 1867 to 1870. Each time they were put down, but their anger was passed down through oral traditions. At the root of their discontent was a toxic caste system imposed by the Spanish Crown across Mexico that placed Europeans and an increasing number of mixed-race *mestizos* at the top and the natives firmly at the bottom, where they remain today.

The invaders exterminated 90 percent of Mexico's original population over the first century of Spanish rule, mainly by importing smallpox and other European diseases against which the locals had no antibodies. A significant number died in combat or from overwork. Those who survived were forced to work in the mines or plantations, under the cynical system of *encomiendas*, or tributes. Under this mechanism, the native population had to pay Spanish overlords with precious metals or labor for the "protection" and the privilege of forcible religious conversion and tutelage in the occupiers' language.

A number of indigenous communities escaped persecution and land grabs by moving to higher, less arable land. In remote mountain regions, they were distant from the seat of Spanish power and could take some solace in the undesirable agricultural conditions, which meant a smaller chance powerful people would want to steal their property. The same Indian villages that revolted in the eighteenth century asserted land claims in the 1930s and later joined guerrilla movements in the twentieth and twenty-first centuries. In a grotesque failure of state building, successive Mexican rulers found it too costly to build schools and roads in these regions. The political elite took little interest in the country's original people; the state has generally only asserted itself in these mountainous areas via military actions to repress leftist movements, exploit the locals, or support mining companies that signed lucrative contracts on Indian land and then didn't share profits.

Still, after an active push by indigenous groups and leading intellectuals, and seeking international approval, the Mexican government amended the constitution to recognize the country's "pluricultural composition" and guarantee the protection of indigenous languages, cultures, and forms of social organization. In reality few protections are in force beyond granting some indigenous communities the right to practice limited autonomy based on ancient "uses and customs."

Perversely, being left largely alone had an upside. Mountain peoples could frequently elect village authorities according to local traditions. For the most part, the most remote populations remained aloof from national party politics. They also did not assimilate. The mountain Indians continued to speak their languages, wear their tunics, carry babies on their backs, farm communally, and dispense justice through councils of elders. They carried on making offerings to the corn and rain gods.

◇◇◇◇◇◇◇

I went to San Cristóbal on the eve of the twentieth anniversary of the Zapatista uprising. I took a short flight to the capital of Chiapas state, Tuxtla de Gutiérrez. From there, I drove ninety minutes on paved roads. Yet on arriving, making contact with the Zapatistas was not so simple.

Having harnessed the media so astutely in the 1990s, the Zapatistas now rejected most requests from journalists, lumping them in the same category as multinational corporations and Mexican politicians: outsiders not to be trusted. This reticence contrasted starkly with the heady early days of the rebellion, when the militants aggressively courted the media, leaving communiqués for reporters in garbage cans or in trees in San Cristóbal before developing a robust list of subscribers to their website. Over time, though, as the movement lost momentum and international support, the EZLN came to see journalists as less useful. They now granted few requests for visits to their jungle bases.

As a member of the gringo capitalist press accompanied by a videographer from the mainstream Mexican media, I had two strikes against me. Raúl, the videographer, had enjoyed access at the start of the rebellion, but over the years the rebels had begun to rebuff him. The Zapatistas did not respond to my e-mailed requests to attend the anniversary celebrations, nor the *escuelitas*, weeklong seminars held for specially vetted guests, who tended to be NGO employees or Europeans who clearly stated their sympathy for the cause. Raúl likewise failed to win an invitation.

Plan B was to show up at the blue cattle gates guarding the communities in the forest and sweet-talk the masked guards into letting us in. The EZLN's ad hoc republic operated out of five control centers, called *caracoles*, or snails. Just as snails do, the people had withdrawn inside their protective shells, fatigued with the outside world and its empty promises. No one could say exactly how many sympathizers were left. The last public appearance by the Zapatistas had occurred a year prior, in December 2012, when forty thousand supporters marched silently through various towns in their signature masks. The date was symbolically chosen for the end of the Mayan calendar cycle that had lasted 5,125 years. New Agers had descended upon Chiapas expecting to experience either spiritual awakening or doomsday.

The putative former head of the Zapatistas, Comandanta Ramona, had died of cancer, and little was known about the current leadership. Speculation about Marcos, who had not been seen in public lately, was common. He'd put on his last media stunt seven years earlier, zooming out of the hills on a black motorcycle for a tour across the nation. Marcos had intended to forge partnerships with other social movements, but little came of the six-month tour, and now rumors circulated that he was sick, too obese to travel, or about to die. (None turned out to be true.)

The Zapatista commanders let few outsiders into their enclaves and tightly controlled what went on inside. The only hints about living conditions came from leftist sympathizers, either NGOs that provided medical supplies and documented human rights abuses, or the carefully vetted leftist activists invited to take part in stage-managed visits. What they described was a tightly disciplined community where alcohol was not tolerated, members had to seek permission to leave the community even for short trips, and all internal disputes were settled by governing councils.

Left to organize our own passage, we sought the help of Víctor Lopez, the director of a human rights center called Fray Bartolomé de las Casas. Frayba, as it is colloquially known, takes its name from the sixteenth-century Dominican friar who championed natives' rights. The first permanently stationed bishop of Chiapas, he was horrified by Spanish atrocities against Indians and did his best to stop them. His push to end the encomienda tribute system angered representatives of the Crown, however, and the Church recalled him to Spain. The human rights center was founded in 1989 by San Cristóbal's controversial bishop of forty years, the late Samuel Ruiz, who took up his predecessor's defense of Indian rights. Many of Ruiz's rural catechists went on to become leaders of the Zapatistas, prompting accusations in government circles that the good bishop was actually an organizing force behind the movement. Nonetheless, the government accepted him as a mediator for the ill-fated San Andrés Accords. Ruiz always insisted, right up until his death in 2011, that while he sympathized with the cause for equal rights he did not support violent means.

Frayba carries on Ruiz's spirit. Víctor and his small staff made regular forays into the caracoles to investigate the trucks mounted with machine guns that patrol the communes. While having "liberated" large tracts of land, the Zapatistas didn't have complete command of it, because hostile government supporters surrounded their settlements. Frayba collected data on paramilitaries allegedly in pay of local political bosses linked to the government. The men ambushed militants near the entrances of their settlements in order to intimidate or murder them. Then there were government soldiers that dismantled Zapatista communities by force, often with fatal consequences. Sometimes loggers and ranchers tried to chase the Zapatistas away in order to cut down and carry off the valuable timber or simply seize their land.

Having witnessed the movement's evolution over the years, Víctor was well positioned to offer an expert perspective, albeit through a sympathetic lens. He believed that, while the EZLN were controlling about their public image and discipline, they had more respect for human rights than the average bribe-grabbing government official. They also, he felt, exhibited an unusual political maturity. Their abandonment of military offensives after the San Andrés Accords showed that they could readily admit to mistakes and move on, a rarity among political movements of any cast.

Víctor said some of his staff at the human rights center had sought medical attention at the Zapatista clinics. They reported that health care, while rudimentary and lacking many vital drugs, was more accessible and effective than in other rural parts of Mexico, where procedures as commonplace as childbirth could turn fatal. As for education, each community now had a schoolhouse that delivered lessons in indigenous languages, which was virtually unheard of in Mexico. The curriculum presented the Zapatista view of history, with a heavy emphasis on colonial exploitation, and also covered farming techniques. Only someone fluent in Tzeltal could evaluate the quality, and the government wasn't allowed in to conduct a literacy survey. "But it's certainly more relevant to indigenous people than the government's standard curriculum that talked about things like traffic lights," said Víctor. Another unusual feature was the emphasis on educating girls, a novelty in a rural society that normally assigned women a social position not far above animals. Female Zapatistas were encouraged to assume positions of leadership and command, from the armed forces to civilian councils.

Ironically, the biggest threat to the Zapatistas' existence was not paramilitary harassment or land grabbers, but their own young people, who were abandoning the closed society to seek economic fortune elsewhere, much as Eduart wanted to abandon the Kanun in Albania for modern ways. Youngsters born after 1994 didn't necessarily share the utopian vision of their parents. A small plot of land on which to grow beans and talk of self-sufficiency was not enough for many of them. Moreover, the Zapatistas' rejection of the government subsidies on which indigenous villages long depended had made life harder. A good portion of the 850,000 Chiapas residents who had migrated to other parts of Mexico or the United States were from the Zapatista highlands. Young people sought jobs and a less regimented lifestyle. Migration eroded social cohesion by exposing those who left to new political views, and the Zapatistas essentially excommunicated anyone who migrated too far afield or spent too much time away. If you left, you couldn't return, or even communicate with family. They also expelled those caught possessing alcohol and accepting public funds. While the threat of exile could serve as a brake against petty crimes, the harsh punishment fractured families and entire communities, exacerbating the effects of immigration.

◇◇◇◇◇◇◇

I wanted to witness these dynamics firsthand. Víctor advised trying our luck at Oventik Caracol, a one-hour drive from San Cristóbal, and then pressing on another "few" hours to Morelia, further into the highlands. This caracol did not have access to the Internet so Víctor typed up a letter of introduction, though he warned it was a crapshoot whether they would allow us past the gate: "They do not trust easily."

It was December 12, the day Mexicans celebrate their patron saint, the brown-skinned Virgin of Guadalupe who embodies both indigenous beliefs and practices on the one hand and Catholicism on the other; she is one of the few symbols with the potential to unite the country. As the legend goes, her apparition revealed itself to an Aztec convert to Christianity, and miraculously seared itself onto the Indian's cloak, which is considered a holy relic today. The Virgin of Guadalupe is particularly loved in indigenous areas that have embraced conversion; one hundred years ago, Emiliano Zapata's revolutionary army carried her banner into battle. On this, her fiesta day, we saw pilgrims dressed in white running for miles on the shoulder of the road, carrying torches and placards of her face from village to village.

The feasting at some rest spots on our way to the caracoles seemed more pagan than Catholic. Revelers wearing jaguar costumes and bull masks danced in the road to the beat of drums. From giant vats, women ladled servings of pox, pronounced *posh*, a potent homebrew of cane alcohol. Several men passed out on the ground from excess, having never made it to church. Those who were still standing seemed unlikely to be upright for evening Mass.

As we approached Oventik, the number of partygoers thinned, no doubt owing to the Zapatistas' famed ban against drink. Festivities halted completely when we reached the billboards at the edge of the enclave.

Black and red lettering painted on a road sign broadcast a revolutionary message:

> You are in Zapatista Rebel Territory
> The people rule
> And the government obeys

Just beyond the sign lay a cluster of crude wooden buildings, which looked like a movie set for a Western, except for the murals covering the facades: a rainbow of snails in bandanas, masked women whose faces formed the kernels of corn husks, and portraits of Zapata.

A thin girl of about fifteen manned the cattle gate at the entrance, clipboard in hand. When we approached, she quickly pulled on a black ski mask embroidered with the letters EZLN, but took it off to inspect our documents. She donned the mask again for the arrival of the next carload of visitors, then waved them through quickly, maybe because, with their dreadlocks and German accents, they seemed suitably leftist. Meanwhile, the girl frowned over our papers.

Each caracol has a "junta of good governance" whose membership rotates regularly in order to minimize corruption and give everyone a chance at leadership. Women are especially encouraged to join. According to the teenage guard at the gate, the Oventik team was in planning meetings for the big anniversary celebration and could not receive us. But apparently our papers passed muster, because we were free to wander the camp and visit the "Che Guevara" gift shop. The Zapatistas don't have many opportunities to earn income, and revolutionary-themed souvenirs are money-spinners. A visit to the handicrafts collectives is de rigueur for Zapa-turistas, the girl at the gate said.

"How much are you going to spend?" she asked, pen aloft to record the amount.

The store was piled floor to ceiling with refrigerator magnets, mugs, pens, T-shirts, ash trays, shot glasses, sugar bowls, all bearing a portrait of Marcos and the symbol of the revolution, a red star. A British shopper vacillated between a doll of Marcos on his horse and a red scarf of the type rebels use to hide their faces.

"Both are very popular," said the salesman behind the cash register. "The bandanas also come in pink."

We walked to the cafeteria, which was stacked high with crates of Coca-Cola, a seemingly odd choice for a movement in revolt against global capitalism. Then we checked out the pharmacy, which was mainly stocked with diarrhea remedies. Those who preferred traditional cures could choose from the plastic bags of medicinal herbs from a shelf in the back. We peeked into the one-room schoolhouse, where the blackboard scrawls hinted at the content of lessons: "What is the state?" and "Battle." The words were written not in the Mayan languages in which the students were taught, but in Spanish, perhaps for the benefit of foreign visitors who would attend the anniversary party.

Walking back to the car, we cast a final glance at Oventik. It seemed so small, and so carefully stage-managed. The misty drizzle lent a ghostly feel to the scene. The soundtrack of Mexican village life ordinarily hums with ranchero music, barking dogs and conversation, and bullhorns advertising market day. Oventik was eerily silent: no radios, only soft voices. Women peeped from cracks in doors of houses on the empty lanes as we approached, saying nothing. I left the settlement none the wiser about its defiant and insular residents.

◇◇◇◇◇◇

Our next destination was Caracol Four, which Víctor said was less of a Potemkin Village than Oventik. Being five hours deeper into the rural highlands, it couldn't rely on tourists taking a day trip from San Cristóbal to shop for souvenirs. I suspected that the poetic Marcos had chosen the caracol's full name: "Heart of the Rainbow of Hope, Whirlwind of Our Words." Most people called it Morelia, after the nearest town. Once a major center of military operations, the caracol had fallen on tough times due to migration and exposure to what the Zapatistas called "bad views." Further, residents had been subjected to organized intimidation that no doubt weakened the revolutionary resolve. Coffee growers aligned with the ruling PRI party had recently trespassed on their property, hauling rebels away and beating them.

We drove through fog and past cedar and pine forests that grew thicker as the elevation increased. Oddly, we saw no signs of the military units that harassed the EZLN: no checkpoints, garrisons, helicopters, or armored vehicles. We reached a cluster of withered corn stalks and barefoot boys kicking a soccer ball so tattered that it barely bounced. The municipality, Morelia, was controlled by the ruling PRI party, which made life uncomfortable for the caracol inhabitants next door. When we asked for directions, the soccer boys pointed sullenly and vaguely to a dirt track leading out of town. At the end of it was the familiar blue gate, staffed again by a teenage guard, although this one left her face uncovered. She had Mayan eyes, almond-shaped and heavily lidded, and spoke fractured Spanish. The much-vaunted Zapatista educational system hadn't prepared her to read Mexico's national language, and she could not make out the words in Víctor's introductory letter. She slipped away to consult with the junta, bare feet leaving imprints on the wet soil. "Decisions cannot be made individually," she explained. "We have to be careful whom we let in."

She returned an hour later, with the news that the junta would receive us "for a few minutes."

The settlement looked like a more weathered version of Oventik. There were the usual revolutionary murals, masked women holding guns, snails in bandanas. One depicted a gray city of tumbling skyscrapers, presumably a vision of collapsing capitalism. The dormitory building sported a painting dedicated to the "Martyrs of January 7, 1994," when the army stormed the community and killed three militants.

A woman sat outside, embroidering an image of Comandanta Ramona on a cloth. She avoided eye contact. Two teens came out with a basketball and then hurried away.

We sat on a hard wooden bench outside the assembly hall, under a portrait of Zapata holding a big gun. Then it was time for us to go in for three separate interrogations, each by a foursome sitting behind a heavy wooden desk. Each group asked the same three questions.

"Who are you?"

"Why are you here?"

"What do you want to see?"

Finally, a silent, barefoot woman ushered us into a meeting room of eighteen people: the Junta of Good Governance that ran affairs in this wary community. They were dressed like everyone else in the community; the men wore jeans and frayed sweaters, and the women traditional flouncy skirts and *huipil* embroidered tops. Their faces were uncovered, yet they declined to state their names or be photographed. They were cordial but unsmiling.

"We can't trust anyone," explained a bearded man. "Bad ideas are not welcome here."

"We don't need others," asserted the serious fellow next to him.

I wondered why the women remained silent. The bearded man seemed to read my thoughts. "I am talking because the women in this room don't manage Spanish well. But dignity of women is very important to us."

He paused, which I took as a sign to ask questions. Where was the movement going? What was the aim over the next twenty years?

"We seek work, food, schools, health, freedom, liberty, justice, dignity, land. A caracol goes very slowly but protected. The government has a different life. We seek what we need ourselves. It is not easy to trick us again. We don't want outside ideas. Exploitation and discrimination are our enemies."

Another pause. "Do you have more questions?"

I did—many. How could they stop young people from leaving? Could they produce enough food to adequately nourish the children? Wasn't drinking Coke a contradiction? Shouldn't the money be spent on milk? What was their goal beyond continued separation from mainstream society? How long could they resist the temptations of modernity, the restaurant job in America, the proximity to urban pediatricians, the taste of beer? Would ranchers and loggers succeed in chopping down their cedars?

Yet I didn't voice these questions. To do so would have seemed impolite, or irrelevant. They didn't have to justify their way of life to anyone but themselves. The caracol was a Zapatista utopia, made by idealists, not angels, and it was riven by contradictions, just like any social movement. Its smallness contrasted with its residents' bold aims: democracy, peace, and equality. They were now operating in relative obscurity and poverty persisted. At least they were able to preserve their land and language. But how long would that last?

Like the people of the Kanun in Albania, the Zapatistas lived in a limbo where they were not fully integrated, but not fully immune from the commercialized world that they reputedly rejected. The modern world couldn't make room for these people, and still, it was always encroaching. They drank foreign soda and sold souvenirs to white tourists, participating in a global market that they couldn't completely ignore.

Yet in a country laid low by narcos and criminal impunity, these people were actually trying to keep the peace. They had chosen to cut themselves off, perhaps not fully aware, at first, of the deprivations this would entail. They had managed to rise above the exploitation and corruption. On some level, a very deep one, they were blessed: they had the mountains to protect them. Maybe that was as good as it could get.

◇◇◇◇◇◇◇

The Zapatistas may have pulled back from the spotlight, but their example inspired autonomy movements in the mountains of adjacent indigenous states. Most didn't amount to much. For instance, Triqui Indians in the tiny town of San Juan Copala, in Oaxaca state, declared their independence in 2006. The authorities moved quickly to squash the movement, mindful of the Triquis' history. They had risen up in defense of their territory in 1735, and again in 1832, 1843, and the 1970s. In order to quell this latest attempt, paramilitaries in league with local authorities abducted militants, cut off the electricity in the town, and set up a blockade to prevent the entry of food, medicine, and teachers. There was a brief international outcry after two human rights activists were killed trying to break the blockade in 2010, but that withered. Many of the seven hundred villagers gave up and moved away.

A more sustained movement arose in the state of Guerrero, in La Montaña. Guerrero is best known internationally for the resort of Acapulco, that playground of celebrities and high-octane nightclubs on the Pacific white sands. Yet the mountains 150 miles from the yachts are home to Mexico's most destitute hamlets: scattered adobe settlements of Me'phaa, Nahua, and Mixtec Indians. The landscape along the pitted road that climbs from the sparkling coast into the Sierra Madre del Sur—a different chain from that in Chiapas, though it has the same name—has changed little over the centuries. Ancient cornfields rise into pine forests with trees reaching sixty feet high. The tropical air grows fresher and the foliage denser as you ascend. Its tallest mountain pushes 12,149 feet into the sky. La Montaña comprises some of the country's roughest terrain, a land of hurricanes and landslides, where cattle can't graze and settlements are cut off for months during the rainy season. The forested slopes and gullies make agriculture difficult beyond communal subsistence plots of maize and beans. And heroin. The vicious narcotics cartels found the climate and isolation ideal for growing poppies. Harassing anyone who tried to stand in their way, they cultivated fields and secured a trafficking corridor from the mountains to the coast.

As in Albania, the simple harsh life in La Montaña suggests an entirely different world and era. Similar to Alpine communities, the community takes precedence over the individual. Certain customs are largely unchanged from pre-Hispanic times, namely collective farming and village councils that impart justice. Far from government eyes, village leaders assigned communal labor, based on the ancient *tequio a la faena* that obliged adult males to collectively work the fields, build homes, and guard settlements.

The people of La Montaña, like those of Chiapas and the Triqui territory, had a long history of resistance, dating back to 1531, when Yope Indians angered by Spanish seizures of their lands went on a rampage. They burned houses, and killed Spanish gold prospectors and a representative of the Crown. They then sacrificed 250 Indians from another tribe who had collaborated with the colonists. More uprisings followed. The conquistadores finally subjugated the Yopes in 1553 by exterminating most of them. Those who escaped took refuge in the higher ground of La Montaña or dispersed, some going as far as Nicaragua. Other indigenous groups joined the new highlanders in order to avoid the tributes and servitude imposed by colonial overlords.

More defiance followed, including two guerrilla movements led by schoolteachers. One was active in the 1960s and 1970s, and the other arose in the 1990s. There was so much unrest, in fact, that the Mexican historian Armando Bartra described the history of the region as a "dog biting its tale," for the repeated cycles of repression and rebellion and repression.

In late 2013 I went to La Montaña to see the dog biting its tail once again. The growing heroin addiction in the United States had encouraged more activity and violence by the narcos. Disgruntled indigenous villagers were organizing what they called "community police," or in less generous terms vigilante squads, to round up and kick out the drug cartels and corrupt police who were harassing and extorting ordinary villagers. I spent a couple weeks following the self-defense units and their leaders, the middle-aged brothers Bruno and Cirino Plácido Valerio. The siblings with thatched hair and sandaled feet were farmers from the Mixtec ethnic group, and their impassioned oratory inspired other farmers to take justice into their own hands. These self-appointed guardians rode shotgun in pickup trucks and patrolled the hills in pursuit of *malos*, or bad guys.

The cartels were just the latest of a wide array of exploiters that had historically preyed on the Indians here. The list of malos was long: crooked police, rapists, extortionists, cattle rustlers, political bosses, land grabbers, robbers, drunks, mining companies, bribe takers, and narcotics smugglers. Mexico's dysfunctional law enforcement and the remoteness of the Indian communities made them ideal victims for profiteers. Some of the worst offenders were the very people assigned to maintain the peace: soldiers and police officers. A typical ruse was to stop an *indio* coming in from the fields with firewood or crops, and claim there was an arrest warrant for him. Then the extortionists would impose a "fine" of $200 to erase it from the computer. It was an exorbitant sum for someone who lives off the land, but the alternative was jail without trial.

My first stop was to get a historical perspective from anthropologist Abel Barrera, who grew up in La Montaña during the 1960s, when authorities dictated that Indians had to cross the road if they saw a white man coming toward them. Abusive security forces molested the women. Doctors treated them with scorn, calling them "pigs" for not bathing frequently. Barrera was so upset by the bigotry and exploitation that he became an activist and founded a human rights center, Tlachinollan. His efforts to document rapes, arbitrary arrests, torture, and forced disappearances have won him a garland of international accolades from the likes of Amnesty International and the MacArthur Foundation.

I interviewed Barrera at his offices, and traveling to the meeting afforded me a vivid encounter with the inaccessibility of mountainous Mexico. There are no airports in these parts, so to reach his office I took an eleven-hour bus ride from Mexico City through gut-rattling switchbacks and precipitous heights. The passengers sitting across the aisle smelled of wood smoke and soil, the universal hallmark of peasants who live off the land and lack running water. They spoke only fractured Spanish.

Barrera's center in Tlapa de Comonfort, a municipal seat at 3,609 feet above sea level, is filled with stacks of files containing complaints against security authorities who were sometimes in cahoots with the drug cartels. The way Barrera tells it, indigenous mountain dwellers across Mexico share similar traits, regardless of their particular ethnic group. Maya, Mixtec, and Nahuas all prize hospitality and will share their last tortilla with a visitor. But they will resist fiercely if someone tries to seize their land. "This is something historical, enriched and actualized by talk of human rights," he said. He held up a stack of claims to press the point. "The ancient community is the dynamic for resistance. They say, 'Here are my roots, my ancestors, my umbilical cord.'

"When the government builds highways, Indians will say, 'But here are sacred waterfalls.' The engineer will respond, 'Do you want a road or your belief?' This despotic approach makes people defensive. There is a warrior spirit to defend their way of life and their land. It's always been hard to impose the government here."

The breaking point for people in La Montaña, he said, came in 1995 when "law enforcement" went beyond quotidian injustices. That June, police ambushed and massacred seventeen *campesinos*, or peasants, at a political meeting. Then an eight-year-old girl was raped and murdered. On October 15, Cirino Plácido decided it was time to take action. Inspired by the Zapatistas, who had risen up the previous year, he summoned campesinos from thirty-six communities to the Santa Cruz del Rincón, a typical highland pueblo. It consists of one dirt road, one church, and about 450 small houses.

Cirino measures just four foot eleven inches, but he looks bigger when surrounded by rapt farmers. Cirino had become well known in the region as a magnetic orator, and people walked for miles, rode on horseback or the flatbed of trucks to hear him speak. According to those present, so many came—some out of curiosity, most out of anger—that the village square was inundated. As in an ancient assembly, the elders sat in a circle and shared their stories. They wore the uniform of campesinos: loose trousers, straw brimmed hats, and huarache sandals. Many were descendants of the preconquest Yope warriors, whose valor was still exalted in tales told to children.

Cirino's followers founded a volunteer force to guard trucks and cattle. Under this new system, each village assembly chose a commander and policemen, who went on patrols or manned checkpoints on the mountain passes. They stopped suspicious vehicles and chased interlopers away. Matrons lugged chili stews and tortillas in old paint buckets to the barricades.

Amazingly, the community policing was legal under a federal law that allows for limited autonomy in some indigenous areas. Called "uses and customs," it preserves traditional mechanisms that aren't seen as unduly challenging the state's integrity. Security forces harassed the community police from time to time—Cirino was detained on a couple occasions—but for the most part the geographic distance from the cities and poor roads provided de facto autonomy.

For the first years of its existence, the community police force did rounds throughout the territory, turning over suspected robbers to regional authorities. To their frustration, many detainees bought their freedom, a common practice across Mexico. That's when the community police set up their own justice system, called CRAC (Regional Coordinator of Community Authorities). Those found guilty of crimes by community assemblies were sentenced to physical labor, which usually meant building roads or working the fields. Punishment also included "reeducation" meetings.

As CRAC grew, splinter groups broke off. Ego eroded unity against their main opponent, the Mexican state. Lacking the rigid discipline of the Zapatistas, rivals accused each other of patronage and abuse. Cirino retreated from his public role, assuming the mantle of elder statesman at the settlement of Buena Vista while other men took control of CRAC.

Attention shifted to Cirino's younger brother, Bruno. He gained some international notoriety in 2013 for moving to the Costa Chica, three thousand feet down the mountain, where he joined with mestizos and businessmen to run narcos out of town. Implementing the community police model, Bruno drove from village to village in his white pickup truck, organizing self-defense squads. They favored a sinister look: wrestling masks or sacks with eyeholes crudely cut out. The units commandeered high-caliber weapons and SUVs with tinted windows seized from malos. These car chases frequently ended with a bad guy getting hauled away without due process of law. Prisoners would be locked in a room at the back of a house until a kangaroo court pronounced them guilty or innocent. If found guilty, detainees were handed over to government authorities, or ordered to leave town.

Like Marcos on horseback in 1994, this was candy for international journalists, who breathlessly documented the daring new movement. *Time* magazine ran dramatic and menacing portraits of the masked community police. The Mexican government and most political analysts in the country viewed them as reckless vigilantes, although several mayors welcomed the cleansing of their towns. In mounting one of the strongest challenges ever to the otherwise untouchable narcos, these scrappy farmers achieved what the incompetent military could not. Copycat citizen militias proliferated all over the country. At one point, observers counted them in half of Mexico's thirty-one states, from near the border with the United States all the way down the Pacific coast. In an attempt to co-opt the vigilantes, Guerrero state's then governor, Angel Aguirre, issued the men beige T-shirts, baseball caps, and radios. But like everyone else, he failed to control them fully.

◇◇◇◇◇◇◇

The media tended to confuse Bruno's policing operation with the efforts of his older brother. While Bruno drove eight hours a day to oversee his growing command, granting interviews to whoever asked, Cirino was largely unseen by international media. Cirino didn't approve of his brother's chaotic operation. I had followed Bruno around for a week, and now I wanted to talk to Cirino, for which I needed his brother's help. It took a full day to locate Cirino. The mountains blocked cell reception, so we relied on a modern game of telephone, passing messages from a lowland phone to someone in a truck who was going up La Montaña. Eventually, we received the reply that Cirino would be happy to receive me in Buena Vista, his hometown. Too small to appear on the road map, the hamlet was a traditional Mixtec community where most people got around on horseback or foot.

I hired a driver named Uriel Sánchez, who was a reporter based in Acapulco, where his beat was cartel violence. An urban mestizo, he was not familiar with La Montaña, and we wondered how we were going to communicate with the locals without an insider translating. We also wondered whether we would get stuck in the mud. I packed cookies and water and changes of clothes for a couple days in case we got stranded, a likely prospect as the wet season was underway. The Mixtec call themselves Na Saabi, or People of the Rain, for good reason.

The Spanish word for storm is *tormenta*, and that's what we drove into as the Nissan sedan climbed into the soaring Sierra Madre. We could barely see through the windshield and got soaked when rolling down the side windows for a better view. The car sunk into the bog too many times to count. After a while mountain regions begin to remind you of one other, and in this case, the jarring switchbacks and brown mud prompted memories of Albania.

I was now traveling to another mountain culture in the throes of a single, encompassing conflict, though it was of an utterly different nature than the one in Albania. In Mexico, again and again, indigenous people fought for equal treatment, control of their land's resources, and autonomy. Sometimes they were resisting the government, sometimes the narco bosses; in either case, the struggle was clear and direct, though the prize seemed always out of reach.

As we ascended, the landscape transformed. The trappings of the state—electrical poles, tarred surfaces, and roadside bars—disappeared. The distances between villages widened; cultivated coffee shrubs gave way to dense vegetation that clung to the rock face. Through the fog appeared the odd wood shack fringed by banana trees, and then only mud, a sludgy trap that threatened to immobilize the wheels of our car. A billboard appeared out of nowhere, promising improvements to roads and electricity. "Yeah, right," Uriel said, swerving past a pothole the size of a kiddie pool. After three hours driving through the deluge we saw our first human, a campesino leading a donkey loaded down with soaked timber. We stopped, and he advised not to go farther. "The road is ugly."

Then we hit a town called San Luis Acatlán, right near where the Yopes staged their 1531 revolt. I told Uriel about a historical account I had read. A colonial officer, Diego Pardo, wrote a desperate letter to representatives of the Crown in Mexico City, pleading for help in putting down the rebellion. The warriors in deerskins were pillaging unchecked. The survivors among the white population had fled the carnage, which Pardo warned could threaten the stability of all of New Spain.

Uriel only half listened. He was rethinking our mission, worrying about damage to his axle and the imminent approach of dusk. We still had four hours to go, which meant we would hit Buena Vista at dark, an unsavory prospect considering the rampant banditry and strict curfews. We agreed to reassess the plan at the next town. There we would seek a more roadworthy vehicle, or wait until the weather cleared.

We drove up to another town, Hidalgo, as darkness fell. With a population of ten thousand, it felt like a metropolis after the empty stretches. The owner of the grocery store on the main drag, a muddy lane, said she knew of someone with a four-wheel-drive vehicle who was willing to drive to Buena Vista. The man occasionally ran supplies up to Cirino's hamlet. "You have to find someone they trust so that they don't shoot," was her advice. She sent a young boy to fetch the driver, and minutes later a man in a grimed hat pulled up in Chevrolet SUV, asking for $1 a minute, an exorbitant sum in this region, but as he explained no one else would be willing to drive up to an armed barricade in this tormenta. We shook hands and lurched off, after Uriel paid the woman to watch his car. He scrawled his telephone number "in case of emergency," which provoked a harsh guffaw. "Are you kidding? Phones don't work here."

The driver chatted amiably as though ours was a routine situation. Given the conditions in the region, it probably was. La Familia Michoacana, a particularly vicious cartel, was growing poppies only seven miles away, he said. But we needn't worry. Cirino's people kept the narcos, as well as miners who wanted to extract gold, silver, and zinc, at bay. The previous month, the driver said, a mining truck bearing equipment passed by. Cirino's people briefly detained and interrogated the occupants, and they never returned, presumably out of fear.

We carried on for about half an hour in the dark and then, suddenly, the ghostly beam of the headlights registered men with rifles standing at a heavy chain. Uriel explained our mission through the car window and we got out. With a perfunctory "take care," the driver sped off. The guards led us to the sole lit building, a one-story cinderblock house with a generator chugging loudly somewhere inside. Cirino stood in the doorway. He was unfazed that we had turned up half a day late. Exhibiting the legendary hospitality of rural Mexico, he insisted that of course we must stay the night, since no one should drive during a nighttime rainstorm.

The house had only two rooms, and we set up camp in the larger one. The only furnishings were a black vinyl couch and a purple striped hammock. Cirino's wife, a typical señora whom he said did all the cooking, had already gone to bed, but he offered us sodas and candy bars from a shack next to his house. The shed also served as an informal bank that made cash loans. A blackboard showed who owed how much to whom. The average debt was about thirty-five cents. No alcohol was sold; like the Zapatistas, they banned the demon drink as well as recreational drugs.

We went back in the house and Cirino stretched out on the hammock in the receiving room. His hypnotic voice rose as he told his story. Cirino was born to a family that picked coffee. His father had hoped he would become a doctor or engineer, but such lofty ambitions were extremely unusual, and in the end unrealistic, for a campesino from the mountains. Cirino dropped out of school after seventh grade in order to work in the fields alongside his three brothers. Hungry for adventure, he spent a few years in Mexico City working as a baker, a bricklayer, and eventually as a municipal policeman. In Mexico City, he gained insights into the bigotry and corruption of the legal system. He decided to go home. Yearning for the mountains, Cirino returned to La Montaña and began contemplating how to resist what he called "this historical process of denial."

The collective nature of mountain culture, he said, provided a perfect vehicle to organize a struggle. "Mestizos in other parts of Mexico are more individualistic. We in La Montaña think collectively with an 'us,' not a 'me.' We believe in consensus and the *pueblo por el pueblo*." People by and for the people.

"We are two times Mexicans because we are the original people in this country. But we don't write the history. They impose their education and culture and language on us and try to take our lands. Many people ask, 'Why does this region have such a violent history?' Well, for five hundred years they have discriminated against us. But this is our birthplace and culture and they can't take that away from us."

As he spoke, I thought about the writing of Yi-Fu Tuan, the father of humanistic geography, who captured, in far less accessible language, the same notions of attachment to place and historical roots. Tuan reminds us that simple, rural societies have a different concept of nature than urbanites. The former rely on harvests rather than paychecks, and they believe in sun gods and that rain forms part of the cosmos. A single oak tree can hold great meaning. Writing about the effective bond between people and place, Tuan argues that the modern state's boundaries are too arbitrary, its area too heterogeneous, to command this sort of attachment. "Awareness of the past is an important element in the love of place," he writes.

I was about to share this reflection with Cirino, but someone knocked insistently at the door. Cirino got up for a whispered exchange with a guard from the barricade. It went on for some time, and then he took a mattress from a back room, slid it toward me, and threw Uriel a blanket on the couch. "Get some rest. We'll continue in the morning."

◇◇◇◇◇◇◇

At 4:30 a.m. a rooster announced that sleep was over and the village erupted into human chatter and the aroma of wood smoke. Dawn revealed adobe houses with thatched roofs tilting precariously on the soaked soil—dwellings made of earth and in danger of returning to it. This gave the settlement an unsettling air of impermanence. Mist hung in the lush hills beyond, where a thread of peasants walked to the fields, small as crickets from this distance. Barefoot women in ruffled skirts and huipiles, long braids competing for space with the babies slung on their backs, carried plastic buckets of water from the river below. A line of people waited to use the outhouse, a rickety hut with a hole in the ground. An aggressive goose tried to block everyone from entering. Dodging past, I noticed that chickens had spent the night there and left four eggs on the soiled floor.

Someone was playing a *corrido*, a genre of narrative ballads set to a polka beat. Since most of the villagers were illiterate, music and storytelling served to pass down grievances about authority. First introduced in the 1850s, the corridos often have an insubordinate subtext, paying homage to outlaws. The narco-corridos glorifying drug bandits are a popular strand, even among Mexicans who abhor cartel violence. Guerrero had developed its own style, with lyrics featuring the words for bullets, police, fights, gunmen, shooting, and killings. This particular song was by a local band, Los Donnys de Guerrero, about a schoolteacher-turned-guerrilla leader, Lucio Cabañas. He hid out in the Atoyac Mountains not far from where I was brushing my teeth. The song portrayed the revolutionary as a fearless David taking on Goliath:

> *Tanks and war planes*
> *rose over that mountain*
> *seeking Lucio Cabañas. . . .*
> *Lucio Cabañas yelled at them*
> *I am going to fight you!*
> *I do not fear the government*
> *I carry fine weapons . . . and I am going to die trying*

Back in the house, Cirino entered the main room where we camped out offering two clay mugs of coffee and an explanation for the late-night knock on the door. The guards had encountered youths from other pueblos lingering outside the village. They were now safely locked up and we could interview them shortly. But first, breakfast. Cirino led us to the back terrace, which looked out at the mountains. A table fashioned from pine planks held bowls of corn tortillas, green sauce, and fluffy scrambled eggs.

I hesitated, assuming these were the eggs from the outhouse floor. "They're delicious," Cirino insisted, pushing them across the table. "La *vieja*, my old lady, she is a great cook."

He scooped a portion with a tortilla. "We are people of few words, but watch out. We grow belligerent when crossed. The people in the capital are scared of us."

With that, he abruptly lifted his shirt. A scar snaked from chest to abdomen. He explained that in 1995 he was driving through the mountains of Veracruz, a neighboring state, to meet with other indigenous leaders including Zapatistas, when someone shot the tire of his Subaru. The vehicle rolled down a hill and Cirino broke many bones. The force crushed his lungs. "I was vomiting blood and my kidneys were coming out." He was rushed to the hospital. Two others in the car died.

Cirino dabbed his mustache and called his wife to clean up. He wanted to show us the prisoners, as well as an assembly devoted to the abysmal health conditions in the village. We drove along a dirt track to a butter-colored church, which served as the headquarters of the community police. Ten campesinos stood in front holding machetes and hatchets, their lunch of salted beef hanging on ropes to air dry.

Indigenous highland communities in Mexico frequently have an ambivalent relationship with Catholicism, which was imposed upon them by the cruel Spanish. The Mixtec, like the Maya, had over the ages developed a syncretic system as a way to cope with forced conversion. Pretty much every town in La Montaña has a church at its center, whose congregants cling tightly to their brand of religion, whether syncretic or something closer to doctrinaire. No such pretense was entertained at this house of prayer, which had been converted to purely secular uses: meeting hall, police station, and jail. Murals covered the walls, painted in the two-dimensional style of ancient pictographs, showing battles and bird gods. The scenes bore blood and ochre hues, the faces in profile. The shotguns in the codices seemed oddly modern for a precolonial scene.

"These are not the originals, " Cirino said when asked about this anomaly. "The Europeans stole those, and put them in the British Museum."

We headed to the basement to see the jail, where two unhappy teenagers were locked in a cell the size of a walk-in closet. Thick bars lent the scene the aspect of a medieval dungeon. The wet floor gave off a sharp odor of ammonia, which might have been why the youths were standing despite their evident exhaustion.

The taller of the two, who couldn't have been more than sixteen, explained that he had been urinating on the road when he was picked up.

The guards thought he was a rapist waiting for a victim. The other prisoner said they were from another pueblo and had gotten lost in the dark. "We didn't do anything," he said, looking at the ground.

"That's not true," the guard countered sharply. "They were drunk. They will be reeducated for three months if found guilty."

He explained that the boys would "in due course" face a jury of elders without the benefit of lawyers. This didn't seem to me the fairest practice. These "courts" relied on hearsay and grudges. Cirino, however, argued that his judicial mechanism was more equitable than corrupt government system, where you could buy your way out of trouble with enough influence and pesos. "Anyway, it's how we've always done things here," he concluded.

Onward to the assembly. A nurse was visiting from the nearest clinic hospital, three hours away, in order to discuss maternal and infant mortality. Women normally give birth in the fields or on the dirt floors of their homes. Maternal mortality was officially 50 per 100,000 live births, or about ten times that in developed countries. Cirino said it was actually about double that amount in this region because the government health system didn't keep proper statistics. Infants fared poorly, too. About 18 in 1,000 babies died in their first few months, usually from diarrhea, respiratory infections, or simple malnutrition. That was triple the number in the United States.

We moved upstairs to an airy classroom where twenty elderly campesinos, mostly women, sat in a circle with the guest speaker. Wall charts illustrated the location of ovaries and the nutritional value of pineapples and hyacinths. One picture depicted a breech birth. None in the circle looked younger than seventy; every able-bodied individual was working in the fields. These were the rural grandmothers, the midwives, who delivered the babies and stroked the sweating foreheads of mothers who bled to death.

Cirino proved himself a good listener, head cocked with concern as everyone went around the room, voicing complaints. No one spoke Spanish so Cirino softly translated by my side.

"Do not try to turn the baby around in the womb yourself," the nurse advised.

Victoria Clemente Jacinto, a shriveled great-grandmother of seventy-six years old objected: "The government blames us if the baby dies."

The circle erupted into a chorus of mockery. "What government? Ha! We only see them at election time."

"Like a macho dog looking for a bitch in heat. He leaves as soon as he impregnates her," chimed the man sitting next to me. The women whooped.

Suddenly the group turned to me, shouting out complaints. Wrinkled hands touched mine, grasping in greeting and hope. Cirino tried to explain that I was a reporter, an abstract notion for peasants who don't read newspapers. They thought I could convey their grievances to the authorities. They flashed identity cards so that I could note their names and demands. *We need an ambulance. We need sewage pipes. We need money. We want dignity. We need, we want.* No one had cows. They needed milk for the children. Sewage ran into the creek. They needed potable water. It went on and on. Everyone had a turn.

Cirino listened, sadly. He had heard this all before.

A clap of thunder signaled a fresh onslaught of rain. Uriel whispered that we had better start down the hill before the deluge hit. Cirino walked us to his vehicle. He had to stay until the end of the meeting, but one of his armed guards would drive us back to the big town. "Don't forget us," he said.

During our drive back to Acapulco, two tropical storms met up in one of nature's freak convergences. We only found out later that much of La Montaña had been cut off as a result of flooding for the next two months. Houses were washed away and the whole region was hip-deep in mud. The government sent military cargo planes to rescue tourists from Acapulco's high-rise hotels. But for weeks, no one reached out to the remotest parts of La Montaña.

As we hurtled through falling trees and axle-deep puddles, I thought about Cirino's double bind. They seemed worse off than the Zapatistas, who had taken control of their medical care and education. By full withdrawal into the jungle hills, the Zapatistas had broken centuries of addiction on a distant and dysfunctional government that didn't care about them. The people of La Montaña had been inspired by the Zapatistas but only followed their example halfway. The lack of organization and of powerful advocates like bishops and *internationalistas* conspired against them. Even the weather and heights were more forbidding.

Yet both shared the same quandary: isolation without full political autonomy. The earth's natural barriers had created an isolation that deprived them of the lowland privileges and political clout. But the modern world still managed to intrude in harmful ways—stealing their lumber, raping women, denying them control over their forests. It was hard to imagine the two communities willingly aligning to the rest of the country without some give from the lowlands. And that didn't seem likely. History and the corrupt government had been unkind, and uncaring, and would no doubt continue to be.

Marcos once wrote, "In Mexico, there are revolutions and change, but for the indigenous nothing changes." This seemed painfully true in Mexico's violent mountains.

3

Holding the High Ground of Nothing

"The war is in the mountains," he said. "For as long
as I can remember, they have killed us in the cities
with decrees, not with bullets."

—Gabriel García Márquez, *Love in the Time of
Cholera* (1985)

If the enemy has occupied (the mountains) before
you, do not follow him, but retreat and try to entice
him away.

—Sun Tzu, *The Art of War* (sixth century BC)

Every time I went to Colombia, people explained the nation's long civil
war using their hands. They might run their palms over raised maps
that showed elevation, or draw the country's outline in the air. I often
met civilians who were afraid to utter out loud the name of the Marxist
FARC guerrillas. Instead, they'd make a hushing noise and silently point
upward, alluding to the mountains where the brutal insurgents lurked,
and to the immensity of the Andes range. The longest continuous chain
on earth, its mountains soar more than 10,000 feet and cut the nation
in half. The Andes had enabled the rebels to fight for fifty years, longer
than any other modern insurgency. The FARC, or Revolutionary Armed
Forces of Colombia, roamed in an elevated territory of jungle and deep

gorges, measuring some 115,000 square miles. There are no roads, and the fog and vegetation are so dense that visibility is often just a few yards. You couldn't find a better guerrilla haven. As a result, the conflict still holds Colombia in its grip. In the words of a former national director of planning, "It is as broken a country as they come."

In September 2012, Julio, a guerrilla deserter, waved his fingers as he explained the terrain to me. I was visiting the country to explore whether peace would ever come, and was canvassing a wide array of think tanks, diplomats, and fighters from both camps. We sat in a nearly empty cinder-block house in a shanty area overlooking Bogotá, the capital, where Julio had moved after forsaking the high jungle. The living room was illuminated by a bare light bulb and a flat-screen television that flickered with the evening news. Julio rocked on a chair meant for nursing, an incongruous perch for a former marksman.

He explained, almost apologetically, that the awkward furniture was obtained cheaply. Work was hard to find, and more appropriate seats would have to wait. Nonetheless, city life made him content. His kids could drink milk and attend school, and he slept on a mattress rather than the earth. There were no government air strikes to interrupt his dreams; he no longer spent his days fearing death.

The latest round of peace talks between the FARC's commanders and the government was just beginning, under foreign mediation in Havana and Oslo. At that point we didn't know that a peace accord would be agreed upon four years later, in 2016, but the prospects were promising. The rebels were on the ropes, thanks to an $8 billion infusion by the United States government over the previous dozen years. This money was meant to stifle the drug trafficking that funded the FARC's struggle and supplied 80 percent of the cocaine that went up American noses. With this American cash, the Colombian military had improved intelligence gathering and purchased helicopter gun ships that could quickly deploy and resupply at high elevations. The army grew more precise in its aerial bombardments of jungle camps, inflicting psychological as well as physical damage. All the legendary FARC commanders were dead: the founder, Tirofijo, which means Sureshot, who was born Manuel Marulanda Vélez, and his three henchmen, Raul Reyes, "Mono Jojoy," and Alfonso Cano. Demoralized, eight thousand guerrillas had turned themselves in over the past decade, sometimes walking hundreds of miles to police stations. That was half the entire insurgent force.

I asked: What about the other half? Could a truce work this time, where two previous ones had failed? Julio's hand came up again and made a slicing gesture to draw the geography. On one side lay an area the size of California where most of Colombia's 48 million people lived. On the other, only two million people, including the last holdouts, resided in a region of similar dimensions to Texas. Most of the remaining fighters had been born in mountain jungle camps and knew nothing but war. Why would they stop the narcotics smuggling that enriched them?

FARC fighters had so little contact with the outside world that both their Marxist ideology and their fashion sense were frozen in the early sixties, when the iconic Che Guevara photograph that now adorns T-shirts and posters first spread across the world. Scrappy hair poked out from their caps. They still echoed his rhetoric about a peasant utopia. "We were in our own world," confessed Julio. Geographic isolation from leftist social movements in the cities calcified their myopic worldview. Unlike other Latin American guerrilla movements, such as those in El Salvador or Mexico, the FARC lacked opportunities to exchange ideas with human rights activists or foreigners, other than the ones they took hostage.

The physical isolation resembled that of Albania's highlanders, in that the FARC simply could not be drawn into the mainstream life of the nation-state whose borders they existed within. Like the Albanians trapped within the Kanun's ancient rules, the FARC couldn't see past the peaks. Yet while Albania's steepest topography allowed for the persistence of an insular culture, Colombia's made possible a subculture of more recent vintage, though that subculture was equally alienated from the status quo.

Despite the government's gains—or, perhaps more accurately, the rebels' losses—it was still struggling to pacify the FARC's traditional strongholds. Julio reminded me that the guerrillas were so fond of the terrain that they capitalized the word for mountain, *montaña*, in their communiqués. They signed missives "From the Mountains." Civil wars are often waged over issues of identity—racial, ethnic, religious, economic— all of which are at least somewhat fungible. But attachment to a specific piece of land is not.

As every military strategist has argued, mountains are the hardest places to conquer. No conventional force in history has defeated quick-moving, high-altitude rebels with intimate knowledge of the terrain and the support of its inhabitants. Mountain geography is all to the guerrillas' advantage. An outside force is automatically handicapped because it is less mobile and savvy about the landscape. The golden rule of infantry doctrine suggests a three-to-one ratio of numerical superiority over defending forces. The proportion must be even higher in the mountains. Soldiers must be trained to react to not only three lateral flanks but also to threats from below and above. A heavily loaded patrol will lose every time against a light, fast enemy that knows how to exploit the terrain. Speed, more than armor, represents security. Mountains are simply too burly to secure against mobile bands. The French could not pursue the Islamist rebels of Mali when they retreated to the Tegharghar mountains beyond Timbuktu in 2013. Osama bin Laden could not be tracked down in the caves of Tora Bora after 9/11. For quite some time, the Kurds have been harassing the Turkish government from their elevated havens. The list of undefeated highland warriors goes on and on: the Vietcong; the GAM, or Free Aceh Movement, which fought for an independent Islamic state in Sumatra; the Karen fighters of Burma; the Kurds; and plenty of others. Peace, when it came, came with diplomacy and talks, not outright military defeat.

Taking that into account, could the Colombian army possibly exert force over a rough territory that had not been ruled from the capital for half a century? Julio suggested that I seek answers where the war began in 1964, in a fabled hamlet at the foot of the Los Nevados range.

"Marquetalia," he counseled. "You need to see Marquetalia to understand the war."

◇◇◇◇◇◇

Since World War II, the average guerrilla insurgency has lasted ten years. That's forty years less than the FARC's. Military strategists continually try to dissect the group's startling longevity. In 2003, Stanford University political scientists James Fearon and David Laitin came up with a useful formula. Examining 145 civil wars from 1945 to 1999, they isolated common factors that, surprisingly, were not religious or ethnic grievances. Instead, the conditions most likely to favor prolonged guerrilla activity were a weak or autocratic central state; mountainous terrain; a sympathetic population that sheltered small bands of rebels; and revenues from contraband, like diamonds or cocaine, to fund the fight.

Colombia neatly meets all the criteria. The war would never have lasted so long if the state had managed to establish a presence over its entire territory, a quarter of which rises over 10,000 feet above sea level. From the time of Spanish colonization in 1525, Colombia's rural land-holding has involved large and dispersed agricultural estates. That feudal system basically remains in place: a fraction of the population owns most of the fertile land, which is worked by tenant farmers. The remainder lives off tiny subsistence plots. A government presence in the mountain-ous hinterland would require a major feat of development and marketing: building roads and bridges at high elevations, and then convincing doc-tors and teachers to move there.

As in Mexico, Spanish colonials enslaved many of Colombia's people and stole much of their lands. Over time, the invaders wiped out 90 per-cent of the indigenous population, whom they called *salvajes*, or savages. Today the indigenous compose at best 3.4 percent of the country's total inhabitants, and most hug the Caribbean coast, the Amazon jungle, or the high slopes of the Andes. As a general rule, the *indios* who dwell in the mountains try to remain aloof of the political violence, and they harbor little fondness for either side. (The FARC's rhetorical championing of the poor has not prevented it from demanding food from the native popula-tion.) Around the world, it's common for national governments to ignore the needs of isolated, unassimilated mountain communities, and for flatland elites to misunderstand their traditional ways of life. I saw this dynamic in Albania and Mexico. But here, the problems go well beyond customs, laws, and land rights. There are essentially no government ser-vices for the country's poor highlanders, indigenous or mestizo.

The insurgency has roots in a vicious rivalry between Liberals and Conservatives that has shaped the lives of Colombians, from those who live in the capital to the inhabitants of nearly every far-flung village. Grievances over land ownership, the harsh treatment by plantation own-ers, and the 1948 assassination of the Liberal candidate for president, Jorge Eliécer Gaitán, politicized the peasantry and unleashed a decade of strife that left three hundred thousand people dead. Colombians refer to this carnage as la Violencia. A power-sharing agreement in 1958 failed to defuse the distrust, and Communist and Liberal peasants formed self-defense units to arm themselves against Conservative-sponsored paramil-itaries. Peasants forcibly displaced from their lands and treated harshly by plantation owners went on long marches to largely uninhabited and neglected rural areas of the country, declaring five "independent republics."

The most famed autonomous enclave was Marquetalia, where 1,200 peasants took over an abandoned hacienda, or farm, in the foothills of the towering Nevado del Huila volcano. Their leader, Tirofijo, easily tapped into their desire to own property and be left alone. During colonial times, the area was populated by the Páez tribe that had fiercely resisted the Spanish, and at first they served as guides and cordial neighbors for the newly arrived farmers. According to the official history of the FARC, these armed colonizers, the precursors of the FARC guerrillas, hauled their pigs, sheep, salt, and coffee on mules; they killed their dogs, to prevent their barking from giving them away. They created a commune, cleared the land, and began to extort landowners in the area for cows, milk, and vegetables. This practice of "taxation" set the stage for later financing of the guerrilla movement.

The definitive biography of Tirofijo, by historian Arturo Alape, stresses the role of topography in the rebels' choice to settle in Marquetalia and in the FARC's endurance in the vicinity for the next fifty years. Entitled in Spanish *Los Sueños y las Montañas*, or *The Dreams and the Mountains*, the biography describes the guerrilla commander as a son of the earth, who intuited how to exploit the terrain for guerrilla purposes. Born in a rural southern district of Colombia, "Marulanda was a man of the Mountain," writes Alape. "He was an inhabitant of the density and also intimately knew the secrets that bury and flourish in its geographic depths."

Despite his intimacy with the rough land, the peaceful experiment with autonomy was short-lived. With the Cold War in full swing, the notion of another left-wing bastion in Latin America prompted anxiety in Washington. The United States feared in Marquetalia a replay of Fidel Castro's retreat into the Sierra Maestra mountains of Cuba, from where he organized his revolution. In May 1964, with the backing of Washington, crack troops from the Colombian army attacked Marquetalia with air support. Marulanda and the forty-seven other armed inhabitants camped at the site fought back but, out-gunned and out-numbered, were forced to flee higher up the peaks. From there, Tirofijo later declared all-out insurgency.

Most historians agree that the conflict would probably not have escalated if the United States had not exerted pressure on Bogotá to attack. If the colony had been left alone, it might have withered away or remained a localized irritation. Instead, over the next few decades the guerrillas built up a fighting machine of thousands that fanned out across the entire country, with tenacious strongholds especially in the south. The insurgency in its first two decades capitalized on the frustrations of peasants excluded from a political system that discouraged legitimate opposition and did little to alleviate their severe living conditions. At its height, the FARC claimed more than eighty fronts, each consisting of 95 to 300 combatants.

Successive right-leaning governments were unreceptive to the FARC's demands for comprehensive land reforms that would redistribute the oligarchic elite's property. Over time, the insurgents lost sight of their lofty goals. In the 1980s, ideology took backstage as the FARC mutated into a criminal organization, labeled "terrorist" in Washington, a moniker ideologically motivated but true with respect to the rebels' abuses of human rights. The FARC extorted the very peasants and Indians that it claimed to liberate and gang-pressed many of their sons into its military wing, threatening to kill the parents otherwise. The FARC kidnapped more-affluent civilians, such as politicians and businessmen, for ransom.

Ensuring the survival of *la lucha* (the struggle), the mountains served as fertile grounds to grow and transport coca leaves, which were converted into the cocaine that has provided much of FARC's funding since the 1980s. The ever-entrepreneurial revolutionaries brought in even more money by diversifying into mining gold and other precious metals in their lands. This activity was illegal according to Colombian law, but then, so was the insurgency in the first place.

Confusing matters, two smaller guerrilla groups with similar Marxist-influenced ideology emerged: the ELN (National Liberation Army) and the more urban-oriented M19, or 19th of April Movement. Competing drug cartels and right-wing paramilitaries collaborating with the army joined the mix. Each group committed atrocities; in total, approximately a quarter of a million people were killed, and six million displaced—a number surpassed only by Syria today.

Explaining the FARC mentality, Julio, the former guerrilla, had told me that a lot of fighters like him who joined the movement didn't have the faintest clue about its ideology. They simply wanted a steady supply of meals and adventure. His story was typical of others I'd heard. He grew up miserably poor and orphaned deep in the peasant highlands. From a young age, he made pennies ferrying people across the river on a raft, but it washed away in a storm and he sought work mashing coca leaves at a nearby farm. FARC forces often wandered into the fields to chat with young men like him, and to buy the coca paste. One day, lacking anything better to do, he accompanied them into the mountains. Life was "fun" for a while, especially the bush dance parties and camaraderie, but eventually he tired of the dangers involved. The most immediate reason for his flight was a business transaction that went sour. On the lam, Julio eventually gave himself up at a government demobilization center, received a small honorarium for cooperating with authorities, and was now trying to figure out the next stage.

Yet the weakness of the central state and the economy—and the landscape itself—worked against prospects of peace. By the time of my visit, in 2012, most of the paramilitaries and the M19 had demobilized, the cartels of drug barons like Pablo Escobar had been replaced by smaller smuggling groups, and the ELN was largely irrelevant in its stronghold by the Venezuelan border. All parties were cautious about prospects for a truce between the government and the FARC since two previous ones, in 1985 and 2002, had broken down. Among the think tank fellows and diplomats with whom I spoke in Bogotá, the consensus was that if they didn't get it right in this round, the military stalemate would continue endlessly. Even if the commanders meeting in Cuba and Norway agreed to stop fighting, henchmen back in the bush might prefer to hold on to their weapons and continue to pursue lucrative illicit activities. Not everyone was willing to bow out like Julio had done. If demobilization meant a crummy job shining shoes in the capital, there was little chance that every fighter would give up terrorizing civilians and profiting from illegal businesses.

And then there was the simple fact of geography. Rogue armed bands could seek sanctuary indefinitely in the untamed Andes if they wanted to. FARC fighters were not necessarily indigenous to the southern strongholds that they still held, unlike the Mexican indigenous who staked ancestral claims on their small plots. Yet FARC militants had settled and roamed in these territories for so many decades that they felt entitled to the land and its fruits. Such men would require enormous concessions to give up their freedom and control.

The FARC had become expert at warding off government incursions. They used tree canopies as shields from rain and detection. The thick forests and clouds blanketed inclines, preventing army surveillance aircraft from spotting movement in the vegetation below. The fighters' primary tactic was the night raid, a hit-and-run surprise attack by small bands swift enough to improvise on the spot without needing to radio a command center for instructions. They knew the mud paths so well that they could prowl without night-vision goggles or flashlights. They stationed plain-clothed spies in the sparely scattered homesteads, who warned the guerrillas if government soldiers approached. Then the rebels packed up their hammocks and dispersed further in the thicket. Unlike the army, they didn't need maps. They knew each river and trail, often using rock formations as compasses.

As Jacobo Arenas, the ideological leader of the FARC, recorded in his diary published in 1972: "It was never easy to reach those heights. No roads existed. The paths rose relentlessly to places that were practically impenetrable. During the rainy season the pass became a dangerous bog for animals and people. For hours on end one would not encounter a human house. The icy wind and permanent cold during the ascent numb the body and quickly deplete energy. It was there, on those giant summits, harassed by armed peasants who caused numerous losses, and harassed by the ruthless and steep nature, that the government soldiers were forced to return to their barracks."

◇◇◇◇◇◇◇

Julio's advice to "see Marquetalia" was deceptively simple. The military had recaptured it in 2006, but that didn't make it easy to get there. On previous trips to Colombia, I either visited Bogotá or the coffee plantation heartland, both easily accessible by commercial flights. Naturally no ordinary airline was going to risk missile fire by going to the front lines of south Tolima, the province home to Marquetalia. Going by road was out of the question: while Marquetalia lay 250 miles from Bogotá, there were scant roads and plenty of land mines and hostage takers waiting to pounce.

When covering a civil war, a journalist customarily embeds with one side, and for that you need reliable contacts that trust your bona fides and can guarantee safe passage. I didn't know any rebels besides Julio, who in any event was not the best conduit to the movement, having betrayed it; the terms of his amnesty mandated that he show government troops the hideouts of former comrades. Several colleagues had more reliable associations, but an approach through their intermediaries might have entailed months of waiting while my credentials were scrupulously checked. (Leftist organizations in Latin America, and especially the FARC, commonly assume gringo journalists are from the CIA.) Even if the proper field commander could be tracked down by cell phone, or was satisfied while Googling my name that I was sufficiently impartial, a visit could entail trekking in waist-high grass among anacondas, or being pinned down for months by combat, or contracting cerebral malaria far from a qualified doctor. Bearing in mind the FARC's penchant for hostage taking, I didn't want to arrive unannounced as the Colombian politician Ingrid Betancourt had done in 2002. She was held captive, in chains, for six years, her hair growing past her waist as she waited to be released.

Government forces, however, could ensure an efficient visit to one of the few pieces of rebel ground they held. The same colleague who had introduced me to Julio had a good connection with the army. He contacted one Colonel Gonzalo Moreno in Planadas, the main base of the Eighth Mobile Brigade, the seven-thousand-man force stationed in south Tolima, which had recaptured some territory held by the FARC, including Marquetalia, in 2006. They were keen to show off this symbolic prize and oblige an American taxpayer, whose government had so generously funded the counterinsurgency. The colonel could offer me a sleepover at Marquetalia, barring a major offensive. It wasn't a fail-safe plan, and the trip was almost postponed when the interior minister suddenly expressed interest in traveling at the same time for a photo op on the fabled site. He ultimately decided to cancel for security reasons. Having passed that hurdle, I was on my way. A date was set for September, weather permitting.

Marquetalia sits on a shelf 8,500 feet above sea level, patrolled by eighty soldiers who flew in and out on helicopters because there was no secure ground path to the site. The booby-trapped forest surrounding the locale was rife with potential ambushes and explosives buried under leaves. Because not all helicopters can make the ascent or fly long distances, I would take a number of aircraft over a couple days. First, I would fly commercial from the capital to Neiva, the southern command's hub in a sizzling valley near the equator. From there I would catch a series of military helicopters.

This form of air transport is critical to any mountain combat zone. The first recorded use of a US helicopter in combat was in the mountains of Burma, in 1944, to airlift troops stranded behind enemy lines. Since then, helicopters have profoundly changed mountain battlefields across the world, Afghanistan and Vietnam among them. Along with offering a new platform to shoot from, rotary wing technology addressed some of the logistical problems that dog infantry in steep terrain, above all that poor roads pose challenges to transport, and it takes longer to get from A to B than on flat land. Nevertheless, past a certain altitude—about 10,000 feet—helicopters become useless, since the thin air generally cannot efficiently support diesel engines or heavily loaded aircraft. This is one reason the American military began to use mules in Afghanistan's Hindu Kush.

Even though the Andes reach that altitude, helicopters changed the government's odds in Colombia. Early in the war, soldiers would trek several days to a given position, usually at night, and then risk losing it, since they could not be easily resupplied or easily get their wounded out of harm's way. Helicopters have given the Colombian military the ability to hold ground. Now, wounded men don't have to be carried in litters through mine fields. When someone is badly hurt in the forest, soldiers clear a patch with machetes, and send up flares so that a helicopter can locate the spot and, while hovering, lift the wounded in a basket lowered by cables.

Militarized gun ship helicopters known colloquially as the Arpy, or Harpy, provided a fresh advantage to the Colombian military. In 1986, Colombia received its first Sikorsky UH-60s, known as Black Hawks, from the United States, which are now used by the police, air force, and army to transport troops and materials, as well as for search and rescue. Under another initiative, the Plan Colombia started under the Clinton administration, Washington began to supply helicopters in earnest. Some were sold to the military and others provided for free. Today the fleet numbers about 125, including about 30 Black Hawks. The venture doesn't come cheap. Each Black Hawk costs about $20 million and an hour of flying time runs about $4,000 in fuel. Not only that, but the Colombian military still didn't have enough pilots and mechanics. A pilot needs about five years to train and once qualified is often lured to the private sector.

Modern soldiers generally lug over one hundred pounds of equipment on their backs. This is punishing at low elevations, and even more so at high altitudes where the body is starved of oxygen and has to work twice as hard to breathe. In Marquetalia, the "birds" served as grocery carts, taxis, and ambulances for the men stuck at heights. They ferried every-thing needed on the base: ammunition, eggs, antibiotics, even tick sham-poo for the mine-sniffing dogs. The animals were deemed so valuable to operations that low-sodium kibble was flown in, even as the grunts made do with rice and beans.

It was too risky to take off and land in fog, which can move in with-out notice, grounding aircraft for days. "Be prepared to be stranded," Moreno advised. The weather posed other challenges, too. Owing to its unpredictability, soldiers have to learn to regularize their body tempera-tures, because the weather may range greatly over a twenty-four-hour period and the climate can change radically as they rise in elevation. Col-onel Moreno advised me to bring layers of fleece, wool, and Gore-Tex as protection against "bone-chilling" nights. When I landed in Neiva, the lowlands, on my first leg of the journey, it was beastly hot with static air that felt like someone had opened a pizza oven. Even the trees sweated. The military sent a cattle truck to pick me up at the Benito Salas commer-cial airport and drove to the military base's tarmac, where a pilot sagging from heat exhaustion awaited alongside a Bell LongRanger helicopter.

He handed over a pair of yellow earplugs and ran me through safety procedures in case we crashed. The LongRanger is a light craft, a seven-seater that takes off with a shudder and sways in the wind like a Fer-ris wheel car. My ears popped as we gained altitude and the farmsteads below receded abruptly, giving way to a view of stony waves. The Andes formed more than sixty-five million years ago when the Pacific plate slid beneath South America, lifting sedimentary rocks into folds that from the air resemble a stegosaurus spine. After ten minutes the hard land-scape gave way to a vast emerald expanse. The jungle was dense with flora and fauna, and I could imagine things that slithered and wild cats and men with assault rifles. Suddenly a rectangle came into view, a bowl-like plateau hugged by peaks. With a whirring lurch, we landed on a patch of dirt the size of a football field. Planadas.

Backs bent low, we sprinted awkwardly to the edge of the landing zone, where two uniformed men stood at attention. A colonel with leading-man looks, about forty and trim as a soccer forward, introduced himself as the commander of the base. "Jairo Leguizamon," he said, extending a hand with clear-varnished nails. Colombian military men pay great attention to grooming; many wear braces to straighten their teeth. Leguizamon's had been fixed and matched his pearly manicure. His sidekick, Colonel

Moreno, who had arranged the trip, was a basset hound of a man, with floppy ears and a long oval face. At his side, a glossy chocolate Labrador named Killer wagged his tail and barked in greeting. Trained in sniffing land mines, he was an indispensable member of the team.

Just yards from where we stood were the barracks, one-story buildings of blue and yellow streaked with dirt. After showing me my quarters—the room of a lieutenant who was away at the front—we headed toward the control room for a briefing.

Colonel Moreno was unexpectedly candid about the challenges of consolidating the territory they had recaptured from the FARC. The area had over one hundred scattered villages, all of which had had a major FARC presence during the government's fifty-year absence. Most of these localities housed people whose sons and brothers had joined the movement, either from sympathy or because they were given no choice. They were reluctant to provide intelligence to the government, fearing for the lives of FARC relatives or their own. When the army "retook" Marquetalia, in 2006, the victory proved hollow. The soldiers found only two inhabited houses, while the guerrillas lurked in the surrounding hills, following Mao's mantra: "The enemy advances, we retreat; the enemy camps, we harass; the enemy tires, we attack; the enemy retreats, we pursue." The FARC's low-tech tactics could be continually adapted to changing circumstances. Moreno's description of the FARC's agility and stealth brought to mind the Pashtun of Afghanistan, who also have proved indomitable.

Now under increased pressure, owing to the arrival of helicopters that allowed the government military to remain in place, the FARC had substituted large-scale offensives with the defensive planting of land mines. They would ring a site with explosives and wait for approaching troops. This method was actually killing more soldiers and police than bullets did at the height of the conflict. Colonel Moreno said the guerrillas were the most prolific nongovernment planters of land mines in the world, a difficult claim to prove, although anecdotal evidence suggested he might be right. The previous year the army had deactivated 916 land mines in the area but the rebels simply planted more. The insurgents packed the explosives into tuna fish tins, and sometimes included feces as well, so that bacteria would kill survivors of the initial blast.

We went through a long corridor to a control room crackling with radios. An entire wall was plastered with a satellite map marked

SECRETO in bold yellow letters. Colonel Moreno explained that due to dense vegetation and cloud cover it was difficult to detect the guerrillas' location with reconnaissance planes and satellite imagery. And once the army received intelligence about a given commander's whereabouts, due to inclement weather they might have to wait as much as a week before deploying troops to hunt him down.

Pinned on the wall map were passport-sized photographs of the most-wanted FARC commandos and the nearest positions of government battalions, which bore the perhaps aspirational names of "Dominant," "Phantom," and "Formidable." Colonel Moreno picked up a wooden pointer and ran it over the pictures. If the map was correct, an enemy group was in the vicinity of Planadas as of a week ago. As they traveled by foot or donkey, they couldn't have gotten "too far away."

The photo of a FARC commander, code-named "Sebastian," was crossed out with red felt pen to signify he had been killed. Colonel Moreno made an expansive circle with the stick. "We have soldiers with eight years of experience in this terrain so we're not as blind as we used to be in the mountains, although not as well as the FARC of course. But there are 110 *veredas*, or hamlets, and they all have plainclothes infiltrators. The civilians don't trust us. Isn't that right, Harry?" Moreno turned to a sniper who had just entered the room, a burly guy with periwinkle eyes and yellow hair. Harry agreed. He was the only member of the team to have dated, and then married, a local girl. Their secret romance so endangered her life that he sent her away to Neiva, where he only saw her on leave. Even her father didn't know that she had married a soldier.

Military historians often note that a populace will embrace the government only if it is less dangerous to do so than it is to support the insurgency. During my state-sponsored visit, it became clear that other than Harry the military had gained little credibility with the high-mountain folk. No magic formula to subdue mountain militias exists, although many strategists have prescribed "winning hearts and minds," a phrase coined by the British general Gerald Templer during the attempt to rid the jungle highlands of Malaysia of anticolonial insurgents in the 1950s. Simply put, it means hoping that kindnesses like building schools will prevail where brute force does not. General David Petraeus, whose 2006 manual for counterinsurgency described winning the higher moral ground by protecting civilians and living among them, is one of the more current examples of the idea. However, his strategy in Afghanistan could not overcome the fact that much of the rural population in remote mountain areas backed or was cowed by the Taliban.

Colonel Leguizamon, who had studied at a combat training school for Latin American soldiers in Fort Benning, Georgia, wanted to test Petraeus's method in southern Tolima, but so far he had seen lesser results than the American general had. His number two, Colonel Moreno, admitted that the military had lost potential allies when, upon arrival in Planadas, they occupied the elementary school as their barracks. They later built an alternative school, but many minds, and hearts, had been closed. Fearing that the FARC had infiltrators, the troops were not allowed to socialize with the locals, and remained on base for meals. They couldn't go for a beer or play cards in town. Townspeople could not join the soldiers' Sunday barbecues or games of soccer on the town's only pitch. Only the colonels were allowed to eat out, and then only at one carefully vetted place, the most expensive restaurant in the area, which happened to be on the edge of the landing strip. There they could drink alcohol served in red plastic cups, even though drinking in public, in occupied areas, was not allowed. Harry or another sniper would stand guard five feet away, which made supper a tense experience for ordinary diners.

"It's like the people are standing on the mountains and throwing rocks at us," admitted Colonel Moreno. He didn't exactly blame them, since the state had essentially abandoned them for five decades. But it was "stressful."

The army's most intimate contact with the public was through radio spots calling on rebels to give themselves up and for civilians to resist their overtures. We stopped by the recording booth, where a private with headphones was going through his playlist of propaganda broadcasts. "Don't pay extortions," went one.

"Mr. Guerrilla, present yourself to a military base to demobilize," was the next.

Colonel Moreno particularly liked the following, because it spoke to the younger generation: "Talk with your children. There are people who want to take advantage of their innocence."

I noted that, without incentives, it might be hard to convince the audience to follow these instructions. Colonel Moreno, too, had doubts as to whether the message was getting through. But without face-to-face contact, it was the best they could do.

◇◇◇◇◇◇◇

But neither was the FARC winning hearts and minds. The revolutionary reign in Planadas had sowed terror, not prosperity. At their height, the FARC patrolled in small groups, barging into shops to declare bans on the sales of Coca-Cola, the demon drink of gringo capitalism. They demanded that the deejays at the discotheques play their preferred *cumbia* tunes, and shot dancers whom they suspected of spying. The club still bore bullet holes on the wall. They harassed workers at the barber's and ice cream parlor. The FARC lifted medicine from the pharmacies, helped themselves to chickens at the market, and slapped a "tax" on beer, rendering the popular drink unaffordable for anyone else. The tax is known as the *vacuna*, the vaccination, and it was also demanded in the form of cattle and crops. Planadas's official population of twenty-nine thousand had shrunk to ten thousand due to killings and displacement.

Harry and six other soldiers took me on a tour of the town. Their idea of wooing the populace was to stop at every corner and look around melodramatically with weapons cocked before proceeding down the street. Every step attracted frightened stares and scurrying women, and the streets were nearly empty by the time we reached the main square, a colonial plaza flanked by palm trees and pastel buildings with balustrade balconies. Mules tethered to posts were the only calm beings, placidly snorting in the crisp air.

The men in the helmets and wearing one hundred pounds of gear were mestizos like the townspeople. They all spoke the same language and worshipped the same Jesus Christ. But they still came off as a strange tribe, not just because they originated from other parts of the country, but because the notion of government institutions like the military was so foreign in these parts.

For a decade, municipal officials fled Planadas out of fear that the FARC would kill them, but they had returned a year ago, hanging on the mayor's pink building a sign announcing that the government was the people's choice. Apparently not everyone's, however: the second-story windows had been blown out by a grenade attack on the police station across the street three weeks before. Two cops and a guard dog had been injured. Four feet of sandbags served as a protective barrier in case the assailants intended to return.

I saw the police officer on duty venture from behind his protective barrier to question a disheveled man. The cop explained to me he was stopping the man on account of his appearance: greasy hair down to his collar and an untucked T-shirt, which were the hallmarks of rebels.

"He dresses like a socialist," the cop told me. He handed the suspect a bottle of mango juice to entice him into conversation. They began discussing the state of agriculture. The suspect opined that coffee growers should be paid more. "You see!" the policeman said triumphantly. "That's socialist thinking."

Eventually the cop tired of discussing fair trade practices, and, lacking firm evidence that the man was indeed FARC, let him go. The longhaired fellow sputtered off on his Vespa with a curse. At that point, an aide from the mayor's office poked his head out and with theatrical whispers led me to an iron bench across the street to talk about life under military pacification. Carlos Cardenas wore a red T-shirt with a logo that announced that he worked for the municipal government, unwise should the FARC be seeking victims. He furtively glanced around for eavesdroppers, and shooed away a couple kids playing tag behind us whom he suspected might be miniature spies. He nodded his chin toward a woman with big hoop earrings who was hanging out of a window across from us, smoking a cigarette with ostentatious casualness. Her husband, he whispered, had been jailed for terrorism. Carlos had to be careful what he said in public. "We in the municipal government are not really in charge," he explained, stating the obvious. The kids circled back and Carlos rose from the bench, suggesting to me that it would be wiser to talk by cell phone. He scrawled his number on my notebook.

The light was fading to salmon dusk and it would soon be time for evening Mass. Colombia is a heavily Catholic country, and in many communities the cathedral is a major anchor of social life. Church offers to mediate between the government and the rebels have failed to secure a lasting peace, but individual sanctuaries do sometimes provide zones where worshippers can momentarily forget their earthly struggles. When I arrived at the town's cathedral, the colonels were staging what looked like an invasion of the holy space, gathering with their bodyguards on the steps. They numbered about fifteen heavily armed men including Harry, all of them standing ready for action as the mothers with young children gingerly slid past, eyes downcast.

The brass went inside and sat in a reserved pew. The bodyguards roamed up and down the nave, on alert for potential assassins. There were virtually no other men of fighting age, just government soldiers and children with brushed hair and women in ruffled dresses. The priest delivered a brief blessing, appearing unnerved by the arsenal in a house of God. The sense of occupation deepened when the radio operator in charge of army propaganda took the podium to lead the hymns. I half expected him to play his broadcasts, but he stuck to message, intoning "Our Lord, Jesus Christ," as he strummed an acoustic guitar. The congregation bowed their heads to pray, probably for peace. Or perhaps to be delivered by their would-be earthly saviors, the army.

◇◇◇◇◇◇

Municipal officials like Carlos didn't venture past the town limits because of the threat of assassination or abduction. If they wanted contact with outlying campesinos, they had to lure them to town.

The FARC's enduring demand was for fair distribution of land. So far, the country's lingering patterns of feudal landowning complicated the government's attempts at resolution. Most of Colombia's roads run through the flatlands, where the large landowners hold more than 50 percent of the country's most fertile properties. Aside from not owning their own land, the mountain people felt abandoned because they had no roads over which to move their goods to market.

As part of the campaign to establish good will, the municipality invited a select group of farmers from *veredas* within a four-hour radius to sell products at a pilot market in Planadas. About two hundred farmers donned their best button-down shirts and straw hats and rode on mules or jeeps to sell sugar cane or thick bunches of bananas. The venders were carefully vetted by authorities before they could put plastic nametags around their necks and take their place at wooden tables. While a folklore group in traditional costume did an Andean version of a square dance, creating a festive air, the farmers griped about slow sales. Pyramids of food remained unsold: onions, eggs, plantains, avocados, cassava, tomatoes, beans, and cheese. The average round-trip cost of travel was six dollars, and few had made back that amount in sales. By lunchtime, annoyed families were trussing up hens and filling sacks with other unsold wares.

I chatted with a few of the vendors as they waited for the jeeps that serve as taxis. All had been forced to hand over crops or their sons to the FARC, but they didn't trust the newly returned government either. They were trying to get by without being killed, and were confused about who stood for what when it came to the FARC and the government—a justifiable confusion, seeing that the antagonists had probably lost sight of why they were fighting anymore.

Aside from growing enough to eat, the farming families were vexed by the lack of health care and education. One woman had a stomach tumor the size of a mango bulging from under her T-shirt. The nearest clinic with an X-ray machine was a seven-hour drive away, and she needed to arrange funds to get there. She was also worried how she would pay for chemotherapy or surgery, if it came to that. Thoughts of her own mortality deepened worries about the future of her seven-year-old daughter. The girl didn't read or write, because she dropped out of school. It took her two hours to walk there and two more back, and the mother kept the child home to help with the farm animals. "But what will happen to her when I'm gone?"

Another woman asked me to help her with math. This was the first time she had been to a market and she didn't know how to add. She was shocked when I told her how little she would make selling plantains.

A cluster of people invited me to ride to their hamlet in their beige jeep to see what "pacification" was like. The army had warned me not to leave the city limits without a military escort, but curiosity overcame caution, and I hopped up onto the backseat, crammed next to five people and sacks of oranges that went unsold at the market. My immediate neighbor was Magdalena Gonzalez, a heavyset, sullen woman of around fifty, the civilian "president" of the vereda El Silencio.

"Must be a quiet place," I ventured conversationally.

"Not at all," she replied stiffly, with that pointing-upward gesture, which meant the FARC. "The government is not in control. You never know when they," she looked up at the rock face towering above us, "will show up."

Within five minutes we were outside the town limit, driving up a dirt road, gravel flying out from under the wheels. We passed only one sign of settlement, a wooden shack with a corrugated roof fanned by banana leaves, the archetypal dwelling of rural Latin America. Then we saw only tall weeds, and mountain faces jutting out like huge arrowheads.

Over the next half an hour, the passengers went into elaborate detail about who had left their town and who had stayed, with some debate over people who may have gone for a short period but might return eventually. There were only forty-eight of them now, said a man in a straw hat in front, without turning his head. There were problems with coffee pests and drought, so people made less money this year and left. They couldn't pay the vacuna, essentially a war tax, demanded by the FARC.

Eventually a creek came into view, speckled by the cobalt glint of Morpho butterflies, next to a wooden shed that advertised beer and ice cream. Overhead a billboard declared "We Like Our Mayor."

"We don't," Gonzalez said tartly.

The car stopped in front of a wooden footbridge, which Gonzalez and I crossed to have a look at a building freckled with bullet holes. This was the elementary school, where seventy children were supposed to do multiplication tables in one room, if they could manage the punishing walk there and home again. In any case it was a moot point: the school had closed because the teacher stopped showing up.

Suddenly a man appeared from the trees beyond, a jittery gargoyle who ran toward me and grabbed my sleeve. He wore the plastic sandals of peasants and a sneer. *FARC*, I thought. *He wants to kidnap me.* Gonzalez backed away, and darted across the bridge toward the car, waving vigorously for me to follow. *Váyase ahoritica mismo*, she screamed. "Get away right now!"

I shook my arm free and galloped toward the vehicle. The motor was running and Gonzalez pulled me onto the seat and shut the door. I tilted onto her lap as the car hurtled off. "He's from . . ." She pointed upward.

We passed a mule driver and picked up speed, forcing him to the shoulder of the road. Gonzalez looked at his disappearing frame through the back window as we sped back toward Planadas.

"Pacification," she hissed. "*Estamos en la olla*. We are in a bad situation."

They sure were. These civilian pawns were trapped between a politically exclusionary state and cynical guerrillas. Even if there were a strong local government offering political representation and expression, the state had failed to build roads that could handle tanks and trucks. These peasant farmers were even worse off than the Zapatista or Kanun communities, because they lacked the social cohesion that provided meaning and, to some extent, rules to live by. Thanks to the mountains, the

Colombian peasants living around Marquetalia were marooned and unmoored. While the mountains insulated the Zapatistas, and the people of La Montaña, from viciousness and corruption, to some extent, here the peaks perpetrated the ruthlessness of the FARC and the failure of the state. That robbed the disempowered citizens agency to live with dignity and safety.

◇◇◇◇◇◇

The next day I waited for a Black Hawk to take me to Marquetalia. I was on the landing zone at 9:00 a.m. but rain elsewhere postponed the flight. Four hours later, a black speck whirred into sight.

A Black Hawk can hold eighteen men with equipment. The cargo this trip included fifteen humans, seventeen crates of eggs, ten sacks of onions, ten more of beans and rice, several huge plastic bladders of water, and slabs of meat. Food shipments only arrive every two weeks so soldiers have to carry enough rations to last a fortnight, plus extra in case flights are held up, sometimes for a few days, by the weather. The men piled in and took positions on the floor, gripping straps hanging from the ceiling or leaning against each other for balance. They waved me toward a blue plastic crate next to the machine gunner, who was manning the open door.

Colonel Leguizamon came along for the ride. "Ah, Marquetalia," he breathed sensually. He strapped on his helmet and crossed himself, murmuring a small prayer. "Accidents are inevitable," he explained. He had survived one when the motor failed, but they were only fifteen feet off the ground so no one was seriously hurt. Leguizamon looked toward the window and pointed out the vegetation and ridges that made it perilous to crash-land. Then he gave a thumb's up and we wobbled upward over a cascade of green. The gunner smiled amiably and fished a cell phone from his pocket. "Baby, we're off," he texted to someone. He remained immersed in the screen for most of the trip, missing the dazzling view outside.

After about half an hour he put the phone away and fixed his hands on his machine gun. We swung through a canyon toward a plume of smoke rising from a crest. The aircraft made wide arcs toward the cliff where little waving figures gathered around a circle of white painted rocks.

The craft plunked down, sending pebbles and dirt flying. We ran out through the swirling dust. An assembly line of soldiers tossed backpacks and cargo toward the camp area, one hundred feet away. A worried man in civilian dress whom I took to be a prisoner, flanked by uniformed soldiers on each side, was pushed into the chopper. He was followed by more troops, who jumped in and slammed the door shut. The helicopter sailed off, its whirring still audible after the dot disappeared into the gray haze.

We stood exposed on a slice of ridge 450 feet wide. The precipice was a sheer drop two miles down, and there was no fence. With just a glance I took in the entire camp. The soldiers had pitched tents in a clearing about the size of a football field, fringed by a spooky fairy-tale forest of vines and masts of oaks that hid unseen beings, the guerrillas. The distant triangles of mountains looked like green, purple, and blue shadows in a sky that went on forever. I suffer from terrible vertigo and have never felt more vulnerable. My legs shook. I feared losing my footing and plunging off the edge, down into the forest studded with land mines.

A tempting silver snake of a river lay at the bottom of the slope, but because of mines the troops rarely left the summit to refill water jugs. It hadn't rained in eighteen days, and they were rationing water. A small hole in the ground provided liquid mud to be strained but it had nearly run dry. The men were getting so thirsty that they'd resorted to squeezing drops of moisture from moss and licking it from their hands.

We walked a few yards to some bunkers carved from the earth, lined with tarps and covered with brush, where the commander delivered me to Roberto Tuta, a mortarman and founder of the brigade that had taken Marquetalia from the FARC six years prior. Tuta had wrapped a black do-rag around his head, which emphasized his razor cheekbones and intense slanted eyes. His features gave him away as a highlander; the country's mountain battalions favor recruits from the Andes accustomed to thin air. Soldiers unprepared for altitude can die when fluid rushes to the brain or lungs. At 8,000 to 14,000 feet, most human bodies begin to grow weak; few people can cope at 18,000. The Colombian military has found that dark-skinned soldiers from coastal areas often suffer from altitude sickness and for that reason prefers to deploy men who grew up at elevations. Tuta appeared to have adequately adapted to this altitude, 8,500 feet, but I had a hammering headache that gripped my temples like an iron winch.

Aside from an ability to breathe high up, the guys had spent so much time on this particular slope that they had come to resemble a mountain culture itself, with unique dress (green uniforms), dialect (military slang), and architecture (bunkers and tents). They even had their own mythology, exaggerated tales of heroism and failure. Like mountain clans everywhere, they distrusted those outside this intimate circle.

Tuta said the second "liberation" of Marquetalia by the army was as empty as the first, back in 1964. The military had advanced from a small town called Gaitania to this ridge-top prize, and once again, the FARC had simply dispersed deeper into the wilderness. Throughout the three-year operation, they moved ahead of the troops, laying mines in their wake. The army's elite Eighth Mobile Brigade, men hardened by mountain operations, shouldered huge losses. Of the original 1,100 men, only 80 remained in service today. They didn't have mine detection and removal teams, and when the daily air bombardment drove the guerrillas further into the bush, civilian spies ran ahead to warn the insurgents to plant more explosives, which the troops walked right into. "I'd never seen such a sight. There were legs and blood everywhere," Tuta recalled grimly. By the time the brigade had seized its objective, most of its members had lost limbs or lives. Many survivors stayed on. Because it was so hard to obtain intimate knowledge of the rugged terrain, those who had been there since the start, like Tuta, were forced to remain in the environs. They rarely had furloughs; some, he said, had gone mad. He stared at the sinister emptiness beyond, the abyss of the sky and the tangled vegetation. Just the previous day, the men had found eighteen crude devices buried in leaves nearby. A stumble could cost a man his testicles and legs, if not his life.

With that, we began a circle around the encampment. I needed to use a latrine. Hygiene always poses challenges for the rare woman on all-male military bases, and doubly so on a thin sliver of earth atop a mountain. A lengthy discussion ensued about where I would "move my body," as Tuta put it. In such a confined living space one had to shovel a deep hole right beyond the sleeping quarters and cover it with sufficient soil to obscure the germs and stench. To avoid ambushes during such vulnerable moments, the base was designed so that the sentries had a view of the bathroom area at all times. For modesty's sake, Tuta suggested that I squat behind the sandbags that protected the sleeping quarters from Danger, the resident sniffer dog. True to his name, Danger did not appreciate a stranger marking his territory and he lunged with bared teeth. The dog's handler held him back with a leash, eyes averted, until my mission was completed.

We walked to the edge of the cliff, where an M-30 mortar was pointed at Tirofijo's old house, a silver-roofed cottage about a mile down where his cabal had first decided to launch the war. Tuta confessed that he would love to shoot at it. Then we made our way to the highest point of the saddle, which melted into the jungle. There we encountered a trio of headless dummies in fatigues, draped with rusty tin cans intended to jangle and alert guards to intruders. A crude wooden cross, hammered into the ground just beyond, indicated that the system sometimes failed: five rebels had jumped the sentry while he did guard duty, a couple years back. "He didn't have a chance," Tuta commented.

It was strange to think that a place so open to the elements could feel so claustrophobic. But the encampment reminded me of isolated offshore oil rigs I've visited in the North Sea, only it was worse here because this sky-high island could be attacked at any moment and there was no lifeboat to make an emergency exit. As we walked back to the bunker, Tuta explained that they had destroyed thirteen thousand pounds of explosives found in the area. Land mines prevented them from leaving the ridge, and the simple task of fetching water from the Ata River below became an ordeal. Going down the hill involved a six-hour hike accompanied by Danger, the sniffer dog, and a handheld German mine detector. The men treaded carefully in the footsteps of those in front, vigilant not to slip even an inch. Everyone halted if the dog scented something suspicious. He would circle in an inhaling frenzy until he located the right spot and sit next to it wagging energetically. Then the men set off the explosives and handed Danger a rubber ball in reward. By the time the group returned to the crest, they were so sweaty from the exertion that they needed to drink even more.

Apart from thirst, men had to contend with boredom. Many of them, including Tuta, had been stationed here for six years. Marquetalia didn't provide much diversion beyond texting: the space was too thin to play soccer, given the risk someone could fall off the edge. Troops had to switch off power at night to save fuel. The men rotated in and out every three months and they lived for these furloughs, counting the hours until they could get away. Not surprisingly, many marriages collapsed due to long absences, and Internet flirting with potential new mates had become a popular activity. At every chance, the soldiers consulted their cell phones. The replies were announced by the *BAM BAM* crack of a pistol, the ringtone then in vogue among the troops. The sound made me jump but, as they pointed out, this was war.

The ever-present cyber activity created a huge security risk. The men frequently Facebooked with strangers who, for all they knew, could be guerrillas posing as girls seeking romantic connections. Tuta said officers didn't have the heart to ban phone usage, as that was the soldiers' only link with civilization.

To otherwise break the monotony, the soldiers spent an inordinate amount of energy planning menus, incorporating dishes from Colombia's diverse regions. Alcohol was banned, so flavorsome condiments like hot peppers took on added importance and the meals provided structure in otherwise tedious days. Normally soldiers can burn up to six thousand calories at high altitude, but these men were barely moving around so they were getting fat. They pulled up their shirts to show distended bellies, almost like those of pregnant women.

Dinner that evening was *sancocho*, a thick stew of the chicken that had sat next to me on the helicopter. Due to lack of refrigeration, perishables have to be eaten right away, and then it's back to lentils and beans until the next flight comes two weeks later. The men were desperate for the fresh meat, as well as conversation with a new face. They tried out English phrases learned in elementary school, and everyone asked how to get an American visa. They all wanted to get off the crest, in any way possible.

Tuta fished a paperback out of his pocket, thumbed and dog-eared to the point of disintegration. I thought he was going to read a psalm from the Bible but the book was *Tirofijo: Los sueños y las montañas*, the biography of the FARC's founder, aka Marulanda.

"Don't steal the title or the FARC will kill you," one of the guys joked.

Tuta cleared his throat and enunciated ponderously for dramatic effect.

"'Marulanda had a sense of the Mountain as a totality. He had lived as a refugee in precipitous flight. He had breathed it as though it were a propitious space, for war and for peace. He knew it in his movements of calm and convulsion, of arrival and departure, as though the Mountain would draw in the lines of his hands and reflect a mirror on memory.'"

Tuta put his right index finger to his temple, mimicking a gun as though shooting himself. "That's what we're up against. I wish I could get off this mountain."

With each conflict I reported on, I understood a little bit more about violence in the mountains. This was an impossible, fifty-year-old civil war that had morphed over the decades from a bona fide revolution for self-determination and economic equity into a huge, highly successful criminal establishment. But despite this dramatic shift in the FARC's raison d'etre, the fight remained, basically, the same: It was a standoff between a corrupt, at times brutal government, and armed insurgency-cum-organized crime. Like in Mexico, there was a single layer of conflict, uncomplicated by other factors like sectarianism or clan violence. The conflict was limited to certain areas and communities, and meanwhile, life went on in relative normalcy in the rest of the country.

However, for the people unlucky enough to live in territory occupied by the FARC or other armed forces, the war indeed took over their lives, and seemed, I'm sure, irreparably twisted and knotty. Where there had once been clear sides, now, with various paramilitaries, insurgency groups, and drug cartels entering and exiting over the years, there was just an enormous mess. And it didn't seem to be going away anytime soon.

As night fell, the inky dark rendered even my feet invisible. The soldiers said that sometimes monkeys howled, but tonight they had gone quiet in the fog that clung to the cliff. Even the fireflies had retired their flickers for the night.

The only illumination came from a cell phone: the sentry on duty was texting a faraway girl from his perch on the edge of the promontory. Sound amplifies at night in mountains, and the *BAM BAM* ringtone echoed loudly through the canyons below. Tuta hissed at the guard to turn off his phone. "Look for your hand," Tuta murmured as I squinted into nothingness, a vertiginous sensation. "You can't see it, right? This is like the Alamo. There's nothing out there but guerrillas. But where?"

We switched on our headlamps and walked slowly and very carefully, one foot in front of the other, to the bunkers, tunneled out of the earth and covered by branches in order to blend in with the forest floor. Inside one of the burrows I unfolded my sleeping bag on a plastic tarp skunky with the smell of men who have gone weeks without baths.

Tuta recommended that I relieve myself right outside the bunker, so as to avoid falling off the cliff on the way to Danger's latrine, which was situated deeper into the base. Fortunately I felt little need, as the only liquid the troops offered at dinner was a cup of chicken soup. The two bottles of water that I'd brought remained inside my daypack in case the helicopter couldn't pick me up the next day as planned.

I slid into my sleeping bag and turned off the flashlight. Sand crunched from the guard who was pacing overhead. At least, I hoped it was the guard. Curled up like a squirrel inside its drey, I lay awake, thinking about human predators with keen eyes and soft feet.

◇◇◇◇◇◇◇

The next morning, rain clouds were gathering faintly in the purple distance, but they stayed far enough away that we could fly back to Planadas. The troops went to the promontory and lit a bonfire to guide the helicopter in. A sergeant got on the radio, a boxy thing the size of a toaster, and reported, "Possible enemy three kilometers away," giving coordinates. Soon, another whirling black speck appeared, getting bigger as it approached.

No one wasted time when the helicopter landed. Outgoing soldiers tossed in rucksacks and empty water jugs. Those staying behind snapped final pictures to post on Facebook. We did a couple of loops, perhaps because of the possible enemy three kilometers away, and flew over the rocks in the sky toward Planadas.

As Marquetalia receded to a dark dot, I wondered why they thought holding this forsaken bit of high ground gave them such an advantage. An elevated vantage point enables observation, certainly, but not when such thick vegetation covers the surroundings, and when you are too high in the mountains to resupply easily. There are also downsides to being high up. In *On War*, Carl von Clausewitz examined the case of the higher Alps, noting that they were so difficult to access that it would be "impossible" to place a considerable body of men there. "Now if we must positively have armies in mountains to keep possession of them, there is nothing to be done but to place them in the valleys," he wrote. "At first sight this appears erroneous, because, in accordance with the prevalent theoretical ideas, it will be said, the heights command the valleys. But that is really not the case. Mountain ridges are only accessible by a few paths and crude tracks, with a few exceptions only passable for infantry, whilst the carriage roads are in the valleys."

So, too, establishing a camp in Marquetalia didn't mean much, even with the advent of helicopters, which came after Clausewitz's time and have proved so critical in mountain combat. As long as armed men were motivated by money and power, as long as people preferred the freedom afforded by the mountains, no one would be able to control the territory lying below and beyond. The FARC used the mountains as a convenient and indomitable shield, just like the narcotics cartels and poppy grow-ers of La Montaña and elsewhere in Mexico. Plan Colombia may have pushed the guerrillas to negotiate, but it had failed to make big strides in the war against drugs entering the United States. The mountains would always serve as a bulwark to order and peace.

The army held the high ground, but not much else.

4

The Dammed

Drown or die—what choice is there
Is this all that you fear?
Millions die and millions drown
To maintain the ways of the world

—Siddhicharan Shrestha, "Sankat" (The Crisis)
(1945)

The Himalayas are the adolescents of the mountain world, outstretching their elders in heights but still prone to unpredictable and destructive behavior. The plates lying under their surface work like seismic hormones, pushing against each other to unleash epic earthquakes. The range is the highest and the youngest in the world, spanning 1,500 miles of fragile geology.

It also provides nearly half the world's population with one of its most basic needs: water. *Himalayas* is a Sanskrit word meaning "abode of snow." The roughly fifteen thousand glaciers in these mountains account for the largest mass of ice and snow outside the north and south poles. The melt from the glacial crowns supplies Asian rivers on which billions of people depend.

By some estimates, the Himalayas harbor a water tank of three thousand cubic miles. This precious resource has triggered a contest among the Himalayas' five nations—India, Nepal, Bhutan, China, and Pakistan—to divert rivers for agriculture and to power their booming economies, exacerbating the tensions between these uneasy neighbors. India's

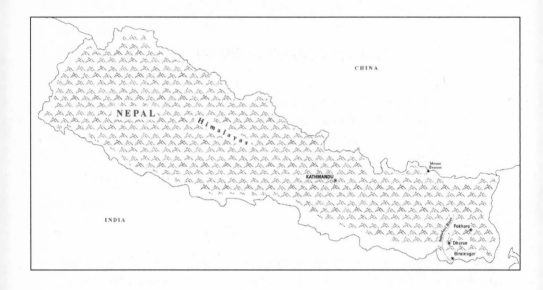

diversion of the Indus, for instance, angers Pakistan and complicates the dispute over Kashmir. The situation is also causing internal problems for each country, as minorities in the mountains resist their central governments' efforts to build hydroelectric dams on their ancient homelands.

One satellite map of the massifs shows little dots representing the sites of dams already constructed, so many as to create nearly solid lines. These are just the ones that already exist. Between them the five nations are planning five hundred more dams in nearly all of the thirty-two major river valleys, which combined could provide more than 300,000 megawatts of electricity. These mountains of concrete would figure among the highest anywhere, and would make the range the most dammed on earth.

There are plans to build another dam along the Saptakosi River in Nepal. (*Sapta* means "seven" in Sanskrit, so named for its upper tributaries.) Also known as the Kosi, it drains some of the world's highest mountains, including Everest. The river rises in Tibet, flows east to Nepal, and crosses into the Bihar plains of India where it joins the Ganges. The indigenous Rai, who make up only 2.8 percent of Nepal's population, have lived above the river's banks for as long as anyone can remember. They worship the Saptakosi and bury their dead near its waters. And they are willing to die to ensure the dam is never built.

◇◇◇◇◇◇

A landlocked country of only twenty-eight million people, Nepal's destiny has been shaped by geography. Mountains cover 64 percent of its territory. Among them are eight of the world's highest peaks, including Mount Everest. The profusion of mountains make road building prohibitively expensive; Nepal is one of the least developed countries in the world, with more than 80 percent of its population depending on subsistence agriculture. It is wedged between the world's two most populous countries, China and India—like "a yam between two boulders," as Nepalis say, meaning that the two giants compete for influence and contracts to build dams for transborder hydroelectric power.

As the gateway to Tibet, Nepal takes in many refugees from that territory. China has been ingratiating itself with the Nepali government, most notably by providing aid after the devastating 2015 earthquake, in an attempt to forestall dissent among the Tibetan exiles living there. However, the Himalayas pose a physical barrier to getting goods from

China, leaving Nepal dependent on India to the south for nearly every necessity. Nepal's main access to the sea is through the port of Calcutta. India's economic heft has fueled Nepali conspiracy theories that its huge neighbor wants to control water resources and rule by proxy as well.

Never colonized by a European power, Nepal has been independent since 1768. Beginning in the nineteenth century, the kingdom of Nepal was ruled by the ruthless Rana dynasty. These hereditary prime ministers sidelined the monarchy and closed the country to the outside. That might explain why Nepal continues to defy conformity: its national flag is the only one in the world that is not square or rectangular; the banner consists of two triangle-shaped pennants on top of each other. The time zone is unique to Nepal, and fifteen minutes off India's, despite the two countries being on the same longitudinal spread. The calendar is fifty-six years and eight months ahead of AD.

A revolt in 1950 restored the crown's full power. After an initial move toward democracy, the monarchy disbanded the parliament in 1960 and banned political parties for the next quarter century. Not until 1990 were they legalized again, when nationwide turbulence forced the kingdom to establish a pluralist parliamentary system. But the unrest grew, and in 1996, Maoist radicals launched a decades-long "People's War." Eastern Nepal became a stronghold of the movement, which found fertile recruiting grounds among landless hill people. Operating clandestinely in remote areas away from the government's eye, activists trekked for miles from village to village to mobilize support.

Following the collapse of the Soviet Union in 1991, the fissure between the Maoists and the more moderate Communist faction, which had first emerged in 1949, deepened. The Maoists were inspired by the Shining Path (*Sendero Luminoso*) guerrillas of Peru, who mobilized indigenous fighters from the Andean highlands. The Maoist rebels hailed from the mountains, fought in the mountains, and hid in the mountains. Beginning in the remote center-west of the country, the insurgency eventually spread to nearly all seventy-five of the nation's districts. Due to porous borders, they easily ran guns and resupplied from India.

The insurgents set up a parallel government and courts, promising to redistribute land and improve lives for the peasantry. Yet like the Shining Path, as well as the FARC in Colombia, they squandered popular support through their brutal methods. They kidnapped children and forced them to fight; they also robbed, murdered, and extorted "taxes" from the people in their lands. The United States declared them terrorists and provided the Nepali military with training, helicopters, and arms to bolster counterinsurgency efforts. Over the course of the rebellion, more than fifteen thousand people died.

In 2006, the parliamentary system was reinstated and a peace accord ended the war. The monarchy was dissolved in 2008, and Nepal established a republic that enjoys the active political participation of the Maoists today. However, their lofty goals to better the lives of rural peasants has not led to living improvements in the mountains where they fought. The isolated villages are just as poor, just as marginalized, and just as suspicious of outsiders who want to seize their land or flood it with dams.

Nepal's high crests and yawning valleys created isolated communities. The nation is home to a diverse quilt of peoples: four main classes and 36 castes, which are divided into subgroups that speak 120 languages in total. The mountains' best-known export were the Gurkha warriors who figured among the British Empire's—and now the Commonwealth's— fiercest soldiers. Those who remained at home passed their bellicosity to ensuing generations, including the Maoist faction.

Your average Nepali has a deep attachment to the highlands. This becomes clear to any visitor to the International Mountain Museum, the only one of its kind on earth. It's located in Pokhara, in the western part of the country, in the foothills of the tourist trekking region. Built to resemble the Himalayan skyline, the exhibition halls feature the lives and costumes of highland tribes, taxidermied wildlife, expeditions, geology, and climbing gear. A Tibetan prayer room allows one to meditate over nature's majesty. Other galleries display everything from trash left on Everest to written ruminations on the mythical Yeti ("probably just a brown bear").

The topography inspires spirituality as well as museum going, and many of the indigenous animists worship one peak or another. Quite a few of Nepal's holy sites are located in high places, next to rivers, that other mighty geography feature.

Among the rivers with headwaters in the Himalayas, the Kosi is the angriest in the monsoon season. Indians call it the "Sorrow of Bihar" for the load of silt and debris it carries, which causes devastating floods. The river last unleashed its sorrow on August 18, 2008, when waters breached an embankment and drenched the lands of 2.3 million people in Bihar, the northern heartland of India. More than 250 died.

Not surprisingly, the river figures in folklore as a spiteful woman, or a monster whose various arms cut channels through fields. In some places she is viewed more benignly, as a free-spirited virgin determined to remain single. Women beg her not to get mad and sprinkle sweets and turmeric, a symbol of marriage, to scare off annihilation.

For the highland Rai, who live hundreds of feet above her banks, the Kosi Ma, or Mother, offers everything essential to life. She provides fish to eat and water for bathing, tea, and gardening. Her glacial waters purify the soul. The Rai believe they cannot survive without the Kosi Ma.

For that reason, villagers were horrified to hear about plans to build an 883-foot-high dam that would submerge their native territory. The awkwardly named Joint India-Nepal Saptakosi High Dam Multipurpose Project would involve a concrete-or-rock-filled dam, a barrage, and canals that would provide 3,000 megawatts of hydropower. It would control floods and aid irrigation downstream. However, most of the power would go to India, an affront to the 60 percent of Nepalis who lack electricity. Neither government has mentioned compensation for the estimated seventy-five thousand oustees, the quaint Indian term for people displaced by dams. All oustees would be Nepali, and India says that is not its problem. Nor has anyone addressed potential devastation in the not-so-unlikely event of an earthquake, which could potentially damage the foundation and cause devastating floods.

◇◇◇◇◇◇◇

Near the end of 2015 I visited Nepal to learn more about the Rai's growing opposition to the Kosi project. This indigenous group that would lose traditional lands was not the only opponents. So were many experts in engineering and water management, whom I interviewed in Nepal's capital, Katmandu, before traveling to the proposed dam site.

"We're damned," sputtered Dipak Gyali, a former water minister in a previous Nepali government whom I consulted about Kosi. Despite the pun, he was furious. Gyali pointed out that India's designs on the river added nationalist fury to an otherwise local dispute. Criticizing India's terrible record of compensating oustees, he acknowledged that Nepal had made the same mistake by not engaging the Rai. Gyali rattled off a dizzying list of places in the Himalayas where protests that had surged against big dams had the potential to grow violent: Tibet, Nepal's Upper Karnali, and northern mountainous areas of India, including Uttarakhand, Himachal Pradesh, Sikkim, Assam, and Arunachal Pradesh.

High dams, Gyali noted, can only be built in highlands. In order to harvest water, one should ideally consult the farmers and fishermen who will lose their homes. Otherwise, he predicted, "water will exacerbate other conflicts and poison the well."

Gyali noted UN estimates that around 1.2 billion people, or nearly one-fifth of humanity, inhabit areas of physical scarcity. The looming water crisis threatens to ensnare an additional five hundred million, due to population growth and climate change. Water use has been growing at more than twice the rate of population increase in the last century, and more and more regions are chronically short of water, especially in the Middle East and Asia. The highlands are critical, because that's where rivers originate, and also where they are dammed.

Gyali gave me examples of transboundary water quarrels involving mountainous regions, starting with Israel's defense of the Golan Heights not only to protect its sovereignty but also to hydrate its fields. Egypt once threatened to attack Ethiopia if it built a dam—it would've been Africa's largest—on the Nile. (War was eventually averted and the project went ahead.) Syria and Iraq at various times came close to military confrontation with Turkey over dams that affect their access to the Euphrates and Tigris. India steals Pakistan's water in disputed mountainous Kashmir, according to Hafiz Saeed, leader of the extremist group Lashkar-e-Taiba, which was linked to the Mumbai hotel attacks of 2008. He threatened jihad over India's "water terrorism."

All these disputes, Giyali noted, were transboundary. He expected that most tensions in the future would largely be of a more local nature, like the Rai's.

◇◇◇◇◇◇

Nepal is shaped like a brick, and the site for the dam lay in the Terai, in the southeastern corner. To get there, I needed to fly from the capital to Biratnagar, an ugly industrial hub of jute mills and factories. The city lies near the border with India, on plains that used to be rain forests until they were cleared in the 1950s to expand agriculture and extinguish malaria. Many highlanders who were running out of arable land on the slopes migrated there. After arriving in Biratnagar, I'd head for the foothills. In order to reach them, I'd hire a jeep, drive for an hour until the rutted road ended, and then walk for several hours on a cliff overlooking the Kosi.

At the time, the area was convulsed by unrest, though one not as extreme as the Maoists'. The Madhesis, a minority group, felt that Nepal's new constitution awarded them too little representation. In protest, they blocked entry points at the Indian border and attacked vehicles that tried to pass. Nepal relies on this crossing to import essential goods, and the result was shortages of cooking gas, diapers, and fuel throughout the country. The riots had killed dozens of people and threatened the lives of hospital patients who couldn't get medicine. The newspapers said the humanitarian crisis was worse than that caused by the 7.8 magnitude earthquake seven months before.

Many Madhesis have family across the border, fueling claims by Nepal's intelligentsia that India was fomenting the unrest. Nepalis will tell you in no uncertain terms that India is to blame for all their country's instability. It was India that brought down the monarchy that had ruled for centuries, they say. India armed the recent Maoist insurgency. I even heard people go so far as to blame the last earthquake on India, noting that the tectonic plate beneath it had crashed under the Eurasian plate. A joke was making the rounds: *What's the similarity between an Indian blockhead and the earthquake? They both push northward into Nepal.*

Many in Nepal now believed New Delhi was igniting these protests. India, they said, wanted a buffer against Nepal itself. India had another reason to meddle, several hydroelectrical experts told me: Himalayan melt. About 47 percent of the water used by India's 1.3 billion citizens comes from the Ganges. The Ganges in turn relies on the Kosi, especially during the dry months of February through April. That's when Nepal's rivers contribute 72 percent of the flow.

"What India wants, she can't say openly," asserted Santa Bahadur Pun, one-time managing director of the Nepal Electricity Authority. "It's to control water resources in eastern Terai. You can only build dams high up in the mountains, not in the plains. That's why India wants Nepal in its pocket."

A journalist from Terai offered to introduce me to dam protestors in the mountains and serve as translator. The affected highlands lay off the usual trekkers' path, without the Sherpas and campsites enjoyed by foreign climbers elsewhere. Being nominally responsible for my comfort, the translator, Deepak, wanted to ensure I understood the conditions before we set out. Lodging would be "rudimentary" and the walk "unsafe." Pressed for specifics, he shared that we'd stay in simple teahouses lacking running water. I should not expect clean latrines. As for the hike—well, leave vertigo at home and bring a sturdy walking stick.

The one-hour flight to Biratnagar took us past an icy crown of peaks, so glorious that I momentarily forgot my anxiety about the rioters who awaited us on the other end. "One of them is Everest, I think," said Deepak, leaning toward the window to get a better glimpse. "We have so many mountains I can't keep track of them all." The sight of these lofty heights provoked him to meditate about mountain people, of whom Deepak was one. We had a mutual friend from Kashmir, and Deepak said they had struck an instant rapport as highlanders.

"Mountain people have a different perspective," Deepak explained, in almost the very same words as the Frenchman Jean Lassalle, the head of the World Mountain People Association. "Hill people have to be more resilient and robust. You're always curious about what's on the other side. It's the opposite for the plains people, like my wife. She was scared when I took her to my village. The house was on a slope. She feared a landslide and could not sleep."

The mountains grew browner and greener as we neared the eastern Terai, and then a sharp jolt of landing brought us onto the earth. Passengers pushed to deplane first and grab their bags off the tarmac, where they'd been dumped unceremoniously. The driver I'd hired, a thin middle-aged man named Govinda, was there to greet us. We briefly discussed how to power through Ituri, the highway town that connected east and west Nepal. Hostile Madhesis were blocking this major artery. Govinda managed to fill his tank with black market petrol but was worried that the protestors might pounce upon us with sickles and long knives. They recently set an ambulance on fire and burned a man to death. If road conditions were really bad, we'd jump out and take an electric rickshaw instead.

Serendipitously, we had arrived during a mysterious hiatus in the upheaval. For no apparent reason the protestors were allowing traffic to proceed normally. Govinda gunned the engine in case they changed their minds. Leaving town, we rode on a dusty dirt track through what was left of the rain forest. The villages grew less frequent as the miles stretched on. Every now and then we passed huts with thatched roofs, inhabited by squatters who came down from the hills looking for work.

The jeep took us to the end of the rutted road, to a small highland settlement at the confluence of the rivers Saptakosi and Koka. Called Baraha Chhetra, it is one of the holiest of Hindu sites. A white-domed shrine pays homage to the place where Barah, the boar avatar of Vishnu, the creator of the universe, slew a demon named Hiranyakshya who was troubling the locals. Legend has it that only virtuous people can lift a big stone that sits in front of the temple, and that bathing in the river will free them of sins. The village proper has just a few hundred full-time residents, who largely support themselves selling food and trinkets to pilgrims. So lucrative is the religious commerce that many live for a whole year off the proceeds of the main festival in February.

The village consisted of one lane, lined by two-story homes of tin and poles with open hearths and dirt floors. We dropped our rucksacks at an "inn" that rented beds. The top story loft was for sleeping. The bottom floor doubled as a snack bar and stable for ducks, chickens, dogs, and a cat missing its eyes. We had to step over pigs lying in the doorway. Trash littered the banks all the way down to the water, where pilgrims were taking purifying dips. The architecture looked Tudor—wattle and mud-framed by exposed structural timbering. The farm animals roaming on the dirt floor by the open hearth added to the medieval atmosphere.

We took a seat at a rough-hewn wooden table and ordered milk tea. A rooster wandered in and left fresh excrement beside us. I tried to ignore the cat's oozing visage. A youth drove a motorbike right up to our table and stared.

"You stand out," Deepak said, stating the obvious.

Other people came over to talk. Everyone carried the surname Rai, meaning they were from the ethnic group of the same name. The earliest inhabitants of the eastern highlands, they have Tibetan features and eat pork, a rarity here. Most Rai are animists who worship stones, the river, mountains, and ancestors. They drape themselves in gold jewelry with naturalistic themes like leaves and moons. Scholars generally describe the language as Tibeto-Burman.

Nepalis often identify themselves as being from the hills or plains, rather than the nation. That goes for the Rai as well. As in other mountain areas like Albania and Mexico, the best hopes of escaping the grinding poverty of the mountains lay in migrating to the plains for work and schooling. There was a significant downhill migration by families who sought better conditions for their kids.

The Gurkha fighting force offers one way to make a living, and even earn foreign currency. For nearly two hundred years, these squat and hardy warriors have particularly thrived in foreign mountain battlefields, including Afghanistan, Malaysia, Borneo, and the Falklands. "Better to die than live a coward," is their slogan. The word *Gurkha* derives from the hill town Gorkha in the country's center-north.

The Rai are one of the four Kirat hill tribes mentioned in early Hindu texts and today form the elite of the Gurkha fighters. Rai currently make up a significant number of the 40,000 Gurkhas in the Indian armed forces and 3,500 in Britain's. Over the years, many Rai Gurkhas have earned distinction for bravery. Among the most decorated was Agansing Rai, who was awarded the Victoria Cross of the British Empire for leading a noteworthy 1944 operation in Burma that wiped out foes on a ridge. By virtue of their ferocity and geographic remoteness, the Rai have enjoyed relative autonomy under successive Nepali governments.

Tourist shops in the capital frequently sell the ceremonial curved knife, called the *khukuri*, associated with the Gurkhas. The formidable blade can measure up to twenty inches long. Nepal's famed mountain warriors wield them efficiently to sever spinal cords and throats. Ordinary hill peasants use this traditional tool to slice potatoes or cut wood.

In Baraha Chhetra, everyone alluded to the Rai Gurkhas. The same fighting spirit was being summoned up against the dam, albeit with words and not the legendary knives. One of the people we spoke to was Mar Bahandur Rai, a forty-three-year-old who sold soda and candy from the bottom floor of his bamboo house. Like many residents of the village, he had migrated from higher up in the hills in order to profit from the religious commerce of Hindus, and he was still attached to the land of his ancestors. He said the engineers called the dam site Sunakhambi, or pillar of gold, because it would make them rich. Rai had doubts, though. He depended on the river from the moment he awoke and splashed water on his face to the rice that he ate at each meal. He worshipped the serpent goddess Naga that lived in its depths and worried that she would grow angry. "No one should try to tame the Kosi," he said nervously.

◇◇◇◇◇◇◇

We set off the next morning right after a breakfast of biscuits and spiced ginger tea. The adventure to reach the other side of the gorge began along a steel suspension bridge over the river, spanning several hundred feet. Each uneasy step made the cables sway violently. I avoided looking down at the abyss three hundred feet below and moved as quickly as possible to reach the other end. Getting off the bridge provided little comfort, however. Terra firma consisted of a narrow ledge three feet wide; any misstep would mean plunging into the turbulent river below. Streams flowed from higher up, creating a muddy slick. I crammed my walking stick into the pebbled soil for dear life.

At least the weather was spectacular. Early December is a kind month, breezy and dry, and I shed my parka after a few minutes as the sun warmed to a perfect walking temperature. To avoid vertigo, I kept my eyes trained ahead, but couldn't resist the odd peek at the gorgeous vista: bamboo rafts poling along the swirling green water and hills lush with juniper. Pigs and goats roamed with abandon, sometimes blocking our way. During these standoffs, one had to calculate the chances of being forced off the path. I almost lost my footing one time when a playful baby goat butted me right at the precipice's edge. We humans walked in single file, Deepak leading the way and shooing the farm animals as best he could. About a mile into the walk he turned and motioned for me to stop. The planned site of the dam lay below. It looked like work had already begun. Laborers had extracted a mound of river stones for construction, and piled bamboo stripped from the forest for frames.

In the mountain areas I had visited elsewhere in the world, trails were generally empty. Rarely did I encounter more than one other person. Here, however, the paths were sometimes as crowded as a city street. The corridor was the main thoroughfare into the hills and it was thronged with children going to school and women carrying reed baskets of firewood on their backs. Others were on their way to harvest corn or to go to market or to fetch water from the river in plastic buckets.

The human thicket evoked thoughts of Mira Rai, Nepal's preeminent running star. She said she developed her skill growing up in the eastern highlands, carrying water uphill and traveling two days on foot to market. She strengthened her lungs and legs on long-distance patrols as a teenaged soldier with the Maoist guerrillas.

Life is hard in the mountains, carrying everything up and down all day, but the walkers, wearing plastic sandals and saris, were amazingly agile. Some clocked six hours a day on foot. Foreign trekkers don't come here and everyone stared at the strange apparition (me) in hiking boots and a puffy jacket. The Kosi rushed below with a disapproving roar. "The river is angriest up in the hills," said Deepak. "She grows calmer when she reaches the plains."

After about two hours, we reached four bamboo and wattle buildings, precariously perched on the precipice. The forty-something owner of one of them, Indra Maya Rai, invited us in for spiced tea that was boiling on the hearth. Her much older husband squatted over a bowl of rice wine.

She mistook me for someone from the dam-building consortium. "Will we get compensation?" she asked anxiously. "I heard India is taking away our river." She grabbed a kid goat that strayed near the fire and plopped it into my lap. It curled like a kitten, nibbling my sleeve. "No one tells us anything. They don't care about us. Do you like your government? I don't trust mine."

Rai brides normally live with their husbands' families. Indra was born farther up in the hills but married a man here, thinking that his extended kin offered better economic prospects than her fellow villagers. Arable land is scarce on rocky inclines, and many families had run out of plots as their families grew and new generations were born. Birth control was uncommon until a couple decades ago, which meant that people now in their seventies might have had eight children, who then had several of their own. The pressure on agricultural land, and desire to live closer to schools and jobs, pushed many people to move lower down the slope. Some went much farther away: many men spent long years as migrant workers in Qatar, including Indra's husband, who had recently returned home.

Indra, her husband, and their three children lived in a rickety hut where she sold tea and rice wine to the many people walking by on their way to school or market. They had a couple of goats and grew millet and vegetables in back. The river could be capricious but so far it had been good to her family, providing fish, and water to irrigate the plot. To stay in its good graces, she went down to the banks every autumn to light incense. "You make a wish to the river god and when it is fulfilled you make an offering of coins and flowers. Otherwise we will get drowned."

But no offerings would stop the dam engineers. She was panicking about where to move once the river swallowed her land. Indra didn't consider herself terribly political. During the Maoist war, she'd remained neutral, and was somewhat cynical about the adversaries, who mainly visited if they needed food. "We were caught in the middle. The army came seeking petrol. The Maoists would come in a group, stay, and then go away. They asked for money but we didn't have any. They wanted to extort us and oblige us to provide a man to their forces. They wanted my husband to join. He told them, 'You can kill me but I won't leave my family.' They meant well, however. They took care of the poor people and went after the rich, going to their houses to disturb them."

It was clear that the threat of the dam was politicizing her. She straightened up, voice rising with rage, hands clenched in fury. "We will throw stones. We will kill them and are ready to be killed. We are organized. Everyone is ready to fight."

The husband spoke up. "I think—"

She cut him off. "He's a simple man. He's not good at talking. We don't have another option. It's better to die fighting than to go hungry."

I drained my tea and gently placed the goat on the ground. It ran back toward the fire. Indra scooped up the animal and tossed it at her husband. She did a *Namaskar*, a sign of respect where one brings palms together before the heart and bows. I returned the sign and wished her luck.

◇◇◇◇◇◇◇

We walked for another hour, occasionally stopping to chat with others on the trail, all of whom said they would fight the dam. Finally we got to Simle, a cluster of twelve homes that comprised the metropolis of these remote parts. The settlement was even filthier than the previous one. We dropped our bags off at a house that rented rooms and I decided not to eat lunch after visiting the outhouse. The toilet was worse than Deepak had warned: so piled with human waste that there was no space to squat. We sat at a table smeared with animal droppings and drank milk tea while someone went to fetch Ganesh Bahadur Rai, the septuagenarian leader of the protest movement.

Ganesh led a settlement of two hundred farmers called Pokhare, not to be confused with the trekking town Pokhara, further to the west. He was by all appearances a celebrity here, too. Boisterous laughter and flirtation heralded his approach. The dapper figure that came into view was graceful like a ballroom dancer, dressed in a tope and pin-striped gray blazer. He didn't look seventy-six.

We sat on stools outside a kiosk. Ganesh took out a pack of Bijuli, a low-quality brand of cigarette whose name translates as "electricity."

"Ironic, right? We're talking about hydropower," he guffawed. He took a deep drag with eyes closed. "If we lose this river, maybe the Nepali people would never drink their own water. We cannot survive without the river. Everything relies on it: finances, birds and insects, fish and irrigation. We need it to bathe and make tea and irrigate fields. We would be helpless."

Ganesh ran through his life story. His family had lived here as far back as anyone remembered. They were humble people who grew pulses and ginger, raising cows for yogurt and milk. He was largely self-taught. The first school opened in the area when he was twelve, but he had to drop out shortly thereafter to help on his parents' farm and collect firewood. "There was an expression, 'Whether or not you go to school you will plough the fields.' That applied to me." He married for love, was widowed, and married a second time through arrangement. They had eight children, for whom he struggled to provide by subsistence farming. Ganesh got his "real education," as he called it, from the Communist Party, which recruited him to lead the local ward. "They taught me to read—Marx and Engels," he said with some wonder, adding, "We're simple people but once we get onto something we are dedicated."

Village assemblies formed the backbone of the Communist movement in the hills. (This was the more moderate Communist wing, not the Maoists. They preferred to recruit fighters, not speech makers.) Ganesh found he had a talent for organizing. He roamed in his sandals for hours in order to mobilize protests and hear grievances. In these remote settlements, anyone with charisma could assume leadership in the political vacuum left by the absent government. The hamlets basically ruled themselves, with their own councils. Authorities didn't appreciate his activism, however, as political parties were still banned. In 1971 they threw him into a flea-ridden jail for a month for pursuing "subversive" activities. That stint failed to dampen his organizing zeal, and upon release Ganesh became the default person in charge, mediating in disputes over marriage or land. "Naturally, someone takes the lead. I feel modest saying this, but in most cases it's me," Ganesh said.

The campaign against the dam began in 2003. Engineers started coming to the area and handing out business cards. Ganesh and a couple other elders agreed that relocating seventy-five thousand people was not a good thing, but it was surprisingly hard to organize opposition at first. "Some people didn't understand what a dam was," he said. Eventually, they learned, and Ganesh organized committees in each of the eighty villages. The new movement linked up with villagers from the barrage farther downstream to stage rowdy rallies of five thousand demonstrators.

I asked about threats of violence. Was that an exaggeration? Ganesh lit another cigarette and waved his hand no. The crowds were so angry that armed police deployed at protests to prevent them from getting out of control. "People are willing to die for this cause," he said. "Their anger is genuine. They are worried about their livelihood and that we would no longer call the river our home. This is a nationalist fight. We are going to lose our resources, our sovereignty. India wants power, and the government says yes to whatever India wants. I have to calm down the citizens when the officials come here. They would have shown their bravery. Nepalis are known as brave soldiers, and we have Gurkhas in our group. They know how to fight.

"Here, it was easier to reach consensus than in the big cities," he said. "It's related to the nature. Long distances separate our communities. It's rare when we meet, so we don't feel forced upon each other. Yet everyone knows everyone. In a city you only get a tea in a small cup but here in a big cup."

"But my cup of tea here was small," Deepak objected jokingly.

Ganesh chortled. "The city ways are coming here, too." He looked up at the peaks beyond. "Come to my place and I will offer you free tea, in a big cup."

I dithered. Dusk was approaching and I didn't want to walk back in the dark.

"I'm leaving now," Ganesh said briskly. "I have to attend a ceremony for departed ancestors. The ancestors cannot wait. You can stay the night at my house."

◇◇◇◇◇◇

Ganesh said it was only a half-hour walk to Pokhare. The old man hurried ahead, gingerly darting through the boulders. Twenty years his junior, I clung to my walking stick to keep from falling over the edge. The only time we stopped was to gaze at a furrow on a peak across the river. It looked like a giant had slashed the forest with a knife. "The landslide happened with the earthquake," he said. "I thought the world was coming to an end."

Nearing the crest, we met two old ladies with firewood on their backs. They wore gold nose ornaments shaped like fish.

"What are you doing running up and down these steep hills?" one said in greeting.

The other peered at me closely. "Is that a man or a woman?"

Ganesh explained that I was from "Umrica."

"I've never met a foreigner before," she said. "It's like a comet fell from the sky. How do you speak with it?"

He said Deepak translated.

"I never heard of such a thing," she muttered and took off.

We wound through the switchbacks, each revealing a fresh vista of blue pines and rhododendron. The rushing sound of water kept us company. We went higher and higher, until we caught sight of a sparkling tributary in the valley below. A few simple houses of bamboo lay on its banks. As we made the descent to Pokhare, a man wearing a ski hat with a pom-pom caught up with us. This was Ganesh's brother-in-law and the village priest, Tahal Mom Rai, seventy-two. They were cellmates when jailed for their Communist agitation.

"We slept like matches in a box," Ganesh chortled. "The lice jumped from one to another."

"They jumped from *you*," parried the priest.

Was he willing to go to prison again, to fight the dam?

"At some point you'll realize this old man is serious," Ganesh chided me. "Forget about jail. I'm ready to give my life for this cause. This is not a selfish cause. It's about our nation and its resources."

We reached the valley. Rhododendron and bamboo trees lined the path. Ganesh touched a stalk, and said it could be sold for fifty cents, if he could get it to market. The trees gave way to a field of green bushes, measuring chin high.

"Indians pay a lot of money for this plant!" he exclaimed.

"Is that? . . ." I asked Deepak under my breath.

"Hashish," he answered quietly.

"Five hundred dollars a kilo!" Ganesh marveled. "We started cultivating this year. Grows beautifully in the mountain climate. We're saving the profits in case the dam displaces us."

We passed a woman drying cannabis leaves on a bamboo platform.

"Hey, don't leave it there," Ganesh shouted at her. "There's a rumor the police are coming. They will destroy it."

We came to the heart of the village, four mud houses built on log stilts. Cows were tethered a distance away, to free the living quarters of excrement. The outhouse for humans was immaculate, its porcelain squat scrubbed clean in anticipation of 120 guests invited to the ceremony.

The priest in the pom-pom hat explained the ritual that was about to begin. Ganesh's nephew had recently passed away, as had another man's wife. The departed souls were still lingering about so the ritual, called a *puja*, would help guide them to heaven. Going there was cause for celebration; praying and feasting would last two days.

Their sect, Kabir Panthi, was Hindi in origin, introduced by a Gurkha from the village who had stumbled upon the creed while deployed in India. The sect's primary spiritual practice was the avoidance of meat, and the Gurkha liked the idea of a vegetarian diet, both for kindness and hygiene. He passed on the word when he returned home.

The men showed me the temple, a cinderblock rectangle with few adornments. It was still under construction and lacked windows. A fresh breeze wafted inside, mixing pleasantly with the incense smoke. We sat on the cement floor cross-legged while they showed me a picture of their saint, Kabir, a fifteenth-century Hindu mystic who began life as a Muslim. Ganesh laughed when I requested permission to take a photograph. "You are civilized. I never ask," he said, to the chuckles of the priest. Aside from worship, the temple served as the place to store protest materials and to plot agitation. The priest unfurled a black banner that read, "WE DON'T WANT KOSI HIGH DAM. THE PEOPLE SHOULD NOT BE DROWNED."

The village loosely interpreted Kabir Panthi's creed, adapting what they believed in and jettisoning that which contradicted their own Rai animist traditions. They still buried the dead, rather than cremating them. Losing ancestral burial grounds to floods made it doubly hard to accept the dam, the priest said. "What can we worship if we lose their graves?" And they practiced piety on their own terms; for instance, the priest was allowed to marry. From what I could gather, in addition to abstaining from meat, purity involved prayer and compassion. Another tenet was living simply without too many possessions, not hard to do since no one had much money.

Since the temple still wasn't fully built, the death ceremony was to be held in a villager's house about three hundred feet away. Going there, we passed four statues carved from wood. Their angular features resembled the Easter Island heads, but far smaller. Were these related to the sect? "No," said Ganesh dismissively. These were to sell to tourists in the towns. "We leave them outside to get an older appearance."

We fell into step with guests arriving at the house, a simple bamboo structure. The women wore gold bangles and moon-shaped ornaments around their necks. They tied folded clothes called *patukas* around their waists. The priest dotted sandalwood paste on their foreheads as they bowed in respect. We sat around a huge campfire just outside the house where the older women stirred brass vats of rice and vegetable curries. The aroma mixed gloriously with the fresh smell of pine. The guests sat on logs and scooped up food from round plates with their right hands. I wasn't hungry but they insisted. "Guests are second to god," one woman said, pushing cauliflower toward me. "We should give prosperity to guests."

The aunties wouldn't stop pressing food. Everywhere I turned a woman was holding a banana leaf with potatoes on it or mango paste. A woman with a gold circle hanging from her nose snuggled next to me and took a selfie on one of the rare cell phones, giggling.

Watching the cooks slice with the traditional khukuri knives made me think of Gurkhas. I asked Ganesh why Nepal's mountaineers made such good warriors.

"The nature makes them tough," he posited. "Also, they drink a lot of rice wine. That encourages the fighting spirit."

The children were allowed to stay up late and they romped about, butting each other like goats. They piled onto one another and jumped rope. The older boys hit a volleyball about.

Ganesh pulled over a boy of eight and ran a hand over his hair. "He's first in his class," Ganesh said proudly. "He wants to be an engineer. It's every Nepali parent's dream to have an engineer in the family. But this one won't build dams, right?"

The boy nodded solemnly.

Smoke curled from the campfire. Stars came out, vivid in the cloudless sky. The men lit cigarettes and pointed out the mountains they worshipped: Pangnam (Setting Sun), Hangwa (King's Abode), and Tangkira (Broken Head). One man asked, "Are there hills like this in America?"

"Of course they don't," one of the women snapped at him. "Everything is flat there."

The priest blew a conch shell to signal the start of ceremonies. Everyone filed into the house and sat on the floor. They covered legs with blankets and leaned against pillows. The musicians hypnotically beat *dhol* drums, chanting and clapping cymbals. Some went into a trance. The hymns reminded the souls to leave this world.

Teachers who worked in a village across the river joined the group. Educators are revered in Nepal; a learned man has social currency in a community where the majority doesn't read. The others made room for the teachers near the conch blower, a place of honor. They patted the floor for me to join them and handed me a blanket to keep my legs warm. We spoke during breaks in chanting.

"I worry about the dam," one whispered. "Even if they got compensation to buy new land, the community would be broken apart. This is not just a matter of property. It's birthplace and a connection to the ancestors. Gatherings like this would disappear. We would become scattered; there would be no possibility for all of us to live in one place like this. The language would disappear if our neighbors are from other groups. Our children might follow their customs. Rai culture would die out."

The other teacher agreed. "I've heard people talk about violence. They would have no other resort."

◇◇◇◇◇◇

The ritual went on all night, but Ganesh suggested I get sleep before the next day's festivities. I curled up in the loft of his house, on a wooden pallet with my pack as a pillow. My down jacket served as a blanket. The air was cold but pure. I thought about the valley, locked in its little mountain cocoon, self-reliant and happy. It was painful to imagine waters surging over it. Would the graves float to the surface? Would rites like the one I witnessed die out?

The pressures on the Nepali Rai exceeded those in other mountain areas I visited. The Albanian adherents of the Kanun, the Zapatistas, the Colombians living in FARC territory—none faced the threat of wholesale dislocation, and none were threatened by their central state's pursuit of wealth and power. In those ranges, just the opposite was often true;

the government mostly left the mountain people alone, though often with problematic consequences. In Nepal, from high ground in the capital, Katmandu, at 4,600 feet above sea level, the government showed the same callous disregard toward the rural mountain communities as plains rulers in the other countries I trekked through. The Rai, like hill people else-where, lacked decent services, and a say over their territory. It was as if they didn't exist in the minds of officials, who were under India's thumb. The Rai felt as ignored as the Maya of Mexico, but the situation in Nepal was far bleaker. The Maya at least could remain on their land. The Rai's struggle was as existential as it was physical; their culture would be swal-lowed up along with the land itself. Their language and religion would slowly disperse into the new status quo around them until they forgot the words and prayers.

◇◇◇◇◇◇◇

In the morning, women were at their places at the campfire, making milk tea. Guests filed in and out of the prayer room, eyes heavy from lack of sleep. The ritual ended around midday. With the departed safely en route to the afterlife, worshippers gathered for a picnic lunch. The women handed out leaves heaped with popped rice, bananas, and circles of sweet fried dough. Everyone squatted in the sun and took selfies with the strange foreigner. The children wrote Nepali script on my notebook. I sang them the ABCs of English. The scenery was breathtaking, the atmosphere so tranquil. Eden before the fall. "It's so idyllic," Deepak said sadly.

Suddenly Ganesh stood up. So did the other men. Joy drained from their faces. They pointed at the peak above. A plume of smoke rose. And then a second.

"It's the soldiers," the teacher said grimly. "They are destroying the hashish fields."

Agitated conversation followed.

"What do we do?"

"Hide the dried plants."

"Burn the crops before they come?"

"They're hours away. We have time."

Ganesh huddled with the men. They decided to do nothing. Hope-fully they could bribe the police to leave the field alone.

The party was over. No one wanted to eat any more. The visitors got up to leave. They handed leftover food to the aunties and anxiously walked away. The teachers watched the distant smoke grimly.

"Our misfortune is to live in these hills," one lamented quietly. "If we don't drown we'll burn."

Soon enough I found myself on a plane out of Nepal. I pondered the teacher's comment. It struck me as a pithy encapsulation of the layered woes confronting the Rai. At bottom, the problem of daily existences, exacerbated by a neglectful state. Above that, unrest elsewhere in the nation; the Madhesis' protests, which magnified the pressure on the state, had not abated. Then there was the meddling of Nepal's neighbors. And at the top, the region's looming water crisis. For Ganesh and his people, the future seemed uncertain at best. Maybe all that would be left of the Rai would be entombed in a diorama of the International Mountain Museum, a quaint display of textiles and gold nose hoops and nothing else.

5

Mountain Thistles

THE CAUCASUS, 5,559 TO 18,000 FEET

> There was one nation that would not give in, would
> not acquire the mental habits of submission—and
> not just individuals among them, but the whole
> nation to a man. These were the Chechens.
>
> —Aleksandr Solzhenitsyn, *The Gulag Archipelago*
> (1973)

> We grew up free as eagles, princes of the mountains.
> There is no threshold from which we will shy.
> There is no God except Allah.
>
> —"Death of Freedom," anthem of the secessionist
> Chechen Republic of Ichkeria (1992)

In 2013 I was invited to talk about the Boston Marathon bombers on a
television program. Two nihilistic brothers had set off pressure cooker
bombs at the finish line, killing three people and causing catastrophic
injuries to others. Tamerlan and Dzhokhar Tsarnaev were, to all appearances, inspired by Islamic jihad overseas. Much was made of their heritage: their parents were from Chechnya and the family had spent time in
Dagestan. Both of these places were Islamic republics in the Caucasus
Mountains, and both were home to resistance movements against Russia.
The television interviewer sought insights. What did these faraway mountains have to do with a sporting event on the eastern seaboard?

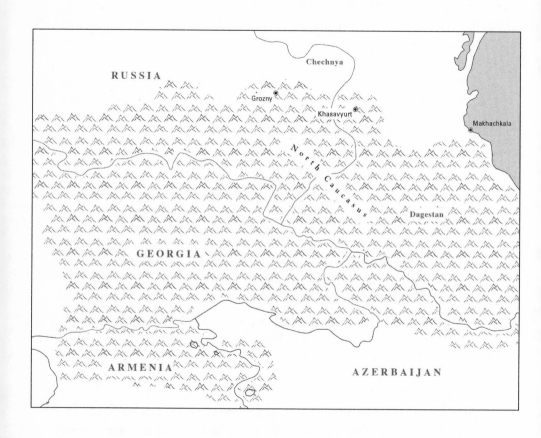

I had only two minutes to deliver a brief history lesson on the region's ethnic violence. I hastily discussed the proud clans that had continually resisted the Mongol hordes in the thirteenth century, the tsars' expansion into the Caucasus, and then the modern-day Kremlin's interventions. The cliché, perpetrated by Chechens themselves, portrays the warriors as wolves that hurl themselves on attackers. The connection to Boston was one of happenstance, I told the host. The brothers were alienated in their adopted country, and taken with the seeming glamour of their mission. But the cultural roots from which they sprang ran deep. The Chechens have always felt greater allegiance to their valleys and kin than to the Russian nation of which they were a part. They had their own religion, and they desperately yearned for their own homeland. Russia treated them as second-class citizens. It is hard for Chechens to belong anywhere but Chechnya, and Chechnya was not free. The brothers carried a sense of isolation and animosity with them across the ocean that, however irrational, led them to identify with a vague Muslim cause. A lot had to do with topography, I wanted to add. But the producer indicated that our time was up.

◇◇◇◇◇◇◇

The North Caucasus, which soars up to 18,000 feet, sits between the Black and Caspian seas, serving as the land bridge from Asia to Europe. Since imperial times, competing powers have desired control of the region, both for access to the water and to use as bulwarks against their foes. The tsars made sure Russia commanded the north, while Iran and Turkey claimed the south. The more recent discoveries of oil and gas in the region have made the mountain chain even more valuable.

Yet the jagged peaks of Chechnya and Dagestan have never been easy to conquer. An invader must contend not only with the vertiginous slopes, but also with the warriors from clans living between the crags. The mountains don't look like most of the rest of Russia, where miles of flat steppes stretch monotonously, clouds hanging oppressively low. Looking at the north Caucasus from the air, the range runs like a gray stone scar, interspersed by canyons and patches of deep green. Thick forests of birch and fir make it doubly hard to infiltrate, as do winter snows that block passage on paths, and sometimes roads, until spring. These gnarly granite and limestone massifs brusquely shaken from the earth's crust twenty-five million years ago have long engendered suspicion among their inhabitants of what lay on the other side of the hill. The remoteness of each valley has yielded a mosaic of tribes defined by land and lineage, dozens of different ethnic groups that, for at least as long as historical records have been kept, have zealously defended their own patches. Each community in both Chechnya and Dagestan had a clearly delineated territory, governed by a council of elders and defended by bands that could spring into action at a moment's notice. They would move quickly from the valleys into the mountains, from where they struck their enemies. First documented eight hundred years ago, these methods are still in use today.

Many built stone villages in the Middle Ages as fortifications to deter sheep rustlers and invaders. One can still find surviving lookout towers and walls. The clans fiercely prized their independence, both from one another and from outsiders. Chechens greet each other with the phrase *"marsha oylla,"* which means, "Come in freedom." That could well be the slogan of Dagestan's thirty ethnic groups as well.

The two adjacent republics comprise only 25,200 square miles, or 0.4 percent of Russia's 6.6 million square miles. Yet combined they account for 150 *teips*, or loose kinship circles in Chechnya, and about 30 ethnic groups in Dagestan. The inbred clans have over history competed for power, and many today operate as political units, sometimes with their own militias. The mountains have everything to do with this social fragmentation. Due to the fractured geography, Chechen and Dagestani societies have traditionally not been overseen, with success, by a central state (or a series thereof), but instead by particular groups often linked by territorial and kinship ties. People feel bound to this extended family or community, and not the formal government. The mountains have long provided physical barriers to religious as well as social assimilation; it's not simple, as a practical matter, for a youth to abscond into greater Russia. Much like in Colombia, the mountains have also nurtured armed insurgencies. And as in Albania, there exists in the mountains a vendetta culture, wherein community conflicts are resolved through violence; as with the Kanun, this culture doesn't mesh within Russia's legal system (such as it is). Not surprisingly, Chechens refer to their heartland as *Derstan*, meaning both Homeland and the Mountain Country.

The communities in the region have not been shaped by terrain and clans alone. Islam was first introduced to the North Caucasus in the seventh century and began to take firm hold in the eighteenth and nineteenth centuries. Politically active Sufi Muslim brotherhoods, called *murids*, united resistance against the tsar's expansion in the nineteenth century. This was the only time that the disparate tribes came together under a nominal leader, the fierce and bushy-hatted Imam Shamil, from Dagestan's Avar ethnic group.

Even then, the 1834–1859 rebellion did not standardize religious observance, which due to large distances between villages varies greatly even today. Some faithful simply worship at home. Others allow dancing and smoking, anathema among more dogmatic Muslims elsewhere. While the physical isolation of the Caucasus allowed for more religious freedom than in the plains, however, in the Soviet era, no one escaped oppression and persecution entirely. And as in Colombia, many of the ingredients for insurrection exist here, among them a brutal government, poverty, and mountainous terrain. Add to that historic grievances of an ethnic nature, and you have a rich recruiting ground for modern extremists.

◇◇◇◇◇◇

The Russian use of the word *Caucasian* confuses Americans, who associate the term with "white." Ironically enough, the Slavic elite calls Caucasians чёрный человек, *chorniye chelavek* or black person. The wording implies "dirty," or even "nigger." Bigotry aside, the term is imprecise: a lot of Chechens look as fair and red-haired as the Irish. Even the darkest Dagestanis have more of an olive Middle Eastern complexion. This reducing of Caucasians to a contemptible "Other" fuels local resentment, as does the fact that for many years Russia had a sort of apartheid system whereby Chechens had to obtain special permits called *propiskas* in order to live in the capital. As with so many oppressed groups, the North Caucasians' collective identity is built around past humiliations and resistance. Heroic epic songs called *illi* passed down over the ages extol moments of courage during historical clashes with aggressors.

Over the past one hundred years, efforts by people of the North Caucasus to gain independence or at least substantial autonomy have continually failed. The Mountainous Republic of the Northern Caucasus only survived from 1917 to 1920 before the Bolsheviks crushed it. Similar misfortune befell the Chechen-Ingush Autonomous Soviet Socialist Republic, which lasted only a decade after its founding in 1934.

Its death was dictated by Josef Stalin, who banned all religions, Islam included. Mosques were closed or dynamited, although the Soviets were never fully able to dislodge religious and clan leaders' power. Stalin looked suspiciously on the Chechens and accused them of collaborating with the Nazis. He figured the best way to deal with this annoying ethnic group was to get rid of it. In February 1944, he abolished the autonomous republic and deported nearly the entire populations of Chechnya and neighboring Ingushetia—about 478,000 people—to Central Asia and Siberia. In methods similar to those employed by Stalin's enemy the Nazis, deportees were herded into freight trains and crushed together during the freezing three-week journey. Many died along the way, their corpses hurled from the compartments onto the icy earth. Others perished in the harsh conditions in exile. For the survivors, trauma was heaped upon trauma. Deportees had to report to police stations and could not travel freely. Authorities banned the Chechen language. The exiles were only allowed to return in 1957, after Stalin's death. By that time, a third of their population had died. The homecoming did not relieve suffering for many survivors, who came back to find their houses occupied by others, including, most insultingly, ethnic Slavs from the plains.

When the Soviet Union splintered into fifteen independent states in 1991, a nationalist rebellion to establish a separate Islamic state in Chechnya broke out. The new countries included Georgia, Armenia, and Azerbaijan, which lay in the Caucasus. Understandably, the predominantly Muslim people of Chechnya felt entitled to their own country as well.

A number of Chechen separatist leaders, descended from the embittered generation exiled by Stalin, emerged. Prominent among them was Dzhokhar Dudayev, a dapper former Russian air force general who declared the separatist Chechen Republic of Ichkeria (an old Turkic word for the area) in October 1991. For the next few years Chechnya had a de facto independent state.

But the territory was too strategically important for Moscow to grant it autonomy, and in December 1994, the Russian military unleashed an onslaught, deploying forty thousand troops and blitzing the Chechen capital, Grozny. Over the next two years it rained munitions upon the city, reducing it to a charred wreck.

As the republic descended into chaos, warlords gained prominence. To complicate matters, Islamic fighters of the hard-line Wahhabist creed came from the Middle East to take part in the struggle against Russia. Their puritanical streak, referred to locally as Salafist, contrasted with the local Sufi Sunni approach, which treated faith more as a peaceful means toward self-improvement.

Russian forces withdrew in 1996, and the warlords rose to take their place, controlling the area they claimed through violence and patronage. Chechnya's assorted kinship groups historically competed for local political power. Rival clans formed their own militias and the region was rife with kidnappings, organized crime, and brutal infighting. With the absence of strong, centralized Chechen leadership, hopes of an independent state frayed.

Russia's offensive occurred just as Al Qaeda was extending its reach into the mountains of Afghanistan and Kashmir. By the late 1990s, it was spreading further still, and this period marked the turning point from secular nationalism to radical jihad in Chechnya. The foreigners who had arrived to help fight Moscow had another motive, of course: to preach international jihad and find and train new recruits. They courted warlords and their militias and further splintered the weakened nationalist movement. The newly arrived political Islamists imposed a harsh form of religion. Nonetheless, the disaffected younger generation, with no job prospects, no outlets for its frustrations, and an enormous hatred for Moscow, was ripe for radical recruitment.

One man played a decisive role in furthering the fanatical cause: Shamil Basayev. This Chechen field commander took his first name from the nineteenth-century resistance leader and the style of his beard from Osama bin Laden. In the 1990s, he grew close to the Saudi-born Sabu Ibn al-Khattab, who fought the Soviet occupation in Afghanistan in the 1980s before moving on to Chechnya. Thus radicalized, during the 1990s Basayev attacked civilians as well as security forces in and around Chechnya, including the Budyonnovsk hospital siege, where over one hundred patients and staff were killed in a mass hostage taking in southern Russia. Basayev also provoked the Kremlin to wage another war against Chechnya, when he and al-Khattab staged an incursion into Dagestan in 1999, the year Vladimir Putin became president. Once again, the Russians shelled Chechen towns relentlessly.

At the same time, the Kremlin courted Akhmad Kadyrov, who served as the region's chief mufti, or spiritual leader, during the two wars. Kadyrov had been born in Kazakhstan during the Soviet exile, and at first harbored little love for Moscow. He went so far as to declare a jihad against Russia in the early 1990s. But Moscow's Faustian offer proved irresistible. Kadyrov distanced himself from the Wahabbist fundamentalists and threw his lot in with the Kremlin. He became the new Moscow-backed president of the republic in 2003. This was an extraordinary course not only for Kadyrov, but also for Putin, who normally preferred force. But realizing he couldn't subdue all the warlords, he chose instead to divide and conquer, knowing that Kadyrov could muster support within his teip, the Benoy, which was one of the more influential clans. The Kremlin promised to shower Chechnya not with artillery but with money. Chechens would be allowed to worship Allah and veil their women. Chechnya went on a binge of mosque building, with financing from other Islamic states like Turkey and others in the Arabian Gulf. As a measure of calm returned under Kadyrov, hard-line fighters, including Basayev, moved operations eastward into the more rugged mountains of Dagestan. From there, Basayev plotted further spectacular attacks. His grisly résumé included the siege of a Moscow theater in 2002, where over 170 people were killed during the raid to free 850 hostages. The year 2004 was particularly busy: his bombers blew up two planes and a metro station in Moscow, killed Kadyrov in a bomb planted in a sports stadium, and took hostages in a school in Beslan, leading to 340 deaths. Basayev's terror campaign only stopped when he died in an explosion in 2006.

Three years after the elder Kadyrov was assassinated, his son, Ramzan, assumed the role of Chechnya's president. The second war officially ended in 2009 when Russia declared its military operation over. Yet a small group of extremists moved to more rugged bases in Dagestan, using the mountains to hide. While their fighting forces were greatly depleted, the insurgents continued to kill policemen and set off bombs in Dagestan, Chechnya, and the Russian capital. In 2010 guerrilla commandos stormed the Chechen parliament and bombed a Moscow metro station. Attackers struck again the following year, setting off explosives at the Domodedovo airport in Moscow. And it was likely these very same extremists that inspired the elder Tsarnaev brother, who was the mastermind of the Boston attack.

◇◇◇◇◇◇◇

I first went to the region in the late 1990s, and returned in 2011. I was intrigued by how the landscape had shaped the clans and Islam, the two paradigms that fostered insurgency. According to the official version promoted by Moscow, Chechnya had unified under the leadership of the Kadyrov family. The rebels who operated in Chechnya by now had fled east to the rougher mountains in Dagestan, which couldn't seem to achieve any unity among its clans. The key to pacification—or not— might lie, I surmised, in how high and fractious the topography was.

I flew south from Moscow 990 miles with a translator and a checklist of sources to meet: human rights defenders, government representatives, religious leaders, agonized mothers whose sons "went to the woods," the euphemism for joining the jihadist armed underground.

It was noteworthy that we felt reasonably safe upon landing in Chechnya, seeing as how only a few years earlier, the republic's capital, Grozny, had arguably been the most pulverized city on earth. Grozny translates as "terrible" in Russia. It first adopted this moniker as a garrison town during the nineteenth century Caucasian war, and has remained true to its name. The last time I went there, in 1999, the bombardment was so massive that I couldn't get closer to the city than an hour's drive away. Not that the word *city* applied at that point. Like most capitals of mountainous regions, Grozny is situated in one of the flatter areas, at an elevation of only 578 feet. This made it easy to attack from the slopes above. The Russians destroyed nearly every building. Half of the 470,000 residents had fled, preferring to squat in comparative comfort beneath tarps in refugee camps or in railway car shelters in the next republic, Ingushetia. Those who remained in Grozny hid in rancid basements lit by candles. They slept in their clothes and darted out during lulls in shelling to scoop water from ditches. Undetonated mortar rounds were stuck in their yards, and in the walls of their homes. Fires raged amid the shattered cement.

But the Russian military couldn't destroy the rebels' hideouts in the mountains. There the insurgents stood watch on nine-hundred-year-old towers overlooking ravines, staging ambushes on the few roads as Russian patrols rolled by. Just like in Colombia, that area was off-limits to the government, then and still today.

Compared to the nineties, however, it was now a cinch to reach Grozny, which had graduated to the UN's list of fastest-growing cities, admittedly an easy qualification seeing that it was rising from nothing.

Although the Russian troops had by now withdrawn, the republic was heavily militarized, thick with Chechen uniformed men who manned checkpoints on the main roads. We drove past villages that last time I visited were coiled with razor wire and lined with snipers, into a rebuilt city so pristine it felt like a theme park, literally. The gate to Grozny bore an eerie resemblance to the entrance of Universal Studios in Orlando, with the same unnatural yellow color and triumphant arch. At checkpoints, I half expected the police to ask for our tickets and hand out maps of the rides. Inside the fantasy city, empty skyscrapers that still hadn't rented out space caught the sun's rays like crystals.

"None of this was here four months ago!" gasped the translator. In a dramatically short period, the city's sewage, water, electricity, and heating systems had been repaired, along with 155 miles of roads, 13 bridges, and 900 shops. After years of privations, luxury reigned, we noticed. Even sushi bars were in ample supply. I counted seven salons on one promenade alone and just as many boutiques selling Prada knockoffs. The spa Egoiska (Egoist) carried hair dye from France. A woman fresh from the gym—*the gym!*—showed off an Italian bag she had bought for $350. Then she asked the cosmetologist about Botox treatments.

The centerpiece of Grozny's rebirth was its central mosque, an extravagant confection of Swarovski crystals and minarets soaring 140 feet high. It can hold ten thousand people at a time. The regime had gone all-out to build this grand symbol, trucking in rare white marble from Turkey. They named the mosque after Kadyrov and claimed, incorrectly, that it was the biggest in Europe. It was certainly among the most ostentatious in Europe, and jarringly unlike the simple minarets dotting the Chechen countryside.

Indeed, nothing in this ersatz Grozny reflected Chechen mountain culture. It was all gilt and artifice, not the earthy stone of the highlands. The younger Kadyrov's regime celebrated a Chechen renaissance, which was, paradoxically, a repudiation of local identity in nearly every detail. In the city's decorative statues that guarded the main drag, they'd even forsaken wolves, the symbol of Chechen manhood, in favor of lions.

Most of the money to rebuild and build was coming from Moscow, a result of the Kremlin's calculation that bankrolling is more effective than bullying to quell restive spirits. Subsidies financed about 90 percent of the official budget of Chechnya, which had little to drive the economy apart from a minor energy venture.

Putin's unusual gamble in ceding control to the Kadyrovs could pay off for Moscow, as long as the red-haired clan remained loyal. Ramzan Kadyrov pushed many aspects of Sharia law, oversaw the building of the mosque, and ordered women to be veiled in public buildings and schools. But while his father was a respected cleric, Kadyrov junior was simply a narcissistic thug. Enormous portraits of him billowed alongside the main boulevard. Schools affixed pictures of his smiling visage to the walls in order to inspire loyalty among the young. Ramzan organized opulent parties with Hollywood and soccer stars, more interested in photo ops with the likes of Hilary Swank than, say, creating jobs for the 50 percent of Chechens who lacked them. His appalling human rights record involved squashing anyone believed to threaten his monopoly on power—rival warlords, members of other clans, critics, suspected jihadists. He consolidated power through torture, kidnappings, arbitrary arrests, and assassinations. He could do whatever he wanted, as long as he remained loyal to Putin.

The problem was that Ramzan's style of rule invariably created resentment. The Kadyrovs' Benoy teip was actually the same as Basayev's, but years of oppression had fragmented it into factions that only deepened under this new regime. Ramzan also alienated a large portion of the population with his doctrinaire notion of Islam, which, he made clear, ran counter to the more individualized and flexible ways practiced deep in the mountains. Many women who wore head scarves during the two wars not for religious reasons but as symbols of their resistance now resented that the regime was pressuring them to be covered. Not only did these practices represent a departure from Chechen Sufism in the elevated rural areas, Kadyrov alienated a large part of the population that might have sided with him against their dogma.

My first interviews in Grozny were with three women in their early thirties who were emblematic of that frustration. The trio looked like models—dyed blonde manes and legs stilted on four-inch heels—but they worked jobs that put their lives in danger. Raisa was a translator for Western organizations, Asya a journalist. The third woman was a human rights activist; she asked that I withhold her name. We met at a tea shop, whose feminine décor included mirrors and plastic ferns on the sparkling white walls. They wore head scarves providing varying degrees of cover, and skirts that modestly reached the ankles.

We talked about the variant of Islam enforced by Kadyrov, and specifically the compulsory dress code he'd introduced in 2007. Girls now had to wear scarves in schools and universities. Women complaining to police about intimidation were often dismissed with insults. In a widely quoted television remark, Kadyrov warned that women should behave "properly" or face killing by men.

Not only did these practices represent a departure from Chechen Sufism in the mountains, it also upset the more secular tendencies in cities like Grozny. By endorsing the radicals' approach to dress, Kadyrov alienated a large part of the population that might have sided with him against their dogma.

Raisa, the translator, kept touching her right thigh. She had been shot a few months before by a paint gun. She was crossing the street with a friend to grab lunch when two men approached in a black car. They fired a plastic pellet into her leg and she felt a stab of pain. Pink paint stained her gray skirt. Her friend got blue in the chest. The attackers wore black military-style garb.

"They shouted, 'Put on a head scarf, whore,'" she recalled. "For three weeks I had a big bruise." The aggression was a merciless irony for Raisa, who thought life could only improve after the Russian shelling stopped.

"The dress code is a violation of Russian law," the activist pointed out. "Moscow remains silent to pacify Kadyrov."

As a compromise, Asya, the journalist, covered her legs and draped a *platok*, or scarf, around her neck that could be pulled up quickly if needed. She had to enter public buildings for press events. Otherwise she wouldn't be able to do her job. More defiant friends wore a small kerchief called a *kasinka*. It resembled the headbands in vogue in the 1960s, and had nothing to do with traditional Chechen dress. Or they put on dresses that were long but so clinging one could see the outlines of their skimpy underwear.

The conversation shifted to Natalia Estemirova, a prominent human rights defender who was one of the most outspoken critics of the regime's abuses before her body was found in the woods in Ingushetia with shots to the head, in 2009. Witnesses had seen four men push her into a white car in Grozny and race off. No one has been held accountable for her murder, which followed her documentation of cases that resulted in more than two hundred judgments by the European Court of Human Rights. Kadyrov's militia, known as the Kadyrovtsy, was widely believed responsible, although the supreme leader denied culpability. Estemirova was the latest in a string of political opponents who were assassinated outside of

Chechnya, including rival warlords and the prominent journalist Anna Politkovskaya, who was also investigating abuses. "The security forces don't even care about showing their faces," said the activist. "They don't even try to prove someone has connections with the rebels. They just take them."

Just then the journalist's cell phone vibrated on the plastic table. All eyes went to it, disapprovingly. The screen saver was Kadyrov's portrait.

"I don't like him," the journalist said huffily. "It helps me with access to authorities."

Suddenly they went quiet. A tall man entered the cafe. Wearing a black leather jacket, he had the muscled swagger of a bodyguard. He took the table next to ours and self-consciously studied the dainty offerings on the menu.

"He follows me everywhere," the rights activist muttered. Then she addressed him loudly: "Join us at the table. You can hear us better that way."

The man looked vaguely chastened but to my surprise actually came over to say an awkward hello, though there was no chitchat beyond that. He returned to his table and stared at his cell phone until we felt compelled to leave. He had won the standoff, but the surveillance wasn't benefiting anyone, least of all those who were still yearning for freedom. This new Chechnya was not a free place.

◇◇◇◇◇◇

My goal was to meet Kadyrov, and see if he was really the monster depicted by the women. His exploits were shocking; while many returnees from the war were still awaiting proper housing, Kadyrov was collecting exotic pets, including a tiger. He spent a fortune sending his racehorses to compete in foreign events. I wanted to ask him about the role of clans in the new Chechnya. I wanted to ask why he imposed a brand of Sharia law that was alien to the tradition. He claimed to represent the Chechen mountain clans yet he was an anomaly and puppet of the Slavic plains. Kadyrov, not surprisingly, denied a request for an interview, not even fifteen minutes. I couldn't visit his stable or private zoo.

Instead, the journalist with the Kadyrov phone arranged an audience for me with the mufti. Chechnya's spiritual leader was a close aide of the president and could perhaps shed light on the persistent turmoil. The mufti's office faced the main mosque, but it was a sorry little place compared to the Kadyrov splendor. In America, it would have the bland look of a dentist's office, except that dentists don't deploy bodyguards to pat you down in the lobby. Sultan Mirzayev was called the "Mufti for Life," although "Life" in these parts is relative, because he was pushed out of the job three years later. The mufti dressed the part of a Chechen patriarch, with a short gray beard that matched his boxy sheep fur hat. Mirzayev studied theology in Dagestan before the Soviet Union collapsed, and after the 1994–1996 war he served as a prominent imam in the breakaway Chechen Republic. After Putin sent troops into Chechnya in the fall of 1999, Mirzayev was co-opted along with Kadyrov the elder. From that day, he never questioned the dynasty, at least not in public. He supported moves that outraged the public, like naming the mosque after the Kadyrovs and shuttering cafes during Ramadan.

After some congenial small talk, in which we established that I was not a Muslim but respected his faith, I asked about these developments, which he predictably defended as manifestations of the new public embrace of Islam. This, he asserted, is what Chechens wanted all along under Soviet rule. Then I asked about the paintballs. The mufti looked annoyed. Even though it was not the previous Chechen custom, women should cover their faces and arms up to their wrists, he said, adding, "To walk without a head scarf is a sin." Against all evidence, he insisted that nobody was forced to wear one. They did it voluntarily to celebrate their heritage.

The way he saw it, everything was fine now that Chechens had relative autonomy. Except for the Wahhabists stirring up trouble, the codependency with Russia worked well. "During the Soviet Union it didn't matter what religion, if you were religious you were a political sinner. The Russians had no understanding during the period of the two wars. I had to fight for my religion and culture. We're a prideful people. But now Russia realizes that allowing us to practice our religion and express our culture brings calm. Look, I have three wives. That is not allowed under Russian law but it is my culture. Our religion is creating calm."

I couldn't imagine he actually believed that, though I understood he had to parrot the regime's message. But I wondered how long that would actually keep him safe, and how long the façade of peace and prosperity could be sustained when so many groups felt disenfranchised.

◇◇◇◇◇◇◇

The precarious nature of Chechen "stability" became even more apparent when we crossed the checkpoints into the neighboring republic, Dagestan, into whose crags the most determined guerrillas had fled. Soldiers draped in automatic rifles peered into the vehicle to ensure that our faces didn't match the mug shots of wanted "terrorists."

One of the first places I visited was a dusty market town of 125,000 named Khasavyurt, a *goryachaya tochka*, or hot spot. Khasavyurt's main claims to fame was hosting the signing of a peace accord that briefly ended the first Chechen war, and freestyle wrestlers who have collected eight Olympic gold medals since 2000. In 1858, the French writer Alexandre Dumas traveled with an armed escort of Cossacks through Khasavyurt, encountering mountain bandits along the way. "Seldom does a night pass without someone being carried off for ransom," he wrote, his imagination captured.

Violence still characterizes the region. Khasavyurt is a mile and a half from the border with Chechnya, which at the time of my visit made it a favored crossing for insurgents smuggling weapons back and forth. As a result, the town was the site of numerous "special operations," which entailed heavily armed Russian soldiers swooping down upon the house of a suspected terrorist and either shooting him or demanding that others inside hand him over. We were following a tip by a human rights activist about one such incident, in a second-floor apartment in a back street tenement where a young couple was shot for alleged ties with insurgents. You never knew with these cases—sometimes the authorities had trustworthy intelligence, but more often the notoriously incompetent intelligence forces operated on hunches. That didn't stop them from barging in and firing anyway.

Khasavyurt does not go out of its way to be welcoming. Two combat helicopters whirled overhead as we drove on the earthen main drag past drab low-rise buildings selling sheep pelts and construction materials. We had planned to move about subtly, on side roads, but the taxi driver got lost and yelled out of the car window for directions, which has to be one of the stupidest things to do in a police state. He even shouted, "Where was the latest special operation?" The people who generously answered him either worked for Russian security forces or had friends who did. As we neared the decrepit apartment block to which he had been directed, a military jeep zoomed up and blocked our path. Four beefy operatives pushed into our sedan, filling it with the stink of vodka. They wore blue camouflage uniforms and, holding assault rifles aloft, shouted, "You're under arrest!"

Authorities deem the rebellion the biggest security threat in Russia, and they don't look fondly upon independent journalists who witness their harsh responses. The men commandeered our taxi and marched us at gunpoint into the dreaded "Department Six" anti-terrorism headquarters. We were taken into an interrogation room whose sign above the door read, "For the Wanted." A particularly aggressive soldier barked that we would never get out. The snarling man waved his AK-47 gun as he told us what he thought about human rights (not much). Then two secret service agents sat us under mug shots of the most-sought-after terrorists affixed to the wall, and inspected our documents. They had identical Beatles haircuts circa 1964. One was blond and one was brown.

The questions were simple:

Why are you here?

What do you know?

With my limited Russian, I tried to point out we had committed no crime. To which the growling soldier replied: "Our notion of democracy is different from yours." He touched his rifle for extra effect.

The two agents, meanwhile, played a classic "good cop, bad cop" routine, complete with offering cigarettes (bad cop) and health warnings (the good one). "Take it," the affectedly mean brunet cop said, pushing the smokes toward me. "Don't! Smoking is unhealthy," urged the nice blond one.

I reached for my first cigarette in twenty-six years. Then I tried to distract them.

"Look," I said, leaning forward as the brown cop lit my cigarette. "I have this theory about mountain clans. They're always fighting."

"Definitely in Dagestan!" said the blond. "We have more than thirty warring clans. You must visit the mountains."

"If we let her out," growled the other.

I held forth about the traits of highlanders, starting with tribes in Papua New Guinea. Its rugged hills created a great number of language groups—839—that regularly fight each other. "Mountain people are suspicious of outsiders," I lectured. "Why are Dutchmen peaceful? It's a flat country and they have to get along. When you gain altitude people start sparring, because you can't see what's on the other side of the hill. Think about it. We see this all over the world, in Appalachia, the Atlas Mountains. Some 80 percent of conflict occurs in—"

"Enough!" shouted the brunet cop. "You're giving me a headache." He left the room.

The blond listened intently. Then he recited Pushkin. Every educated Russian of a certain age knows his poems. The line he uttered was from "Prisoner of the Caucasus," published in 1821.

Hurry home, pretty ones
A Chechen lurks across the stream

He smiled, pleased with himself for remembering the stanza. He apparently appreciated anthropology as well as literature, as he launched into a discussion of the physical landscape and its inhabitants. They relied on sheep herding and subsistence agriculture, like so many clan cultures. Behavior was governed by honor codes and loyalty to kin. A man's calling was to defend his group's reputation and feuds were common. The stereotype is of exaggerated machismo and pride, long on bloodlust and short on forgiveness. Prowess with weapons is valued, too.

I noted the local saying, "Giving what you've got is hospitality. Hitting with what you've got is courage."

"Yes," the agent said enthusiastically.

He moved on to history. The very topography, he said, was a powerful means of defense against marauding Mongols and Turkic tribes in the thirteenth and fourteenth centuries. These guerrilla methods then served the clans well during later moments of resistance, inflicting defeat on the Persians in 1744 and on the tsars in the nineteenth century. During the latter conflict, Imam Shamil and his united tribes waged one of the most remarkable guerrilla campaigns in modern history, and their example still inspires local resisters today. Shamil used the religious brotherhoods and spiritual leaders of each clan as an organizing tool, to the excitement of Karl Marx, who called the revolutionary a "great democrat." The agent didn't necessarily agree with that judgment, but he was nonetheless awed by the clans' military prowess.

The ferocious defense of the Caucasus captured the imagination not only of Pushkin, but also his fellow poet Mikhail Lermontov and the novelist Leo Tolstoy, who traveled to the region as soldiers in the Russian army. Lermontov depicted the Caucasians as vicious savages but also lamented the "needless" bloodshed caused by the war. Tolstoy's writing career was bookended by novels set amidst the turmoil, *The Kazaks* (1863) and *Hadji Murat* (1904), the latter about a legendary rebel leader. He compared the Chechens to thistles: "Man has conquered everything and destroyed millions of plants, but this one won't submit." The agent and I discussed mountain societies in other countries. I shared my observations about Albanian blood feuders and the self-defense units in Mexico. There were remarkable similarities. The guerrilla tactics the policeman described reminded me of Colombia. "Geography is a powerful thing," he mused.

Our bonding over scholarly matters had mellowed the interrogator. By now the agent had accepted that the translator and I were not the type of people to strap on suicide vests. "We can never beat the Caucasians," he confided in a moment of trust. He offered us tea and cookies before letting us go.

◇◇◇◇◇◇◇

International security experts believe the older of the two Boston bombers, Tamerlan Tsarnaev, became radicalized during an extended visit to the capital of Dagestan, Makhachkala, a seaside city whose mosques served as organizing bases for militants. While visiting his parents in Dagestan months before making his bombs, Tsarnaev worshipped at an orthodox mosque known for its anti-American sermons. The house of worship was on the radar of Russian forces, which assassinated several of its congregants.

The noisy city of nearly half a million people is filled with ugly apartments built during Soviet times, and equally ugly violence. While the fighters were largely ensconced in the mountains, having escaped Kadyrov, they came down to Makhachkala to get supplies, recruit, and set off improvised explosive devices like the type found in Afghanistan.

After Khasavyurt, all the energy we had left over after pursuing and conducting interviews went toward evading the Russian intelligence services. From the moment the translator and I checked into a bland hotel on a busy commercial street in Makhachkala, we set a strict routine to avoid detection. We hired different taxi drivers for each ride, remained silent in the backseat, and avoided sensitive conversations on our cell phones. We wore head scarves and long black clothes in an attempt to blend in. The photographer was of North Caucasian descent and spoke native Russian, the lingua franca of the region, so she attracted less attention than me, a middle-aged American who spoke stale Russian.

The focal point of Makhachkala is the white-domed Jama Masjid mosque, whose capacity of seventeen thousand makes it—unlike Kadyrov's mosque in Grozny—one of the largest in Europe. Construction was financed with Turkish money; it's one of many mosques in the North Caucasus built recently thanks to foreign largesse. The Soviets closed most of Dagestan's 1,700 mosques, but since the late 1980s that number has been surpassed. Much of the mosque- and madrassa-building here and in Chechnya has been funded by money from Arabian Gulf states, especially Saudi Arabia, which has been sponsoring Dagestanis abroad to indoctrinate them in the fundamentalist Wahhabist creed. The Jama Masjid, however, was of the mainstream Sufi strain now sanctioned by the Russian state. It was a grandiose symbol of the Islamic renaissance in the post-Soviet era, and more importantly, served as a form of social control: authorities could now watch large numbers of citizens in one crowded place.

A couple of days after we arrived, a bombing took place. A few hours later, we took a taxi to see the damage: an entire city block within 1,500 feet of the Interior Ministry had been blasted. Six people were killed and sixty more sent to the hospital with lacerations and burns. The police cordons and chunks of cement lying on the streets would complicate our route, the driver grumbled, but he quickly agreed to swing by the site when we offered to double the fare. When we arrived, we saw a mess of electrical cables sticking through the cratered walls, splintered glass from exploded windows, and distraught people hoping to cross the police tape to retrieve belongings. Incongruously, three tailors remained seated behind sewing machines in a dress shop on the second floor of a damaged building. We had a clear view of them from the street through the blown-out windows. Their calm determination to continue working struck me as absurd, but then again, this sort of thing happened every day in Dagestan.

Back at the hotel, we washed off residue from the explosion and got ready for dinner with a former politician. First we checked our luggage to make sure no agents had rifled through it or erased files from our laptops. Colleagues had recommended our dinner companion, Sabidov Sagida, as an astute observer who was as neutral as one could be in this polarized environment. Now retired, Sabidov had survived an assassination attempt when he served as deputy mayor of Khasavyurt a couple years back. Still jumpy, he suggested the restaurant just off our hotel lobby, as any putative assassin would have to go through various layers of hotel staff—the guard, the receptionist, the man guarding the receptionist, the maitre d', the waiters, the Russian spies hanging around the premises—before reaching our table. We spotted him easily, since he was the only other person in the dining room, which was typical of Russian hotel restaurants: enormous, empty, and decorated with tacky glass chandeliers. A television blared at the highest volume, also customary.

Politicians in Dagestan have two looks: the mullah with beard and *papapkha*, the curly wool hat worn throughout the Caucasus, or the bland bureaucrat in polyester suit and bowl haircut. Sabidov favored the latter. As we took our places at the dirty-linened table, the waiter brought *khinkal*, a dumpling filled with boiled lamb, and salty mineral water. He turned down the television, presumably to eavesdrop more easily on our conversation. Sabidov asked him to turn it back up—the evening news was reporting yet another blast in Makhachkala, this time at a grocery that sold wine. "It never stops," he said, fixated on the screen.

That led the conversation to the rebels, and the fragmented clans that still feuded amongst themselves, much as they did in the Middle Ages. Sabidov estimated the Islamist guerrillas at just a couple hundred in total, and said they were not responsible for all of the violence, although sometimes kin feuding and political Islam overlapped. He opined that, due to the wild terrain and large number of clans, Dagestan was proving even harder to suppress than Chechnya, which had tamer geography and fewer ethnicities. While the mountains presented a convenient refuge for the guerrillas fleeing Kadyrov's rule, the social fragmentation in Dagestan made the likely domination of one kin group impossible. The violence, therefore, went beyond politicized religion and hatred of Russia. Sabidov spooned sour cream on top of the lumps and took a doughy bite. He glanced back up at the television images of bomb rubble. Authorities had to contend with a traditional system of *dzamaats*. These governing organizations sprang from Dagestan's thirty different ethnic groups, all Muslim and many of which are at odds with each other. Dzamaats are based on customary clan law; each operates in a particular neighborhood or village, making decisions and dispensing justice and favors. These political networks consolidated power in isolated communities after the Soviet collapse, to the point that businesses needed their approval for projects and politicians sought their votes. Leaders of the dzamaats, he said, often acted like Mafia warlords. "On the municipal levels, they are fighting one against the other to preserve their political, financial, and administrative power. That's why many shoot each other."

He gave an example from his own life. As a politician, he was in the public eye and therefore naturally vulnerable to assassination by jihadist rebels who targeted people who held public office. In 1999, his little daughter went into the garden and found a bomb in their walnut tree. It would have been tripped if she had stepped on a concealed wire. "My little girl," he said, shaking his head. This was a personal matter; someone wanted to wipe out his family. Five relatives including his brother and cousins had been killed already. Sabidov was supposed to be next. The targeting had nothing to do with ideology, but rather grudges. "They were not terrorists," he insisted. "It was clan-related."

I asked Sabidov what would quell the turmoil. He pushed the dumplings around his plate, in order to represent the territorial divisions. They didn't touch each other. "Nothing. There's no social cohesion or allegiance to a national state. I'd like to say there's a magic formula but it's only getting worse."

◇◇◇◇◇◇

Before the Soviet era, Dagestan had been a major center of Islamic theology. As Imam Shamil demonstrated, the Sufi faith was practically the only thing that could unite the area's diverse ethnic and linguistic groups. But the Soviets closed mosques and forbade public worship during their repressive rule, and the possibility of a return to a religiously unified nation became even more remote with the arrival of fanatical Wahhabist preachers in the 1990s. In Dagestan, as in Chechnya, religious life had fractured such that the fundamentalist radicals were targeting for assassination Sufi spiritual leaders.

At the time of my visit, Ahmed-haji Abdulaev was Dagestan's mufti. A Sufi, he had the support of the Russian state. By all accounts he had reached out to prominent Salafis to foster greater understanding, establishing an Islamic Scholars Board, among other measures. This gesture failed to deter jihadists from gunning down Sufi clerics, however, and the mufti feared he might be next.

Getting through the security at his office required an hour of patience. It was a squat commercial building in downtown Makhachkala, perhaps chosen for having no distinguishing features. There was nothing remotely spiritual about the space, which was policed by security cameras and flak-jacketed bodyguards. They kept their weapons ready while checking our documents, and then escorted us up the dirt-streaked and smelly stairwell to a drab room with shuttered blinds. A drawn-looking man with goatee and a papapkha sat behind a solid desk. His black suit hung a size too large, enhancing his air of vulnerability.

The mufti stood and gave a sort of weak bow. The desk was too big to reach across, and in any event he wouldn't have shaken hands with a strange woman. Normally people offer you tea in Dagestan, but he was in a rush to finish the interview in time for afternoon prayers. He got straight to the point: the Russians were to blame for the violence. If the Soviets and then the Russian regime after them had granted independence to the Caucasian people, there would be peace. Years of denying Dagestanis their religious heritage had caused a breakdown in values. The youth grew up not knowing what it meant to be a good Sufi Muslim. Then they were radicalized by the security forces' draconian crackdowns. "The Russians knock on the apartment doors, they tell them to give up the people inside. So what happens? They shoot. That's why we have suicide bombers."

Even as he pointed the finger at the Russians, the mufti defended government policies of rounding up young men spotted attending radical mosques that were believed to have ties with the armed underground. Only Sufism could cut across all the fragmentation and unite the republic, just as it had in the nineteenth century. But that, he said, was unlikely in the current situation, and maybe the future, too. "The country has been poisoned by outside influences," he said.

My eyes drifted to a picture of Mecca hanging on the wall, prompting thoughts about the Wahhabism imported from Saudi Arabia. The longer I spent here, the more I became convinced that the mufti was right: the continuous meddling from the outside had frayed the culture and left it weak. If the Chechens and the Dagestanis had simply been left alone— by the Kremlin, by foreign preachers and fighters—this mess could have been avoided.

◇◇◇◇◇◇◇

My next undertaking was to meet some of these meddling foreigners. Despite the best efforts of authorities to round up extremists, Salafi influence still endured across the territory, including Kirovaul, a settlement comprised mostly of Avars.

The area has one of Dagestan's highest concentrations of theologians and clerics, of both moderate and Salafi strains, and the half dozen mosques in the town were split between the two creeds. The surrounding district is known for cells of armed resistance. Kirovaul had been the site of recent shootouts between Russian security forces and jihadists, including a woman who blew herself up with a suicide belt when the army approached. An ammunition cache was found in her house. This seemed like a fitting place to examine what the mufti described as the foreign "poison" in the country.

Through human rights groups we contacted the spokesman of the Salafi community in Kirovaul, Said Akhmed Nasibov, about the shooting death of his son and nephew a few months before. Authorities said the murders stemmed from a clan feud. It took us a while to find a taxi driver willing to go to Kirovaul, but once on the road there were surprisingly few checkpoints for an area rife with terrorism. We passed through the radical Kizilyhurtovsky district, into the baked foothills. The village lies at the top of a small plateau, with views of purple mountains and thick deciduous forests where authorities comb for radicals who have killed policemen and Sufi clerics. Kirovaul's unpaved streets of simple white houses are home to one thousand people, many of them widows dressed in black. They were raising their children alone because the men had vanished into state custody, or died in armed conflict. Many dzamaats, like that of Kirovaul, consisted of more than one clan or language group. The introduction of radical Salafi thought divided some communities and unified others. In Kirovaul, deep divisions had emerged. The Nasibovs had converted to the new creed. In front of the family's one-story stuccoed home sat an imported SUV. The vehicle likely cost about $35,000, an unimaginable sum in a village where most people grew their own food. Eggplant and raspberry bushes sprouted on the patio, and a goat bleated somewhere nearby. A bearded man of about sixty, his sunken cheeks framed by a bushy salt-and-pepper beard, came to the door. This was Said Akhmed Nasibov, the patriarch.

A dozen women in mourning black and hijabs awaited us inside. They had strong features, prematurely wrinkled skin, and mouths full of gold teeth, a status symbol. We left our shoes at the threshold and they swept children's stuffed animals from the bed so that we could take seats. The room was filled with carpets—on the floor, on the walls, for sitting, for praying, for decoration. The women turned off the forty-two-inch flat-screen television and brought in a brass tray of steaming black tea, though everyone was soon too busy talking to drink. One after another, they told stories of the police killing or seizing their family members, mostly the males. There had been so many "special operations" that they had lost track.

"They hit a disabled woman one time."

"It wasn't even in the news."

"Was that the latest?"

"It was June 25, 2010. How could you forget the date?"

"I'm getting confused. There have been so many."

"Everyone in this village knows of someone who was accused of being a *boyevik*," said Nasibov. That was the word for terrorist. A toddler sat on his lap playing with the newspaper clipping about his son's death.

This village had produced national champions of *sambo*, a Russian form of judo, and the son, Magomed Nasibov, had won various tournaments himself. On July 21, 2010, the twenty-one-year-old asked an older cousin, also named Magomed Nasibov, to drive him to Makhachkala to pick up a sports bag from his coach. On their way back they were stopped at a police checkpoint, their silver sedan searched. The Nasibov family had already been on the radar of the security forces, who had searched the cousin's house various times and sentenced his brother to two and a half years in jail in connection with terrorist activities. The two Magomed Nasibovs were allowed through the checkpoint, but as they neared home, at around 1:30 a.m., witnesses saw an armored car approach at high speed and unload two bursts of machine-gun fire at their car.

"They shot 171 bullets," one of the women in black told me.

I asked if it was true that they were engaged in a feud with another family, the Malikovs, as the authorities claimed. The Malikovs' patriarch was a town official and he and his son had recently been shot dead. Nasibov the elder didn't address the question, only stating, "We are believers." *Believer* widely means Salafi here. "We want to practice our own beliefs. The authorities don't like that."

Then he laid his son's sambo medals and trophies out on a carpet. The women cried loudly. The nearby mosque's loudspeaker called for evening prayers. Another fatherless girl, around five, put on a purple hijab. The entire group rose to worship, saying to me that they hoped I found what I came for.

I hadn't. I left with an uneasy feeling. Was it true the government was targeting this family as a means of subduing the whole Salafi community? Or was this actually a personal feud? Maybe it was both. Whatever the case, this family was being wiped out. A couple of years after I met them, Nasibov himself was shot dead by masked men. Two more nephews and a male cousin were killed, too. His sister, Patimat, was detained for alleged connections with the underground. At this rate, there weren't going to be many Nasibovs left.

As Sabidov, the politician, had illustrated, the lines between kin violence and terrorism by the state and fundamentalists were often blurred, one compounding the other. The complex interplay between the clans, the government, and the foreign radicals resulted in a toxic cauldron that begged resolution. I thought of what the mufti had said: the state's suppression had fractured these traditional clan fiefdoms in the mountains, leaving them chaotic and vulnerable to extremist influence and base criminals. The forces shaping Dagestani society were centrifugal, not centripetal, as they had been during Imam Shamil's time in the nineteenth century.

◇◇◇◇◇◇◇

The normally friendly lady at the reception desk glared when the translator and I returned to the hotel. "You are trouble," she muttered, as she pushed the room keys over the desk. "When are you leaving?" When we got to the room, we saw what she meant: three security agents with the police-vogue Beatles haircuts had set up chairs outside the door. They were smoking, flicking the ash onto the carpeted floor.

Everywhere, we encountered more Beatles hairstyles. The taxi's rearview mirror showed them tailgating us. They hung around restaurants while we ate shashlik kebabs. They watched us when we visited mosques. They followed us to buy bottled water. And they maintained their sentry outside the hotel room for the duration of my stay.

Every day that we were in Makhachkala, someone was shot, usually a Russian policeman. On September 25, 2011, the night after Vladimir Putin announced he would run for president again, the Russian security forces made a sinister show of force. Dozens of military men in black masks roamed the streets, shaking down drivers at a major thoroughfare. The security forces pulled young men out of their cars at gunpoint, checking documents of anyone who might be suspected of jihadist affiliation. They peeled black film from tinted car windows in order to peer inside.

That same night, we met with a doctor named Yevgeny Zaslavski who had lost his feet in a car bomb intended for a relative connected to the military. After the amputation, he was fitted with prosthetics. In his fifties, he learned to drive, in order to minimize walking. He drove us to dinner, and I saw he was still having trouble working the clutch and accelerator. He barely seemed to notice the shakedowns occurring outside the car. He mused aloud about where we would have dinner. When I asked if maybe he felt uneasy, the doctor looked at me flatly.

"To exist like this is not okay. But you get used to it," he said, with a bored glance outside. He was more worried about securing his fake foot on the brake.

Zaslavski took us to a restaurant that specialized in shellfish from the Caspian Sea. You entered the dining room through a sizeable papier-mâché water vessel. Lanky and mustachioed, Zaslavski wore a flawlessly tailored wool suit. His feet looked real, encased in tan leather loafers. He refused to use a cane, waddling unsteadily. We dined alone in a wood-paneled room upstairs. He ordered a bottle of Armenian brandy, which he nearly finished, and a plate of boiled prawns, which he didn't touch. As we tore into the food he explained why: he was Jewish.

Jewish? *Bis prabl'em*, he said. No problem.

No problem? There was a Muslim insurgency going on outside.

Zaslavski demurred, explaining that, paradoxically, in the midst of all this religious turmoil, Russia's oldest Jewish community was relatively safe because they lived above the clan rivalry. There had been some vandalism of graves and brick throwing at synagogues, but these were believed to be isolated acts by individuals rather than groups. "If they were really serious they would have blown up the rabbi's car," noted Zaslavski. Called "Mountain Jews," the Tats, as they are also known, have lived in the region for twelve centuries. They are so embedded in Dagestan that some Muslims consider them another clan. The Jews in Makhachkala were treated in a neutral fashion because they didn't get involved in internecine struggles.

Legend has it that the Tats came from Persia, although some amateur historians posit that they were Khazars, a nomadic Turkic group that converted to Judaism in the late eighth century. Whatever their origin, the Tats intermarried with locals and adopted many customs not normally associated with Jews, such as cultivating tobacco and fighting on horseback. But they also preserved many of their own ways and distinguished themselves through their prowess with weapons. They were also magnificent dancers, sought after for weddings. The Tats who came down from the mountains to lowland cities preserved these. Their language incorporated elements of Persian; they felt little or no kinship with the Ashkenazi Jewry in the rest of Russia. Under Stalin, they worshipped underground, but today were thoroughly aboveboard.

"Mountain Jews were badasses before the Israelis," the doctor said.

Intrigued, the translator and I made an appointment with the aged chairman of the Jewish community, Shimi Dibyayev, to spend a Sabbath with the group.

In keeping with the Tats' respected position in society, the synagogue is one of the more elegant buildings in Makhachkala, a nineteenth-century brick building whose three stories are carefully tended. Dibyayev was fully armed as he squired me with a limp through the temple. He was ready to take on attackers, just in case other Dagestanis turned on the Tats. "I always carry a pistol and have seven more weapons at home," he said. "When someone upsets a Jewish person, he goes with two guns." I did a double take, because Dibyayev had trouble seeing and hearing, but he assured me, "Of course I'm used to guns. I'm eighty-five years old, what do you think?"

Women and men are supposed to worship separately, but the Tats had adopted the legendary hospitality of the clans and were not going to turn away two foreign guests who had come from far away. We were shown the prayer room in the back, where a couple of middle-aged men rocked back and forth. Much to the annoyance of the rabbi, worshippers peeled off to drink wine with us and play *narde*, a form of backgammon. Over plates of feta cheese and olives, they showed off the fanny packs that men wear to carry pistols. "It's become a fashion statement," one of the younger men explained. Older traditions had endured, such as kidnapping brides. Following tribal practice, the groom and his friends snatch a future bride from the road, sometimes against her will, sometimes with the family's assent, and drag her to the wedding. Generally, in the twenty-first century, she is aware of the engagement but is still mock-kidnapped. They were surprised to hear that this ritual was uncommon among Jews elsewhere.

Most people we spoke to said Jews and Muslims got along on a social level and the radical fringe was just that. "We've been here so long, we're part of the local culture," Dibyayev said, adding, "I've been to Israel and am much more worried about Jews there."

◇◇◇◇◇◇

There were several more bombings over the following days. I wondered whether our hotel was next. It was time to go.

On the flight back to Moscow, I considered what the Chechen mufti had said about religion creating calm in Chechnya. Behind me sat a soldier with a bullet embedded in his face. He moaned through the bandages, and gave off a rotted flesh smell. The passenger sitting across the aisle sprayed Chanel Coco fragrance on her nostrils to obscure the stench.

Back in 1999, during the height of the shelling in Grozny, I'd known a doctor who lived there. True to her Hippocratic oath, she treated everyone who sought help: Russian soldiers, separatists, anyone who had shrapnel or burns. For that the warlords threatened her with death and burned her house. She made it to Moscow with her family, but lacked the *propiska*, the special permission to live in the city required for the *chorniye chelavek*, the black people of the Caucasus.

I would visit the family in their basement apartment because they were scared to go outside. The irony was not lost on the doctor that she was still seeking shelter below street level; this would have made a fine bunker, in Grozny. She would make us a rice dish called *ploff* and her little girl who dreamed of being a ballerina would do a twirling dance. Eventually, we helped her secure political asylum and they moved to Chicago. Would she feel safe in Chechnya today? I doubted it. The jihadists could still hunt her down. Kadyrov was unlikely to reward her with a new house, or practice.

Moscow's cynical investment in Kadyrov may have seemed to be paying off: for the time being, things were quiet in Grozny, at least on the surface (and provided you hadn't displeased the president or his cronies). From the Russian point of view, managing the North Caucasus was certainly easier than it had been during the wars. But giving power to a leader like Kadyrov did not promote unity. On the contrary, the rigged elections, corruption, nepotism, and murder of opposition figures on Kadyrov's watch would only radicalize rivals and clans excluded from his inner circle. This made things unstable for his regime, for Moscow, and, of course, for the people of Chechnya. The freedom of the Chechen people today is as contrived as Grozny's Las Vegas architecture.

Even after the two devastating wars, Russia had not actually conquered the North Caucasus. Instead it installed a fragile puppet state that could blow up any time—in which case, Russia would likely send the military back in. Meanwhile, the extremists had merely absconded into Dagestan. None of this seemed like much of a triumph for Moscow.

The Boston bombers, even with their distant connection, showed how these republics posed a threat across the world. The training of terrorists in the mosques of the North Caucasus is ongoing due to the unrest and the failure of the state to forge a sense of unity.

And things were only going to get worse, for all concerned. Not only was the new regime ignoring Chechnya's underlying problems, including massive youth unemployment and poverty, it was actively creating new ones by imposing strict religious law; oppressing women, journalists, and anyone who spoke against it; and spending government money recklessly. Moscow's favoritism of one clan threatened, not deepened, Chechen unity; it had the same effect on Chechen autonomy.

Chechnya and Dagestan offered a study in contrasts. The former had a strongman, the latter didn't. Yet the republics shared many of the same problems, despite the differing role of the central state in each. The people of these two republics had lost their chance at lasting peace. As in Nepal, the state's blunt intrusion, compounded by foreign influence, was making life precarious and unsafe for ancestral mountain people. If the tsars had never interfered, or if these regions had been granted independence in 1991, the ancient loathing of centralized rule would never have mutated the way it did. Chechen and Dagestani identity was as unmovable as the mountains. Just as the mountains refused to submit to the contours of the flatlands, so too one could never shake the unyielding power of their clans.

6

On the Existential Border

KASHMIR, 5,200 TO 16,000 FEET

The monsoons never cross
the mountains into Kashmir.

> —Agha Shahid Ali, "The Season of the Plains"
> (1987)

Arshad Hussain was pursuing his medical degree in the capital of Kashmir, Srinagar, more concerned with passing exams than with the violence surging outside the library. It was 1998, and the Muslim enclave had detonated into such violence that it was hard to keep track of who was attacking whom. Put simply, Kashmir had been ruled, nastily, by India ever since the British departed in 1947 and partitioned the subcontinent along religious lines, into Muslim Pakistan and Hindu-dominated India. Kashmir, located right on the border between the two countries in a breathtaking Himalayan valley, got stuck on the Indian side, even though it had always been predominantly Muslim. Most Kashmiris, who were a distinct highland people, wanted either independence or to align themselves with Pakistan, which had fought three wars with India over the region. Now, the Indian occupiers in Kashmir were being attacked by rock-throwing youths who wanted independence, as well as by radical armed groups who had a more jihadist agenda.

Like most residents of Kashmir, Arshad opposed Indian rule. But he felt detached from the rioters, and little connection with the extremists who were being armed and trained by Pakistan or Al Qaeda in camps hidden amid folds in the mountains. Of course Arshad couldn't

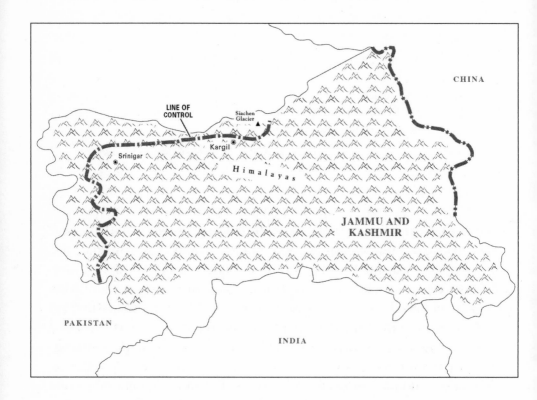

CHINA

LINE OF
CONTROL

Siachen
Glacier

Kargil

Srinigar

H i m a l a y a s

JAMMU AND
KASHMIR

PAKISTAN

INDIA

completely ignore what was going on; the streets were filled with barbed wire and sandbags. India had responded to the revolt by posting even more troops, making for the highest ratio of soldiers to civilians in the world. These security forces randomly hauled men of fighting age out of cars and buses for questioning. Bombs went off daily, cinemas were converted into barracks, and curfews prevented socializing at night. Srinagar was, effectively, a city at war, and one that had destroyed the economy. The foreign skiers and trekkers who used to sustain the tourism industry vanished, too scared to venture into the weapons-infested slopes. This put out of business the purveyors of oriental silk carpets and owners of walnut-carved houseboats that had previously attracted hash-smoking travelers.

Every week in the newspaper Arshad read about twenty, thirty, forty deaths from explosions or cross fire, but it seemed abstract, just numbers. Anyway, he had to focus on passing his postgraduate exams. Arshad was the first in his lower-class family to seek a coveted medical degree, and he couldn't fail. He was so intent on getting high grades that in 1991 he volunteered to intern at the government's sole psychiatric hospital. Kashmiris don't normally see shrinks, he figured, so he'd have many quiet hours to prepare for the tests. No one would come to the clinic; he'd treat at most a single patient per day, according to people he consulted.

But it was not so. In fact, Arshad was shocked at how busy the clinic was. Often he was the only doctor on duty and he couldn't cope with the deluge. Hundreds of patients would pour in over the course of an average day. They were desperate, too; they banged on his office door, which he had to lock during consultations. They sought relief from nightmares, heart palpitations, and panic. The hospital wasn't that easy to find; it lay on a cul-de-sac on an edge of town not serviced by public buses. But they managed to find it. When they got an appointment with Arshad, they begged for remedies to end the depression, insomnia, and fear, always fear.

Arshad gradually noticed a disturbing uptick in suicide attempts. Killing oneself used to be taboo among Kashmiris, whose language doesn't even have a word for the act. Men in particular would never show such vulnerability. But now parents were bringing in sons who had swallowed pesticides or slashed themselves to end their anguish. There was another condition so common that Arshad gave it a name: "Midnight Knock Syndrome." People would panic thinking that soldiers were coming to get them. They weren't just being paranoid: thousands of young men had vanished when Indian soldiers went house to house, usually in the middle of the night, hunting down putative militants. When memories flared of these terrifying nights, many people rushed to the hospital to seek some sort of comfort.

⬦⬦⬦⬦⬦⬦⬦

Nepal, another state caught between two big powers, India and China, describes itself as a yam between two boulders. Kashmir is like a smashed lily with the potential to become radioactive. It has all the virulent ingredients of mountain conflicts examined in earlier chapters—a minority ethnic group; an ancestral, almost sacred attachment to the land; poverty; discrimination; contested water resources; and crags that provide havens to jihadists. Unlike those other regions, though, Kashmir is trapped in a buffer zone between two nuclear-armed nations, India and Pakistan, that refuse to leave it alone. Kashmir's quagmire had become a tangle of interests, all at odds. There was ethnic nationalism, internationalist jihad, a nonviolent independence movement, a state desperately holding on to a strategic enclave, and its neighbor seeking to extend its border. No one could agree on a solution acceptable to all. Ordinary people, the mechanics and housewives and saffron farmers, were powerless in the middle.

Because of this panoply of factors, Kashmir struck me as the most in extremis of all the places I had visited: and the fractious two-thousand-mile mountain border was as psychological as it was political. While misery afflicted all the mountain people I met, Kashmir exhibited the most acute distress of any highland population, if not in the world. The psychological trauma here affected 30 to 90 percent of the population, depending on what study you read. To put things in perspective, even with all the suicidal soldiers returning to the United States, only about 6 to 8 percent of our population has been similarly traumatized. My goal here, unsavory as it was urgent, was to decode all that could go wrong in a mountain culture, and the psychological impact of denied autonomy and identity. The other locales offered me a glimpse into tactics and political organizing. Kashmir showed me how prolonged violence and fear can destroy the soul.

Kashmir's conflict, I knew, brimmed with global superlatives in numerous ways. The border fight is the world's longest-running international dispute. The sheer number of diverse armed groups is dizzying: more than a dozen. Srinagar's ratio of 50 soldiers per 1,000 civilians is among the highest anywhere. Kashmir's Siachen Glacier is the highest-altitude battlefield on earth. With each country nuclear-armed, all-out conflagration would spell an Armageddon that would reverberate around the world.

In an essay entitled "Negotiating Necrophilia," Ashis Nandy, a leading public intellectual from India, asserts that Kashmir "overwrites" almost everything that is written about it. He meant that Kashmir, extreme in so many regards, was especially distinct in one specific way: "Not because of its unique culture, its geopolitical significance, or its breathtaking beauty, but because of its pain."

◇◇◇◇◇◇◇

Mountains are often at least partly a state of mind. When I visited Jerusalem with Anton, my Risk-playing son, we marveled that the Mount of Olives was but a hill. Yet it figured so large in the Bible! Likewise Masada. We scaled the mound in just an hour, yet in Jewish lore the defense of the plateau was monumental. The key is not just height, but how certain places loom in the imagination.

Kashmir rises high as both a mental and a landmass space. The valley's main city, Srinagar, was built at a respectable 5,190 feet above sea level, and the villages on the slopes climb even higher. Kashmiris describe their territory as a vertical island, calling the rest of India the "mainland," as though they were physically cut off. Certainly Kashmir is culturally detached, a minority with a different god and diet. The language is distinct and its speakers drink their chai salty, not sweet. The principal spiritual days of these Sufi Muslims are Thursdays and Fridays, as opposed to Hindu India where worship takes place any day of the week. This sense of apartness contributed to the monstrous pain that Nandy referred to.

I visited "the island" in 2008. By then Arshad was a full-fledged doctor running the psychiatric ward, and I followed him on his rounds. Traumatized Kashmiris were still streaming into the psych ward. Arshad and his few helpers were seeing more than one hundred thousand patients a year, up from sixty-two thousand when he'd started out. The various wars and two decades of constant death threats, torture chambers, disappearances, and indiscriminate shootings had led international mental health experts to pronounce Kashmir one of the most traumatized war zones in the world.

An entire generation had grown up during the separatist struggle, victimized by one party or another. The variety of armed groups, often fighting each other as well as against India—Shia versus Sunni, moderate against extremist—made it hard to trust anyone. Ordinary civilians feared that their neighbors might betray them to any of the various camps. All around them—week after week, for years on end—people were vanishing or being killed. Death tolls varied wildly according to whom you asked. The Indian government reported that more than forty-seven thousand people died over the two decades of violence. Human rights groups said it was double that. That number does not include disappearances, which the rights groups estimate at ten thousand. The government claims most of the vanished went to Pakistan voluntarily, a questionable assertion.

Whatever figure you believe, it's certain that the violence has touched everyone. And the overwhelming emotional distress wasn't just a reaction to traumatic experiences, as in most combat zones. The Hindu-dominated Indian government had instituted repressive policies, smashing at Kashmiri identity itself. "It is an existential crisis," said Arshad.

◇◇◇◇◇◇

The causes of the enduring brutality in Kashmir began with the region's terrain. The Himalayas illustrate the curse of mountain buffer zones—frontiers too sparsely inhabited to be priorities for the plains elite. The needs and unique ways of these communities—they are generally minorities, and often indigenous—are usually overlooked or repressed by the capitals, which in turn fuels frustration. Of course, not every range that serves as a border is a site of conflict. Switzerland in its entirety is one big peaceful buffer zone for the five nations surrounding it. The Pyrenees separate Spain and France without any grumbling from either country, and in fact the two governments collaborated on cross-border crackdowns on Basque separatists going back and forth. Spain and France also share military protection of Andorra, the mountain principality that straddles their borders. This prevents either from overrunning it.

But buffer zones don't work so smoothly in the Himalayas. China and India use tiny Nepal, Sikkim, and Bhutan as bulwarks against each other. As in Nepal, the behemoths on either side of Kashmir bully the minority mountain people, ignoring their interests for strategic gain. Kashmir was historically British India's defense against China; India now uses the territory as a shield against Pakistan. And like Nepal, Kashmir has significant rivers originating in the mountains that its bigger neighbors want to exploit for their own benefit and not the locals'.

I also saw many parallels between Kashmir and Chechnya. In both, the mountain people are Sufis repressed by the dominant religious group. Radicalization has been the result, and has followed the same pattern: the hijacking of what was originally an ethnic separatist movement by international jihadists, aided by the fact that in the mountains, guerrilla fighters can more easily smuggle arms and train recruits. In Chechnya the foreign jihadists came from the Middle East. In Kashmir they were hardened Al Qaeda fighters trained in Afghanistan or Pakistan. In both cases, what was once a garden-variety secessionist movement spread from the mountains to the plains.

Unlike in the Caucasus, however, the conflict in Kashmir is not purely a case of frustrated sovereignty or collision of faiths. The many dimensions of Kashmir's imbroglio had an additional factor—two nations coveted it. Such has been the fate of Kashmir over history. Its attractive location and fertile charms have drawn a mosaic of invaders, occupiers, colonizers, and Silk Road adventurers—Mughals, Afghans, and Sikhs among them—who left traces in what became a potpourri of cultures. At different times the main faith was animist, Buddhist, Hindu, or Muslim. Modern Kashmir still includes most of these groups. The central and heavily populated Valley, the locus of today's struggle, is mainly Sunni Muslim. It was once home to many other groups, including a sizeable population of Hindu Brahmins, called Pandits, thousands of whom have fled due to targeting by Islamic militants. Until the second half of the twentieth century, the various religious communities in the Valley coexisted in relative harmony, to the extent that they even adopted bits of each other's culture. Sufi mysticism as practiced in Kashmir incorporates elements of Hindu scriptures. Worshippers of both faiths pray at the same shrines. Kashmir is the only place in India where Muslims carry the Hindu surnames Pandit and Bhat. Instead of the domes that predominate in the Islamic world at large, many Muslim shrines here have pagoda roofs, an architectural style associated with Buddhism.

When the British left, they exacerbated latent religious tensions by partitioning the subcontinent. Rarely are postcolonial transitions smooth, and this was one of the worst in the twentieth century, characterized by a lack of foresight and planning. As in Palestine, Britain acted as though it was simply ceding a house to new owners, without careful attention to the competing claims. The British left it to the 562 princely states to choose whether to align with India or Pakistan. Kashmir was predominantly Muslim, and the Hindu maharajah, Hari Singh, dithered. He eventually opted to join India following an invasion of Kashmir by Muslim tribesmen backed by Pakistan. War broke out. On January 1, 1949, a cease-fire was struck, with 65 percent of the territory placed under Indian control (Jammu and Kashmir) and the rest under Pakistan's (Azad Kashmir). China claimed another small parcel, Aksai Chin, which led to a separate border war with India in 1962.

The de facto border between Pakistan and India, called the Line of Control, was supposed to be temporary but still remains in effect more than sixty-five years later. A UN-recommended plebiscite—over accession to Pakistan or India but not independence—was never held. Two more wars erupted, in 1965 and 1971. Major fighting followed along the disputed Line of Control, in Kargil, in 1999, nearly sparking nuclear war. Kashmiris yearning for self-determination grew frustrated with Hindu hegemony, rigged elections, and the plebiscite that was never held. The aforementioned unrest erupted, and both countries continued to militarize along the frontier.

The Kashmir conflict is remarkable for its complexity and for the terrain it has played out on. Since April 1984, India and Pakistan have fought sporadically over the disputed Siachen Glacier, which traverses close to the Line of Control. At nearly 20,000 feet high, the icy peak is the world's highest combat zone and conditions are extreme. Most people cannot survive for extended periods at that altitude. Combat conditions are extreme. Oxygen starvation can prevent soldiers from sleeping, and causes them to hallucinate. Some even become psychotic. Indian troops train on the glacier for weeks, spending some portion of it at lower elevations, but even so, during their three-month tenure on the summit they lose an average of fifteen to twenty pounds. More have died from exposure than from bullets; 30 to 50 percent of the fatalities have been from cerebral edema. Due to the fact that the glacier is too high to resupply aerially, porters carry supplies up the rock faces. Evacuation is rare because it would require nearly a dozen people to carry just one casualty out. Frostbitten toes are simply cut off; the injured usually die. Then there are avalanches. In 2012, one buried 124 Pakistani soldiers in one of the worst such incidents since World War I.

Because the glacier is so heavily militarized, and hard to ascend—I would need training and climbing entailing several months—Indian authorities ignored my requests to accompany the troops. That meant I would spend my time thousands of feet lower down, where in any event most of the explosions, fatalities, and cross fire were occurring.

Arshad had recommended coming in winter, to see Kashmir at its saddest. The sky is overcast with oppressive clouds, the streets filthy with diesel fumes and slush. It gets dark early, extending the night curfews that trap people inside their unheated homes. It is always complicated to get to mountainous locales, and each of my journeys entailed a unique and often dangerous logistical obstacle. In Mexico it was landslides, in Albania appalling roads. In Kashmir, heavy winter snows prevented me from going too high into the mountains, where passes and even major roads were blocked. My trip would have to be restricted to the main city, Srinagar, and its environs. But the first challenge involved winning over the Indian consulate in Manhattan. The government was sensitive to criticism about its heavy-handedness in Kashmir, and it regularly kicked out researchers who might embarrass it. Activists were recently expelled for seeking mass graves of disappeared young men. So the phrasing on my visa application had to be sufficiently neutral to avoid setting off alarms, treading the line between obfuscation and outright falsehood. Colleagues had advised it was best not to mention "Kashmir" or "conflict." I spent a couple days debating the wording and settled on the vague "looking at medical conditions in the evolving India." That passed muster, and three weeks later the consulate delivered my passport with a decorative visa stamp.

I flew to New Delhi, where I spent twenty-four hours delayed due to blizzards in Srinagar, fretting that the Indian authorities would discover my actual goal and haul me away. But nobody came for me, and eventually I was flying into the white immensity of the Himalayas. No matter what angle you approach them, the Himalayas are dazzling. While not as tall as Everest in Nepal, the jagged crowns were so high that we flew level with the numerous summits, rather than over them.

Kashmir's foremost bards write about the beauty of their mountains, and the frustrated aspirations of those living in their folds. Perhaps they take the massifs that exceed anything on earth for granted, leaving it to a

South Korean poet, Ko Un, to capture the sheer scale of the world's high-est mountains' peaks:

In the Himalayan world
ordinary peaks go unnoticed.
Only peaks of 7000 meters,
Or 7500,
have been given one name or another.

On descent into the city, a rectangle of earth crossed with rivers and lakes came into view through the streaked Plexiglas window. In the seventeenth century, the Mughal emperor Jahangir gazed upon the Valley of Kashmir and exclaimed in ecstasy: "If there were paradise on earth, this was it." This rapturous ode tends to pop up in tourist ads, as if anyone needs to be convinced of the enchanting scenery. Immensely fertile, the Valley bounded by the Great Himalayas and Pir Panjal ranges is 6,158 square miles of magnificence. Peaks crowned by pristine snow soar over purple saffron meadows, orchards, lakes, and alpine forests. Mulberry trees grow in profusion, feeding worms that spin silk for the region's prized carpets. Mountain goats with the finest hair supply the cash-mere textile industry. The earth pops with delicacies: walnuts, apricots, apples, cherries, and almonds to name just a few. Such luxuries have lured merchants since the days when Kashmir was a popular stopover on the ancient Silk Road that stretched from China to the Mediterranean. Kash-mir's admirers included the thirteenth-century traveler Marco Polo. He was particularly struck by the stunning women and sorcerers who could, he was told, change the weather. Polo was in awe of the inhabitants' spirit, too. "The people have no fear of anybody, and keep their independence, with a king of their own to rule and do justice," he wrote.

Kashmiris may be as strong-willed as ever, but Shangri-La the Valley is not. As we began the descent, I saw that the rectangle was frozen. The pilot landed with a jolt, and relieved applause, onto a tarmac that was white with ice and dark with uniforms. The profusion of security forces reminded me of Chechnya. This being a police state, I knew my every movement had to be calibrated. In the name of optimal transparency, the driver, who had long experience working with foreign reporters, pasted a large "PRESS" sign on the windshield of the rented jeep. As soon as I checked into the hotel, a chilly nondescript establishment in Srinagar, security policemen arrived for a few questions. The hotel was geared toward businessmen, but since Kashmir's economy had collapsed due to the violence, I appeared to be one of the few guests, which gave the hotel staff plenty of free time to follow me into the business center whenever I sent e-mails. I assumed the room telephone was tapped, owing to the fuzzy sound of interference on the line.

I spent nearly all my time in town, because of the snow. My sense of being restricted—trapped, even—was enhanced by the claustrophobic feel of Srinagar, whose surrounding mountains seemed to mock the misery below with their ice-capped beauty.

Due to alarming levels of unemployment, capable translators were in ample supply, and I had the privilege of hiring a twenty-something scholar grossly overqualified for the task. Wajahat was a charming political scientist with excellent English and expertise on ethnic nationalism, who should have been teaching at a university rather than interpreting interviews with psychiatric patients.

Srinagar was once the summering spot of the British Raj, who retreated there to escape the lowland heat. Their refuge was situated at a green edge of town where the mountains provide a spectacular background to terraced Mughal gardens and the mirror-like Dal Lake. Rock stars in the 1960s favored staying there on houseboats with intricately carved porches. George Harrison studied sitar on a floating hotel, and Lou Reed, rarely one to wax lyrical, said that his stay on the water "regenerated manhood and introspection." Bollywood likes to film romantic scenes by the lake, but the violence has scared off the hippie tourists who once flocked to the zone. Shuttered houseboats bob forlornly on the water, which has grown choked with lilies and pollution.

Seen from a hill, the old city several miles away holds equal charm: colorful silk garments fluttering from terraces, the pagoda roofs of shrines, the Himalayas in the distance. Delicate bridges cross the green Jhelum River that cuts through town, banked by old brick buildings with lattice windows.

There was nothing remotely charming about getting about the chaotic streets by car, however. Military checkpoints slowed down traffic, so we had to budget time for random questioning by uniformed patrols. You could wait an hour if stuck behind a vehicle being searched by soldiers. And then there were the protests, which could close off a street at a moment's notice. One time we missed an appointment because of a clash between "stone pelters" and security forces. We made a wrong turn into a street where bandana-clad youths had set up a barricade of burning tires; shops clanged down their gates as the demonstrators hurled Molotov cocktails at a truck of uniformed men. We had to wait until more security forces arrived to tear-gas the lot, and by that time we just went back to the hotel and drank tea in the chilly lobby. The sense of gloom deepened with the low heavy clouds, whose gray matched the uniforms, the dirty snow, and the spirits at the government psychiatric hospital, which I visited nearly every day for three weeks.

I intended to observe the psychic cost of repressed and denied autonomy. But I hadn't adequately prepared myself for such an unfathomable degree of crisis. The clinic had not received sufficient support, and the blue sign in front hung upside down on a last hinge. Inside, it smelled of iodine and sweat. The walls were streaked with grime, the floors with mud. Moaning and dazed patients filled the corridors, kneeling, leaning. Some rocked back and forth and muttered to themselves. People traveled from mountain villages hours away for a five-minute audience with Arshad in the presence of a dozen other patients and their accompanying relatives. Arshad's resources are so stretched that some people got a single, cursory session, with little or no follow-up. The only thing in generous supply, surprisingly, was medication, forty-seven different varieties of antidepressants and antipsychotics whose available supply was listed on a large blackboard.

My first day in the halls, we heard a loud *clunk*: a woman had collapsed on the dirty floor. Her uncle tried to lift her. "She gets like this," he said. Her name was Farida Sunderwani, she was thirty-four, and like so many patients had come from higher up the slopes to see the doctor. Her hamlet had no clinic. She experienced anxiety headaches so severe that she ripped out her hair. She suffered a collapse after a stray bullet killed her husband, and her in-laws kicked her out of the house. Too weak to work, Sunderwani relied on handouts from neighbors and could no longer care for her children. "I have no more dignity," she stated flatly.

I pushed through the human thicket to the consulting room. Arshad was easy to spot: a remarkably placid man of about thirty with thick curly hair who exuded calm amid the bedlam. Like most buildings in Srinagar, the hospital was unheated, and Arshad had forsaken white doctor's garb for a leather coat and scarf. He sat at a table chin in hand, while patients and their assorted relatives swarmed about, all talking at once. In the space of twenty minutes, Arshad took a call on his cell phone from a suicidal patient and handed a box of pills to a woman who thought her murdered brother was following her around. A former detainee, too scared to stay home alone, wanted to talk, as did a widow who fainted at the memory of her husband's shooting. Meanwhile, several men desperate to refill their tranquilizer prescriptions tried to barge into the office. Arshad apologized to me for not serving the salted tea that is traditionally given to guests. "It's a bit busy today," he said dryly.

At that moment the guards let in a middle-aged man with vacant eyes. Arshad lit up with recognition and gestured for him to sit. He explained to me that Abdur Rashid Kawdar was on a suicide watch. Kawdar had wandered like a restless ghost ever since he found his brother's body by the river, his throat slit. Then Indian soldiers killed his brother-in-law. The murders had occurred back in 1991, but Kawdar still feared being caught in a dragnet. Unable to hold down a job, he visited the psychiatric clinic every day.

"There's no sense of security in any conflict zone. Here the political turmoil undermines other things, like their sense of identity. The sense of a solution has not arrived and that creates immense frustration. They are in limbo," Arshad observed.

The word *limbo* was apt. His patients were mostly civilians caught in the middle, on a sort of existential border, a psychological buffer zone offering no resolution or relief.

I asked him how he powered on.

He looked surprised, as though he hadn't considered the matter for some time.

"There is a good question. How do I keep up spirits? Seeing someone get well after six weeks gives me such satisfaction. You have to focus on those cases."

But what about all the people he couldn't help?

He gave an enigmatic smile. "I can't change the political situation."

Indeed, I thought, Kashmiris were right to refer to their district as an "island" in the sky. With its geographic isolation, challenging topography, and desperate, dangerous, unending geopolitical quagmire, it's indeed like a lonely island, cut off from the rest of the world. The hundreds of patients I saw at the hospital were emissaries from Kashmir's ten million shipwrecked souls.

◇◇◇◇◇◇◇

Most of the people seeking help were Muslim women thrust into a bread-winning role after their men vanished. Many of them were from the smaller villages higher up on the slopes. Arshad said the stress of trying to feed their children often was debilitating. The lack of a death certificate made it doubly hard to put the pain behind them and move on. The uncertainty was like a disease, as was the memory of the Knock on the Door.

When they came knocking, soldiers went for maximum surprise and minimal witnesses. They usually appeared between 1 and 3 a.m., when people were in bed and it was too dark for anyone to see what was happening. The troops would drive up in trucks, kick aside barking dogs, and bang and shout and holler until you opened the door. If you didn't let them in, they'd force the lock. Neighbors would cower quietly, hoping they wouldn't be next. The soldiers would demand the man—it was always a man—and if you didn't hand him over they rampaged through the rooms, knocking over furniture, and you, too, if you stood in the way.

They never said where they were taking the men, just marched them off without a chance for a final hug. Mothers would bury their noses in their vanished sons' clothes to remember their scent, until it faded. After a while, they forgot the tone of their voices. Their memories of their sons and husbands became frozen in the identification photos left behind. When I visited the houses of the disappeared, congested warrens rife with open sewers and untrustworthy neighbors, every mother and wife I met showed me one of these unsmiling portraits.

I interviewed several of these women and it was hard to know if they were telling me the whole truth. They claimed their men were innocent. Maybe they didn't know if they were or not. Sons don't tell their mothers everything. Maybe the soldiers had a reliable hunch; someone tipped them off, a gun was traced. But it was well known that the Kashmiri cops and security forces picked up many innocents. They held them as a means of extortion, and sometimes killed them. If a neighborhood was on a transit path of militants, the locals were often considered guilty. They could be used to move messages, the soldiers believed. Some restaurants were known to provide food to insurgents out the back door. But did that justify holding people without trial, or applying electrodes to their genitals?

Most of the mothers didn't have lawyers, not that legal guidance would have helped much in such a dysfunctional and corrupt judicial system. But they did have Parveena Ahangar.

Ahangar was a barely literate housewife who had become politicized after her own son vanished in military custody. Exuding moral righteousness, she had managed to organize a network of six hundred families who regularly staged protests, a sort of combination support group and advocacy movement. Known as the Iron Lady of Kashmir, Ahangar became the darling of international rights groups and was nominated for the Nobel Peace Prize.

By her own account, this portly matron was an unlikely candidate to challenge Indian authorities. She had a sheltered upbringing as the daughter of a contractor, married a mechanic at age twelve, and immediately set about producing five children. She largely did housework until the night her son, Javed Ahmed, a seventeen-year-old with a thin mustache and speech impediment, disappeared. It was August 18, 1990. Javed was at his uncle's place when the police came for him. He insisted it was a case of mistaken identity but they pushed him out the door anyway. Ahangar spent nearly two decades fruitlessly searching for him. She heard that he was injured in an army hospital. The staff said he wasn't there. She couldn't find her son at police stations, either. She went to the district and high courts to demand his whereabouts. Nothing. She kept petitioning. The case dragged on. The government denied it was holding him.

Ahangar was so depressed, and scared, that she didn't speak to relatives for months after her son disappeared. She withdrew from friends. But then she met other women making the same macabre rounds at morgues and jails. They began to organize protests on the tenth of every month. They met at the mosques, in the streets, or at home. Ahangar was detained numerous times but persisted, going from village to village in the mountains to reach out to new families. The act of organizing distracted her from her grief and developed a momentum of its own, propelling her with a force that she never thought possible.

A gadfly in the view of the authorities, Ahangar has the reassuring manner of a grief counselor for those who seek her help. She has puffy circles under her eyes from lack of sleep. She wrapped the translator and me in a pillowy hug when we appeared at her modest home in Batamaloo, a working-class district of many vanished men and frequent marches. It was Thursday, the day to visit shrines, and she was planning to take a carload of mothers to pray for their relatives' return. Four women awaited us, sitting cross-legged on a red carpet in the living room. They wore scarves, long tunics called *phirans*, and anguished faces. They clutched photographs tightly.

The women went around the circle telling their stories. Rafiqa was what they called a half widow. Until her husband was proven dead, she could not inherit his property or claim state compensation. Kashmiri custom only allows half widows to remarry after seven years, but most choose not to in case their husbands return. Rafiqa's husband had been missing for twenty-one years. Every night she set a dinner bowl for him. Her in-laws were tired of supporting her and demanded that she marry their other son.

"Otherwise I must leave the house," she choked. Ahangar cradled her, and gently wiped her face with a cloth.

When the crying subsided, a sturdy woman in a red scarf, Rahet Kowoosa, showed us her fingers. They were twisted like pretzels. Indian soldiers had smashed her hands with rifle butts when she tried to block the vehicle carrying away her son.

Rahet Begum, sitting to her left, spoke up. "At night I feel my son is calling me and I look out the window. My husband says, 'He's not there.'" She pulled out a plastic bag of pills. "The doctor gave me these to calm down. Equirex for the heart. Alpanol, Doxepin, Lansoprazole. I couldn't take care of my youngest son so we married him off."

Wajahat stopped translating. I glanced over. Tears streaked his face.

The last woman in the group remained silent. Everyone turned to her but she looked down at her hands and said nothing. We finished our tea, listening to snow sliding from the roof. "Let us go," Ahangar said.

We piled into my rented jeep and drove by the Jhelum River, banked by Chinar trees. These long-living trees are found in nearly every Kashmiri village; Hindus often built their shrines near them. The oldest is believed to have been planted in 1374, just around the time Islam was taking hold in Kashmir. The dirty green river flows forty-six miles to Pakistan. India was building a 330-megawatt hydroelectric dam on a tributary that would distribute much of the additional power to the "mainland." "They steal everything from us," Ahangar groused.

Traffic stalled as soldiers in flak jackets got out of a truck and approached a young man on the sidewalk. The women pursed their lips, until the cars started to move again. Suddenly the silent mother spoke.

"My son was associated with the insurgents," she murmured. "What did he know? He was twenty-one. It was child's play." She didn't reveal which faction he fought.

The others looked at her. I couldn't read their expressions. She pressed on. She had not seen her son for eleven years. On April 13, 1997, counter-terrorist operatives stormed the house and took him away. The militants later came for his gun. "My heart races all the time. What if they come again?"

We reached the imposing Makhdoom Sahib mosque, perched on a hill near an old fort. Dedicated to a Sufi saint who spread the word of Islam in the sixteenth century, it is one of the most sacred shrines of Kashmir. It had many pillars and the pagoda-like roof so common to Valley shrines. The hill, called Hari Parbat, is hallowed ground for Hindus, too; a temple lay on the other slope. They believe the site was where the mother goddess crushed a demon bothering the locals.

Makhdoom Sahib required a hike up a steep set of stairs. Ahangar stooped and wiped her hands on each step to remind herself of the saint's powers. Once at the top, we had a commanding view of the city below. As we headed toward the prayer area, a veiled woman in her thirties approached Ahangar. She recognized her from the television news. Her husband was missing: could she help her? Ahangar hugged her and they made plans to talk.

The women went inside. They kneeled and rocked back and forth, uttering prayers and pleas. They keened, louder and louder. Other congregants joined in. They wailed out their pain for a good half hour, until they were spent. On the way out we passed a wall covered with multicolored threads, called *desh*. They are hung to symbolize a wish, and removed when the wish is granted. The wall of unanswered hopes stretched for what looked to be almost one hundred feet. The women added a few strands and left for home.

◇◇◇◇◇◇◇

Days later, at the clinic, Arshad was interviewing a middle-aged woman who wore amulets around her wrist and neck, and she touched them during the more stressful moments of the consultation. When she left the room, prescription in hand, I asked about the role of religion in managing emotions. Sufism seemed to play a big part in people's lives; the

Valley was dotted with shrines, and Kashmir was known as the abode of saints.

While religion had been politicized, spirituality still served as an emotional buffer. In fact, Arshad had noted that as the violence dragged on, more people were going to shrines and seeing faith healers, called *peers.* He encouraged the practice, despite what his teachers would have thought about these so-called miracle cures. Arshad called this alternative method "fast track relief." The traditional belief systems were crucial ways to build resiliency, he explained. They were also a way to restore social bonds, at a time when the family and community were torn apart.

"They might not be praying five times, but their belief in God and oneness gives them meaning to life. They are trying to create some sort of meaning to what's happening in their lives, where everything else seems absurd," he explained. "The idea is to connect with a peer to get a unique blessing. It makes them feel emotionally fit. If you've been dealt with unjustly, he will return what's lost, maybe not today or tomorrow but sometime. The saint never refuses you. It's about hope. They had saints long before the Indian occupation. It's a way to connect with a more tranquil past."

Intrigued, I spent the next week visiting shrines. Thursday, the major shrine day, has the air of a market fair. Venders sell sweetmeats while the security forces lurk around the perimeter but don't go inside the sanctuaries, at least not in uniform.

The variety of houses of prayer was vast, from the white-domed Hazratbal, which allegedly holds a hair of the prophet Mohammed, to the shabby Rozabal, shaped like a simple box. My favorite was the Dastgir Sahib, for its ornate interior carvings of walnut and delicate glass chandeliers. Arshad was right: just listening to prayers and inhaling the incense brought down the blood pressure immeasurably.

We also visited some peers. They all had different methods. Some wrote verses on paper and handed out blessed sugar rocks to be swallowed, just as Arshad handed out prescriptions for pharmaceuticals. Others had more esoteric methods. One peer worked out of his apartment in a quiet part of town. The shingle outside the building listed the visiting hours, like a dentist's office. Devotees waited their turn in the receiving room, whose windows were darkened by embroidered drapes. The holy man smoked a hookah on the floor and gestured to everyone to join him. In the far corner, he bent over a young man who was possessed by bad spirits, running amber beads over his face, and intoning phrases from the Koran to exorcise the evil. The patient went into a sort of trance. He was practically asleep when the peer nudged him to make room for the next client. "I'm free of the demons," the healed man told us as he headed out. Sometimes, the peer ran the flat side of a dagger over someone's torso. It went on for hours. The holy man was still chanting when we crept quietly out of the room.

The next faith healer we saw was one of the most popular in the Valley. He was also arguably the most eccentric. "This one is unpredictable," Wajahat cautioned, as we set off. "Some see him as a madman, others as having special powers."

We headed toward Sopore, an area of pronounced militancy that lies on the main road to Muzzaffarabad, the capital of Pakistani-controlled Kashmir. A town of less than one hundred thousand people, Sopore is surrounded by apple orchards and a huge military presence. The well-paved road from Srinagar was a mere thirty-five miles, lined at many points with soldiers. They stood in fields, and on roofs. Convoys of military trucks clogged the road.

Ahad Saeb is immensely popular. We drove up at noon to find about eight hundred people waiting their turn. Some had traveled from high mountain passes in search of blessings. The crowd jostled and rattled the metal door of the house to demand entry. Sandbags lined the perimeter to ward off a less welcome type of visitor—jihadists who sometimes attacked more moderate Sufi leaders.

The peer lived in relative comfort, compared to the holy men in Kashmir who historically meditated in snow-covered caves in the mountains. Then as now, their adherents make long pilgrimages across dizzying glacial trails, securing their steps with wooden staffs or carried on litters.

It was a crisp sunny day, the first in weeks, which lent a particularly festive air to the occasion. Musicians played devotionals on harmoniums and stringed instruments, praising the Sufi saints. A woman swayed as though in a daze. Helpers went around with huge dishes of saffron rice for the faithful. The chain link gate was thick with amulets, gold bangles, and rubber bands. I spoke with a mother of five girls, Rafiqa, who was tying green shawl threads to the desh fence. She didn't know her own age but remembered the year, 1994, when strangers came to the house at dinnertime and shot her husband, Abdul Aziz Malil, point-blank in the head. Why was she here? "I faint and my heart races when I hear gunshots.

Antidepressants don't help. I come here four times a month. At first I feel calmer and then the anxiety starts up again and I have to come back."

The grandson of the peer was standing nearby. Galraiz Mushtaq was only twenty but served as the spokesman for the shrine, a responsibility he assumed with solemn pride. He observed that Rafiqa was typical of supplicants. "The violence creates despair. They come to seek relief."

After a couple hours we made it inside. The holy man sat on a red and black carpet in a wool cap, naked under his blanket. Supplicants kneeled around him in a semicircle. The peer nodded his head, muttered softly, and occasionally looked at the crowd with an inscrutable gaze. The faithful offered bowls of saffron, almonds, cinnamon, and cardamom to be blessed. Most of the crowd was male and they touched him with bags of sugar and identification cards. They addressed him as Baba, wise man. Tears rolled down their faces. "Bless us, pray for us."

Out in the halls servants circulated with salty tea and rolls. A mother introduced me to her teenaged daughter. "She washes her face over and over again and doesn't want to leave the house," the mother said. They visited the peer once a week. The girl crouched, shivering, and said she wanted to go home. "Wait," her mother said. "Baba will make you better." At the mention of his name, the girl relaxed. "Baba," she said, smiling.

I went back into the room. Someone handed the peer a gold pen and he stared at it intently. A plate with blessed sugar was passed around. I took two cubes and made a wish: *May Kashmiris find peace.*

We walked out into the bright day. The warmth was a relief after those weeks in the chilly clinic. People were sunning on the grass and chatting; I hadn't felt this kind of lightness before, in Kashmir. The helpers passed around more food. You could forget there was a conflict, if you ignored the sandbags.

Given the array and ferocity of actors and causes—jihadist pressure, callous government, international rivalry, discrimination, distrust—it's hard to imagine a solution that could break the stalemate. Kashmir was a worst-case scenario, a mountain crisis that sank its people into literal madness. Even if one layer vanished, the others would remain.

Yet for an ephemeral moment, these ordinary individuals could connect with their roots. Not as victims, nor as a citizens lacking political autonomy. Simply as Kashmiris, communing with their mountain saints. They weren't free, or safe. But for at least one afternoon, they could find some brief measure of peace.

7

The Gods of the Valleys Are Not the Gods of the Hills

PART I

◇

THE GREEN MOUNTAINS AND THE HINDU KUSH,
4,393 TO 10,000 FEET

We do deserts, we don't do mountains.

—Colin Powell, former chairman
of the Joint Chiefs of Staff

Duncan Domey almost died during his first live combat mission. This was before he joined the fraternity of mountain warriors who understand combat at high altitude.

Flying in a Chinook helicopter over Afghanistan on March 3, 2002, the mortarman was impatient for action. The chopper had already turned back once due to fire from Al Qaeda forces on the ground. Now it flew in circles in a second attempt to land. Domey felt bored and vulnerable and worried about getting shot out of the sky or crash-landing. He was stuck in the middle of a row of seats, which meant that he couldn't look out the window at the snow-flecked ridges and caves below. This was Pashtun tribal country, an untamable spot in the Hindu Kush, which means "Kill Hindus." These mountains had resisted invaders since ancient Greek times. All he knew was that motivated Al Qaeda and Taliban fighters were waiting to engage the Americans on the ground.

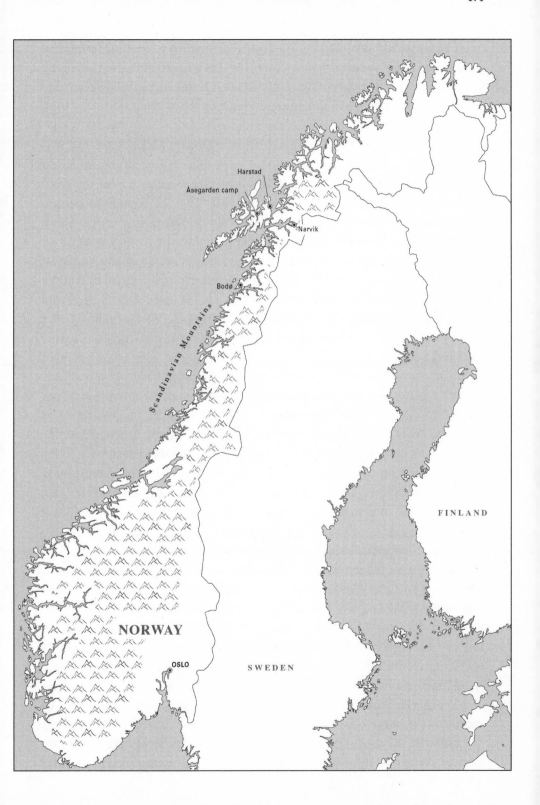

Harstad

Åsegarden camp

Narvik

Bodø

Scandinavian Mountains

NORWAY

OSLO

SWEDEN

FINLAND

The ungainly aircraft finally touched down on the saddle-backed mountain, the rotator blades churning up gravel and dust. Domey stepped out onto a jagged ridge high above the tree line at 10,000 feet. He stumbled on fragments of granite strewn along the arid surface as he took his first steps. It could have been the moon.

Then the enemy struck, but not the one Domey had expected: it was the air itself, so depleted of oxygen that he gasped, trying to get more into his lungs. Inhaling deeply only made him dizzy, so he sat on the hard ground. But he couldn't get back on his feet. The 110 pounds of ammunition, helmet, body armor, M4 assault rifle, sleeping bag, knives, and packages of ready-to-eat meals were too heavy for his woozy body. Two buddies had to haul him up. Domey struggled to walk, stopping every few steps to suck in more air. His chest constricted. He was confused. And he wasn't alone: many of his fellow soldiers wheezed and retched, prostrate on the ground like fish left behind by a receding tide. "We were lucky that we did not have to fight because we were all combat ineffective," Domey later recalled.

In its more mild manifestations, altitude sickness feels like a bad case of the flu, but it becomes much more dire for some people starting at about 8,000 feet. At over 14,000, many of us, soldier or civilian, can't function at all. If the heart cannot pump oxygen efficiently, the body drowns from the inside, as its own fluids fill the lungs and brain. The ideal mountain fighters are raised on thin air, developing big lungs and bodies conditioned to need less oxygen. They are nimble of foot and built like barrels, with a lower center of gravity that makes it easier to maintain balance on a slope. The majority of the American infantrymen here in the Hindu Kush had never climbed this high; their lungs were sea-level small.

Domey was taking part in Operation Anaconda, the United States' first major battle in Afghanistan and its highest ever. The mission: to ring and trap Al Qaeda guerrillas in the Shahikot Valley, near the border with Pakistan. Various militaries around the world have specialized mountain units that train new recruits over three months, bringing troops slowly up to a summit, then down, and up again. But the United States didn't have specialized units, and hadn't taken into account the effect on a soldier of a quick rise from 5,000 to 10,500 feet. The Army seemed doomed to repeat this mistake over the ensuing years.

Some of the most punishing marches in history have taken place on or over ranges so inhospitable that men lost toes to the bitter cold and dropped dead from hunger. "Napoleon could have whipped the Austrians on the plains," Ernest Hemingway wrote after seeing the Italian front of World War I. "He never would have fought them in the mountains." For all his grand theories, Mao Tse-tung could not dominate the 16,000-foot ranges during his long march in 1934–35, and he was carried part of the way while his men died of diarrhea and exhaustion. At high elevation, the elements are lethal. Soldiers not only suffer altitude sickness and frostbite but also perish in the landslides and avalanches that thunder down at the speed of trains.

It's not just the human body that fails in the mountains. Tanks and helicopters are often unable to function in rugged and extreme heights, respectively. Airplanes can't land. Military doctrine dictates that infantry attacks require numerical superiority of three-to-one against defending forces, but the ratio must be higher on slopes. Throughout history, mountain dwellers have repeatedly resisted better-armed invaders not only because they hold the proverbial high ground, but because of their nimbler feet and the rapidly fluctuating, often brutal weather conditions.

Domey and his unit never went through basic altitude training. The weakness he experienced upon landing in the Hindu Kush worsened over the next hours, and the ache in his head deepened to a severe pounding. Normally doctors prescribe fluids and rest for altitude sickness, but the latter was a luxury he didn't have, and Domey had to press on. His mental alertness faded along with the color in his face.

His physical condition remained weak over the following days. When enemy forces attacked the unit, Domey set to work firing his mortar, but he struggled to focus on the precise calculations necessary to fire accurately. He was overwhelmed by exhaustion more intense than the fatigue from typical dehydration and the stress of combat. When an air strike hit too close one night, showering him with shrapnel, Domey wearily pulled his body armor over his shoulder, placed his helmet over his head, and collapsed back into a deep sleep.

I interviewed Domey in 2012, a decade after Anaconda, when I spent a few days at the Army's Mountain Warfare School in Jericho, Vermont. Having gone to Colombia, Chechnya, and Kashmir, I was well aware of the general futility of waging war against mountain fighters, and I was curious about how the United States and other nations approached the problem. Domey was working as an instructor at the school. After Anaconda, he'd applied himself to learning how to survive and fight in the mountains. Having acquired the necessary skills, he was now hoping to teach the next generation.

The United States had lost Afghanistan. The Taliban was resurgent. The country was fractured by struggles among various ethnic groups and warlords. Among other failures, we had put misplaced trust in a corrupt government and tribal leaders. Tactically, had we been doomed from the start? Had we learned nothing from history? Hannibal lost half of his poorly clad men in the campaign across the Alps in 218 BC. The soldiers, more accustomed to the Mediterranean warmth, froze to death or plunged over the precipices. There was the folly of the 1962 Sino-Indian war over the Himalayan border, when China had surprised Indian troops by traversing a glacial mountain the Indian military had believed insuperable, and cut off their supply lines. The 1915 Battle of Sarikamish, when Turkey launched a winter invasion of Russia in the mountains, provides another cautionary tale about conventional forces, unschooled in mountain warfare, blithely heading into battle against highlanders. The list goes on and on.

Many elements in Anaconda were ill-conceived, partly due to a misunderstanding of the enemy. US military planners liked the name Anaconda because it called to mind the biggest serpent in the world, one that wraps around its prey and chokes it. The Hindu Kush enemy, though, proved difficult to encircle and strangle; it was more like a bunch of agile little rodents than one sizeable animal. The Taliban and Al Qaeda fighters, carrying little more than light weapons, knew the trails and crevasses far better than the wheezing American soldiers, who bore half their body weight on their backs.

A booklet first published in 1932, entitled *Passing It On: Short Talks on Tribal Fighting on the North-West Frontier of India*, underscores how little has changed on the Afghanistan-Pakistan border. The Army reissued it for the benefit of today's troops, to offer a lesson about the importance of history. The cover shows pith-helmeted Brits struggling to hold on to ropes to secure a canon on a steep slope. The author, a British general named Sir Andrew Skeen, makes observations about late nineteenth-century Pashtun tribesmen that are remarkably relevant today. To wit: "They come down hillsides like falling boulders, not running but bounding, and in crags they literally drop from foothold to foothold. . . . These men are hard as nails; they live on little, carrying nothing but a rifle and a few cartridges, a knife and a bit of food, and they are shod for quick and sure movement." A seasoned mountain forces commander would study examples like these, and take them into consideration when launching an offensive in the region. But no one with the necessary experience seems to have been involved in planning Anaconda.

Anaconda also suffered from poor intelligence. The Americans found more numerous and better-armed guerrillas than they'd anticipated. Between March 2 and March 16, the 1,700 airlifted US troops and their 1,000 Afghan allies battled 500 to 1,000 enemy fighters. They had expected at most 200.

As I'd seen in Colombia, ground troops in mountainous regions rely on helicopters for resupply and support fire. Visibility, however, often became a problem because of low clouds, and enemy fire and bad weather also held up the choppers several times. Not knowing how long the delays would last, Domey and fellow soldiers began to ration water and limit their packets of precooked meals to one a day. At high altitude, soldiers can burn up to six thousand calories daily. These men were eating less than a fourth that amount, exacerbating their fatigue. A brook lay nearby, but they lacked tablets to purify the murky water and didn't want to risk dysentery on top of everything else. At one point, Domey watched thirstily through his binoculars as a helicopter dropped a pallet of water bottles five hundred yards away. The soldiers on the ground couldn't reach it because of enemy gunfire. "That kind of thing stands out in your mind," Domey recalled.

In March in the Shahikot Valley, cold and warm air often collide, yielding enormous, rapid climatic shifts. The temperature swung from sixty degrees to below freezing in just hours, and the treeless summit provided no shelter from either sun or cold. When quickly rising in elevation, the body sweats profusely, which can prompt hypothermia. Civilian climbers know to regulate their temperature with special fabrics that wick moisture and dry quickly, but the Army doesn't shop at Patagonia. It also can't buy from foreign manufacturers, which strikes Merino wool undergarments from the packing list.

During the afternoons, Domey's cotton T-shirt absorbed his streaming sweat like a paper towel, creating a soaking second skin that made him shiver violently when the mercury sank at night. Snowfall one evening left a frosty blanket more than half a foot high, making a cold mess of his sleeping bag. Wet and trembling, Domey dug a hole to sleep in, using flattened meal boxes for insulation and covering the whole arrangement with his poncho. At least he had a sleeping bag, even if it was soaked.

Men elsewhere on the ridge had shed their rucksacks to save weight; they huddled together at night for warmth.

A picture shot by a news photographer at the time shows an anxious Domey on patrol on a high, dusty plateau. His face was pinched by fatigue and distress. Heat exhaustion and the high sun had reddened it to match the earth. At the time, he says, he was brooding over an irony: he was serving with the Tenth Mountain Division, which despite its name hadn't specialized in high-altitude fighting since World War II.

The division was one of the most renowned in Army history; accounts of their heroic exploits were one reason he signed up. Its original three thousand soldiers, activated in the early 1940s, had been carefully recruited for skills useful in the mountains: they were climbers, hunting guides, loggers, muleskinners, farmers, and Olympic athletes. To prepare for combat in the Alps, they trained in the Colorado Rockies under physical conditions so harsh that the men suffered more injuries from the weather there than while fighting in Europe later.

Domey, who was born in the Netherlands and raised in Massachusetts, had dreamed of fighting in the mountains ever since he was a little kid. He'd grown up skiing in the Alps and watching war movies. He had a romantic notion about the American fighting man, especially the "snow phantoms" of the Tenth Mountain Division, so named for their white outerwear and swiftness on skis.

When he enlisted, he specifically asked to be stationed with the division, not realizing that the word *mountain* was by now a mere legacy. The Tenth Mountain had been moved to Fort Drum, a swampy farm area in New York too low-lying to prepare men for pulmonary edema. It was as level as Holland, albeit colder, better suited for cross-country skiing than rappelling. High-altitude skills were not taught. Politics had motivated the relocation; the base was supposed to revive an economically depressed quarter, and highland combat was no longer a priority for the Pentagon. Domey is a bit sheepish about his mistake, and regrets that he didn't do more homework before asking to be stationed there. "To my consternation, I discovered that we were just another light infantry division, located in a relatively flat area that has very cold winters. We were not prepared for mountains."

While Anaconda eventually succeeded in flushing Islamic militants from the Shahikot Valley, Domey still marvels that American military planners had rushed in with scant thought to the high altitude. "Just because we succeeded doesn't mean we did it well. No one had recent real-world experience in mountain operations, and it wasn't on anybody's radar that they required an additional skill set."

Having witnessed firsthand mountain conflicts around the world, I had come to see how their consequences reverberate far and wide. Now I wanted to explore one of the most obvious potential solutions: military intervention. Were we prepared, if necessary, to quell violence on the mountaintop through military means? And how were other nations thinking about the problem of mountain conflicts? That's why I'd traveled to Vermont from New York: to find the answers.

I went there to decipher why the world's largest expeditionary force, at the start of the Afghanistan campaign, had missed such basics as rope preparedness and breathing at elevation—and if things had changed since. Surely the experience in Afghanistan had provided some insight into how and how not to fight in some of the world's most forbidding terrain, against and among mountain people. What tactics and strategies would ensure success? The United States appears to have lacked a coherent doctrine. Colin Powell made his famous quip—"We do deserts, we don't do mountains"—in 1992, when, as chairman of the Joint Chiefs of Staff, he was reluctant to intervene in Bosnia. He was being facetious, as was frequently his wont. Powell had plenty of other reasons not to get involved in the Balkans. But now, his words seemed prophetic.

◇◇◇◇◇◇

The Mountain Warfare School is lodged among forested peaks in sparsely populated farmland. The center is so poorly marked that even some locals don't know about its existence; "an open secret," is how Domey put it.

I visited in mid-August, and already the leaves were turning auburn and saffron on Mount Mansfield, the state's tallest peak. Mansfield is a mere pimple by Afghan standards; it reaches 4,393 feet at the highest point and can be climbed in a day. It has a flat top that resembles a man's face looking up from a prone position—thus the name. That lends it a tame appearance from a distance, belying its treacherous nature in winter, when gusting snows limit visibility to ten feet and plunge temperatures to minus fifty.

The school lies in a drab rectangular building with a sign on its façade that reads, "The Gods of the Valleys Are Not the Gods of the Hills." The quotation is from Ethan Allen, a Revolutionary War folk hero who helped win independence for Vermont as the commander of the Green Mountain Boys. The legacy of this unruly militia generates great local pride. Most of the instructors are Vermont National Guardsmen who, like their fore-bears, grew up hunting and camping in snow caves. The Army views them as best equipped to impart the right skills for hill terrain.

The American military has three other centers that offer specialized mountain training, in the Colorado Rockies, Alaska, and a hard-core Marines school in California, a place of such steep drops that men have become paralyzed by vertigo during exercises. Vermont is the only center that continually updates its curriculum based on feedback from the field, and the instructors there write Army doctrine for mountain combat.

Normally the Army is cagey when entertaining requests for access, but the Mountain Warfare School was surprisingly accommodating. Its commander, a major named Justin Davis with the girth of a forest bear and the deliberate air of a scholar, admitted, "We don't get a lot of atten-tion." He seemed pleased, even flattered, that a civilian writer was taking an interest. Davis's desk was covered with military patches, mugs, and emblems from other mountain schools he has visited or hosted. Experts and instructors from around the world meet regularly to swap notes on the latest equipment and methodology. There are differences of opinion; Davis said a lot of Europeans tended to be more "old school" with their emphasis on skis rather than ropes.

The major gave me an introductory lecture on climbing ropes and carabiners, the spring-hinged rings that connect and hold lines. "We typ-ically use nylon kernmantle rope with an outer sheath and many inter-nal strands. We use both dynamic, about a 40 percent stretch, and static, or minimal stretch, depending on the application. Length and diameter vary, again depending on the application. An average length is about 150 feet and an average diameter is ten millimeters."

"Right," I said.

Davis appraised me skeptically. "There's a lot of information to take in." He pointed to a table with a pot of coffee, warning about quality. "This is the Army, don't expect much." I poured the muddy fluid into a double-sized mug, which had an insignia of men skiing and rappelling around the word *MOUNTAIN*.

An instructor walked in to fetch a rope.

"Writer," Davis said.

"Know anything about mountains?" the instructor asked. I shook my head "no."

"Neither do most recruits," he said, and left the room.

Davis promised a long weekend of exercises, from slope shooting to cliff scaling. It was summer, so the ice wall wouldn't have ice and no one would be snowshoeing, but there would be lots of knot tying, medical evacuation exercises, and mule-packing with barrels, though I wouldn't see any actual mules. The Army rediscovered mules as a reliable form of transport during the Afghanistan campaign. The animals are found to be more dependable than all-terrain vehicles, which require fuel and attract enemy attention with their mechanized rumbles. The *clip-clop* and snorts of the animals, on the contrary, blend in with the environment. Even the US Army must resort to simpler systems when fighting in the peaks.

First I would meet Domey, as the major deemed it vital to understand the fiasco of Anaconda. Domey was the only instructor who had fought there and he wanted to share what he had learned. We walked through corridors lined with display cases spotlighting the glory days of the Tenth Mountain Division, when men had climbing skills and wore thinner parkas. I paused to examine a pair of leather boots that seemed too delicate to keep out the chill. Domey waited for us, standing at attention in the conference room.

Domey had been promoted to sergeant first class, and in the decade since the photo I'd seen of him in Afghanistan, he seemed to have aged backward, his thin face fleshed out, sapphire eyes bright. He had just returned from seven months with a Spanish division doing ski patrols in the Pyrenees. Domey marveled that the Spanish specialists devote more than half a year to learning mountain combat techniques. In contrast, American soldiers zip through Jericho in two-week intervals. He pointed out that though there are half a million active-duty American soldiers, only about 850 men train at Jericho each year. The Army spends approximately $800,000 annually on the school, apart from building costs and salaries—a fraction of the overall defense budget, which tops $800 billion. Moreover, many recruits train here in summer when it's too mild to prepare for the challenges of three-foot snow and frostbite. "In Spain, we spent days on avalanche and snow pack analysis," noted Domey. "Here it's just a couple hours."

Spain wasn't the only country that had dedicated mountain units much better prepared than the US Army's. So did many NATO allies, as well as Russia, China, India, Switzerland, Pakistan, and Colombia. The US military's official line was that its forces were too large and globally focused to have one division solely deployed to mountain areas. The infantry was expected to fight anywhere: jungles, deserts, cities, and hills. Domey argued that such thinking was narrow-minded, as the Anaconda debacle amply showed. As Domey explained, the key is the lowly rope. Ropes are remarkably versatile; they can hold six hundred pounds, pull a wounded man a thousand feet to safety, and help a unit up bare rock face. Lines can be stretched across crevasses and, crucially, enable medical evacuation, which can be complicated by weather and altitude and requires greater manpower than on lowland. If there was a takeaway from Anaconda, it was that rope affords solutions to the biggest challenge of mountain combat: load management.

So the Jericho school focuses on rope, rope, and more rope—nothing fancy, just the long nylon type used by civilian climbers. Ropes figure heavily in the basic course in rock climbing, land navigation, medical evacuation, and rigorous treks uphill. Everywhere on the school's grounds, I saw soldiers tying them to pine trees, hanging on them from cliffs, and pulling other men with them.

This emphasis marks a profound and perhaps unexpected shift. When the Army opened the school in 1983, it embraced the model of Austrian alpinists, who were exceptionally good mountain skiers but hadn't fought a war for a long while. The instructors at the time didn't take into account that modern soldiers climb rock faces lugging enormous weight. In 2005, three years after Anaconda, the center shifted instruction away from what some instructors derisively call the "Gucci" approach, which emphasizes skiing. Today, Jericho emphasizes mobility and survival, teaching ways to quickly tie lines to haul gear and evacuate casualties, and the singular rifle skills necessary for shooting on a slope.

"Low tech, high advantage," said Domey.

◇◇◇◇◇◇◇

Imagine you're going up and down sharp inclines with forty-five pounds of body armor and sixty-five more of equipment. You do this year after year. It's hell on the back and knees. Davis, who was forty, couldn't jog alongside the trainees anymore due to accumulated leg strain, so we slowly walked toward the practice area through trails thick with wildflowers.

In his free time, he cultivates bees, fishes for trout, and slithers through swamps to observe underwater life. He pointed out a marshy spot where a startled turtle had snapped at his chest, and mentioned close encounters with inquisitive muskrats. Davis unfurled a fiddlehead fern that he recommended sautéed. "Tastes like asparagus."

A lanky man with a posture stooped by too many rucksacks fell into step as we rambled through the underbrush. This was Sergeant Stephen Jennings, rope master and, at forty-nine, the elder of the cadre.

"Hey Justin, how are the bees?"

"Doing fine."

"Got enough honey?"

"Yup."

"We all share the same hobbies," explained Jennings. "Lately it's making honey mead. We're such a close-knit bunch, if one person gets a Subaru, the next day you'll see five parked here."

He plucked a blade of grass that he said worked as bug repellent. "We're country boys. Some guys have passed up promotions in order to stick around here."

"Best job in the world," agreed Davis.

The instructors reminded me of mountain people I'd encountered elsewhere: separate from, and suspicious of, the dominant culture (in this case, the culture prevalent in the US military); committed to low-tech traditions; keepers of knowledge specific to the highlands. Soldiers trained and seasoned in the mountains are their own kind of clan. The teachers here had either fought in the mountains and come back stunned at how egregiously the Army had failed to prepare them, or they were highlanders themselves, comfortable in the intense conditions of high peaks, savvy about how to live and fight there. Whatever their backgrounds, they were all determined to change the way the Army did high-altitude combat. The bonds between these men were forged from shared disappointments and frustrations with the way the elite disregarded their voices and needs, but also from a deep love of the mountains, know-how about surviving in extreme upland conditions, and a sense of being apart from the mainstream.

We reached Castle Rock, a sixty-foot wall of schist where soldiers dangled from ropes to which they were secured at the waist. Their gray camouflage blended into the rock but the tan boots stuck out as they tried, many unsuccessfully, to find their feet in crevices.

Unlike the instructors, these boys were largely unaccustomed to the outdoors. Jennings took in the scene of dangling feet. "This course is like drinking out of a fire hose because of the fast pace. They have just two weeks to master knot tying, medical evacuation, slope shooting, and rock climbing. Many can't keep up and about 25 percent flunk out. We would take them back, but the Army budgets usually don't allow for second chances." Flunking robs them of the special mountaineer badge, and bragging rights at the bar, but doesn't necessarily preclude being deployed to mountains later on.

One kid, frightened from either vertigo or the thought of failing, froze thirty feet up, his feet kicking in the air. The rappelling instructor tried to calm him. "Don't look down. The rope won't break."

A couple other youths found toeholds, but struggled to belay up and down.

"The enemy is not dumb. They see if you're tired," the instructor called out.

Under his breath, Jennings said, "Imagine doing this with a rucksack on your back in the dark with night vision goggles. The NODS [goggles] affect depth perception. I heard about a guy who plunged off a cliff because of the NODS."

Furthermore, I thought silently, what good would ropes really do in the Hindu Kush, other than keep men and their equipment upright? Afghanistan was fragmented by warring clans, valleys that didn't speak the same language, hatred of foreign meddlers, corruption, and the ready availability of AK-47s. In Colombia, I saw how even well-prepared mountain troops couldn't defeat guerrillas. I was skeptical: aside from logistics, what difference could a taut line really make in the wider scheme of things?

◇◇◇◇◇◇◇

The son of a public school teacher, Major Davis admits to "loving all things pedantic." He reads voraciously—mythology, martial arts, military theory, historical fiction. Davis leant me a pile of disintegrating books, calling them "required reading." That night, as the recruits reviewed knot tying, I sat in the lobby of my antiseptic Holiday Inn Express and reviewed the stack.

Nearly all the books related to Afghanistan. The rest of the reading pertained to what made a good mountain warrior when fighting on someone else's turf. Practically no conventional force has overcome mountain guerrillas embedded in the population and terrain. One might argue that the French vanquished independence fighters in the Algerian mountains in the late 1950s. In order to cut off the insurgents of the National Liberation Front from remote villages in the mountains where they recruited and supplied themselves, the French forcibly transferred more than two million villagers to the plains. Cruelty, too, marked the remarkable siege of warrior monks on Mount Hiei in Japan in 1571. The brutal Samurai warlord, Oda Nobunaga, crushed them by leading thirty thousand men to destroy temples and massacre townspeople.

Both of those cases involved egregious human rights abuses that would be considered politically unacceptable for a government like ours. But there are modern successes that don't involve harm to civilians. Erwin Rommel, perhaps the greatest mountain warrior ever, relied on stealth. The Nazi general perfected light infantry techniques in the Italian and Romanian mountains during World War I, detailed in his book *Attacks*. Published in 1937, the account has become the standard of how to use speed and deception to overcome the enemy on its own ground. Throughout the book, Rommel repeatedly sneaks up on the enemy and tricks it into surrendering under the impression that he was commanding a larger force. Time and again, his relatively few soldiers captured huge numbers of enemy troops and hordes of material with relatively low casualties.

Field Marshal Aleksandr Suvorov, the undefeated tsarist general and one of the greatest military commanders ever, used these same methods; he famously said, "To surprise is to vanquish." In 1799, at age seventy, Suvorov dodged the French to lead more than twenty thousand men over the Alps in seventeen days. Besides daring, both Rommel and Suvorov had the charisma to inspire their men to endure intense hardship. They also enjoyed the independence to make quick decisions, a luxury unthinkable in the lumbering American bureaucracy today.

◇◇◇◇◇◇

The next day began with a visit to a gash in the earth, meant to simulate a gorge. Soldiers practiced moving casualties with two lines, fastened like a pulley system. They began by transporting gray rucksacks and then moved on to a live "victim," contained inside a rigid fiberglass cocoon that looked like a sarcophagus. He howled in mock pain, which grew more authentic as the others dangled candy bars just out of his reach.

We moved on to knot tying at a clearing in the forest. The masts of pine blocked out the waning daylight, and I sat on a fallen tree amid feathery beds of ferns and fronds in the dappled shade. About ten soldiers in their early twenties frowned over the carabiners and nylon lines, with competitive glances over their shoulders to see how the others were doing. Knot tying may be low tech, but it is a complex skill. To keep it simple, the school teaches only 15 of an estimated 3,400 varieties; though relatively few in number, they challenge students more than anything else in the curriculum. "They have trouble visualizing and the fast pace leaves many behind," Major Davis said. I sat on a log, observing the flatlanders struggle to tie the knots correctly. Davis was clearly dismayed. He could tie these and hundreds of other knots in his sleep.

◇◇◇◇◇◇◇

Later that day, I spoke with Davis and Chris Bushway, a sergeant with a large air-cast on his ankle from an old war injury. Davis mused about topography in Afghanistan. "It makes it hard to unite the country. You can have two valleys that have communities with unintelligible languages who hate each other."

They talked about what made a good mountain fighter.

"The best mountaineering military are those who are executing true combat in the mountains," said Bushway. "The guys in Tajikistan know how to fight people in the mountains because they live in the mountains. In order to be ready for Afghanistan you need to understand the cultural aspects, how a Hazara looks at things versus a Nuristani."

Davis favored the specialist mountaineers for these conditions.

"You do not win a counterinsurgency by military means alone. From an ethnographic standpoint, we flock to those we know, who make us feel comfortable. Different groups have values that separate them from others. The environment breeds a certain mentality. Mountain men—we are tough, self-reliant. People who live in that environment are used to suffering. I derive a certain amount of pride as a Vermonter. For us this is a lifestyle. A lot of us have gone to other units and we all come back. Mountain warfare is part of our identity."

This was particularly striking, the men told me, at meetings of the International Association of Military Mountain Schools. The simple approach of the Vermonters created a stir among the other participants.

"They have cigarettes and talk during the European presentations, because it's something familiar," said Bushway. "When we talk they are quiet and watch. It goes beyond what they've learned. The Austrians and the Germans tended to be the biggest skeptics at first. They do high end. But they have become our biggest advocates."

Davis added, "To me, we're just some guys from Vermont. To them, we're the guys from the US who have fought in Afghanistan. They listen and watch."

◇◇◇◇◇◇◇

On the final day of exercises, the instructor taught long-range angle shooting. This is the part the guys most look forward to; they get to blast an M4 carbine at metal targets shaped like the top half of a body. We ascended the trail in an all-terrain vehicle. Davis handed me a helmet and dark plastic glasses to protect against flying objects. The screaming engine and the many times the wheels got stuck on rocks brought home the point that mule-back is not only stealthier, but probably more comfortable. We reached the firing range, a cliff with a commanding view of Mount Mansfield, the sun hitting its features picturesquely.

The soldiers had to relearn how to aim, because a bullet shot from a slope travels differently than one shot on flat land, due to the angle. Four men at a time lay on their stomachs and fired downward at a distance of 984 to 2,624 feet. First Sergeant Jared Smith, a fiftyish elfin man of wiry build, tried to soothe their nerves with jokey advice not to fall off the edge. "It's a long drop down!"

The shooters stabilized the weapons on logs while spotters, looking through scopes on tripods, stood over them, calling out locations as the bullets smacked the metal. "High right! Too far left!"

"The point of aim and impact are different than flat shooting, so aim at a man's legs to get him in the chest," Smith explained to one boy with hair like chick fuzz. The soldier squinted through his scope and hit the shoulder of the cut-out human targets. "Good," Smith said. "Good."

A young soldier from Missouri, named, appropriately, Zachary Knott, waited for his chance on the range. "It would have been good to know all this before I went out to Afghanistan. I never knew about these ropes and lines. I could have used them for water supply. Boy, this would have been useful."

Max Bresnahan, another Missourian, weighed in. "Basic ruck packing, it sounds so simple but it can be problematic." The others nodded. "I was carrying far too much ammo. We weren't allowed to procure water, there was all sorts of poop in it. It probably would have worked if you purified it but they didn't let us. So we carried seventy-two hours' worth of water and food."

Smith wandered over to take a break. A native Vermonter, he mused about the challenges of teaching wilderness skills to kids raised on PlayStation who have never seen a compass. Unlike the original three thousand World War II–era soldiers of the Tenth Mountain Division, none in this bunch were Olympic athletes or muleskinners. Most didn't know how to navigate without GPS.

"We're trying to teach a mountain culture to a country that doesn't have it," Smith griped. "In World War II, the percentage of people who lived on farms and ranges was 60 percent. Now it's less than 2 percent. Most Americans don't have outdoors experience anymore. However, the folks in Central Asia understand cold, hunger, and war."

Smith paused to consult one of the tripod spotters. "It's too high. Tell him to aim lower." He turned back to me. "You know what's interesting? I taught advanced techniques to Tajiks without an interpreter. They got it. In a mountain culture, men know it's going to be hard. Koreans also. They are tough physically and mentally. Their food is awful, but I like working with them."

◇◇◇◇◇◇◇

Before I left, I chatted with several instructors about adjustments made since Anaconda. They encouraged soldiers fighting in the mountains to leave behind big bowie knives and pack water purifying tablets instead of heavy water canisters. But when it came to ammo, many men were still carrying eight magazines when they only needed four. More soldiers, by this point, carried ropes and knew how to use them, although it was impossible to quantify just how many, other than the 850 a year trained in the two-week courses here. Muscle memory is critical for any physical skill, be it tying a tourniquet or firing a machine gun, and a soldier must put in rope work regularly in order to remain capable.

The gear had clearly improved. At substantial cost, the Army had replaced earlier models of boots that shredded quickly, and it had been issuing layerable clothing like the sort bought in civilian camping stores, which could wick moisture and adapt to varying climates. Yet commanders don't always know what's available in warehouses, or soldiers don't know how to wear it properly—or their superiors don't let them. ("Sometimes the commanders don't like the look of fleece, even if it has the name and rank on it and can be worn as an official uniform," said Jennings.)

These were all lessons learned from Afghanistan. NATO was winding down operations there and the Mountain School is training for a new possible battleground: the Arctic. Vast troves of energy and mining treasures are buried there, and new shipping routes were opening up due to global warming melting the polar ice caps. Russia and China were forming new brigades dedicated to winter fighting, and Moscow was mobilizing troops along the border with Norway and testing fighter jets near the North Pole. NATO wanted to be ready just in case things blew up there, or in Iran, or on the Korean peninsula, all of which have treacherously cold mountains.

Having determined that it had needed more ropes in Afghanistan, America and its allies were now trying to figure out how to fight in glacial conditions. Barring space, the High North is the last frontier militarily, and no force has the technology to maintain a large force there for an extended period of time.

The glacial climate creates the most extreme fighting conditions anywhere. The human body can adapt to altitudes by producing more red blood cells. But it can't get used to the extreme cold. Machinery fails, too. When the temperature drops to minus 55 Fahrenheit, ballistics malfunction, helicopters can't take off, and vehicles stall. Men lose all depth perception in swirling snow or, on a clear day, scorch their corneas in the glare. While Afghanistan involved combat against irregulars, in the Arctic, NATO was worried about a potential fight against an increasingly aggressive Russia, something closer to a major power. Did both scenarios provide obstacles that made it impossible to prevail militarily?

"Glaciers," Davis said contemplatively. "That's where you should go next."

Seven months later I boarded a plane for the Arctic Circle. It was March, fifty degrees below zero, and the coldest place I had ever been.

PART II

◇

THE LYNGEN ALPS, 6,014 FEET

The most frightening enemy was nature itself . . .
entire platoons were hit, smothered, buried without
a trace, without a cry, with no other sound than the
one made by the gigantic white mass itself.

—Paolo Monelli, on Italian avalanches in World War I

The joint headquarters of the Norwegian military is in a refurbished Cold
War bunker tunneled into a granite mountain one hundred miles north of
the Arctic Circle. It's just outside Bodø, a pleasant port of fifty thousand
people from which cruises leave daily for the glaciers and fjords. Norway
is shaped like an upside down lamb chop, with Bodø at the gusty north
that forms the bone. Bombed during World War II, the town was rebuilt
with a banal uniformity that contrasts with the untamed nature surrounding it. More sea eagles nest here than anywhere else on earth, and
the world's strongest maelstrom swirls violently nearby. The quay looks
out on the unwelcoming sea and mountains, and offers front-row seats to
the aurora borealis, nature's celestial light shows.

Norway writes Arctic doctrine for the rest of NATO and routinely
shares its expertise in cold weather combat with its alliance partners.
Hundreds of mountains cover Norway, including glaciers that jut thousands of feet above sea level. The terrain here is not so different from
Afghanistan, though it is covered with ice.

I drove a few miles out of Bodø on an impeccably maintained road
marked periodically by moose-crossing signs. I was headed for the Reitan
military base, where Norway liaisons with its NATO allies about military
preparedness and tracks Russian activity next door. In case I got lost,
I could just follow the roar of the F-16 fighter jets overhead. A turnoff

led to a red guard booth of the type found at commercial parking lots. I parked and walked smack into the middle of the mountain bunker, along a white tunnel whose halogen lighting outshone the feeble polar winter outside. Eventually I reached an operations room straight out of a James Bond movie. Purposeful men and women in uniforms sat at terminals, inspecting satellite maps of maritime and air activity on a gigantic flat screen (I later learned it was 430 square feet) that hung at one end of the room.

The bunker had been built in the early 1960s to withstand a nuclear blast. Still spooked by the Nazis' occupation, Norway had been worried about a possible Soviet attack. The facility was still on guard fifty years later. Russia's self-designation as the Arctic's sole superpower has created urgency; the melting glaciers threaten not just polar bears but also Norwegians, who, as citizens of the only NATO member that borders Russia, were at the front line of any defense of new and potential sea routes and offshore oil. Russian president Vladimir Putin was rebuilding military capabilities that had collapsed along with the Soviet Union, commissioning Arctic submarines and taking advantage of the open air and sea space to train and test new missiles. Russia had bolstered winter brigades, and stationed more troops along the 120-mile boundary. It had been the first stage of Putin's wider campaign of military aggression. He'd prioritized militarization of the Arctic before overrunning Ukraine and getting involved in Syria.

Norwegian military men jest that their army is only big enough to defend a traffic junction in Oslo. That's an exaggeration—active frontline personnel number roughly 26,000. But it's a fraction of Russia's 766,000. In 2009 Norway moved its joint military headquarters from the south to Bodø to better maintain watch and to train their troops, and those from the bigger countries in NATO, how to survive in these desolate conditions. It turns out that in order to fight in the Arctic, the first thing you've got to know is how to stay warm there.

Mountain experts of a certain rank all seem to know each other; as I learned in Vermont, it's an exclusive circle of specialists that transcends boundaries. What was new in Norway was seeing that extreme cold and mountain fighting techniques are generally taught together, as mountains are often covered by snow. Even among the mavens, the Norwegians are viewed with awe for their know-how and hardiness and are sought after for tips on the latest practices and technological advances. Major Davis was familiar with operations here and had provided me with a list of people to interview and questions to ask, particularly relating to avalanches.

My Arctic visit began with a briefing over lunch in the wood-paneled officers' dining room. The two-star general who commanded operations, Rune Jakobsen, led me to a five-star buffet groaning under piles of delicious salmon as well as three varieties of pickled herring, romaine salad, and fresh pineapple. Heaping his own plate with these healthy offerings, he explained that vitamin deficiency was a big enemy when there are only four hours of dim natural light and you work in a bunker. Once we had loaded up on A and D, the talk turned to military capability and operations.

"If you can fight and survive in the extreme of the Arctic, you can fight anywhere in the world," Jakobsen said. Very few people on earth have the necessary skills, which are extremely specific, and many of them are fairly difficult and involved. In Vermont, I found that the endeavor of the Mountain School created a sort of clan out of its instructors. Over the course of my visit to Norway, I saw that mountain expertise created a bond among soldiers from all different countries.

Jakobsen handed me some materials that detailed activities in the High North, as this area is known. "In planning you always need alternatives, more than in other combat situations." On top of bad weather and avalanches—tactical givens in these frozen mountains—a lot of other things could go wrong, too. For one, Russia might act on its outsized ambitions; there were sovereignty issues, for instance, in Svalbard, a Norwegian island with a Russian community. Then there was the possibility of terrorism, organized crime, and attacks on oil installations.

"We are trying to create a reconnaissance picture to know what is going on and why," said the general. "Tasks include show of military presence, surveillance of areas of interest, ensuring sovereignty, military contingency planning, and exercises in crisis management." The given here is that the rest of NATO would come to their aid. In fact, some American pilots were at the air base during my visit.

Just that day, the monitors had received signals that a Tupolev "Bear" bomber aircraft was twelve nautical miles off the Norwegian coast. A pilot from the United States scrambled to intercept it. Days earlier, spotters had seen three other Bears, escorted by Sukhoi fighter jets. The previous year the Norwegians had identified seventy-one Russian military planes. The number had been steadily rising since 2006, when militarization in the Arctic began in earnest.

"The Russians are showing muscle. There's no immediate threat," the general said. "But the goal is to have continued presence and surveillance and ensure a situational awareness."

After lunch, the men took me out to the military tarmac, where I met an American pilot for whom the conditions were a revelation. As we toured the facilities, Lieutenant Colonel Heath Wimberley, who went by "Cooler," said that he had been flying F-16s for fifteen years. "One thing I tell folks, every day here it's something different. For instance, I got a call from the squadron about some Russian planes. The snow was as deep as the wheels of the car. We don't do that in the States, but we launched. We get a phone call to be airborne in fifteen minutes, even in 20 Celsius."

I shivered in the driving rain; the temperature hovered just over freezing and I was soaked. "Today is like a summer day in Bodø," Cooler said indulgently. "Weather conditions tend to be unpredictable. Rapid changes, heavy winds, rain to snow, and snow to rain. Parachuting in a snow storm is not a good idea," he advised, not that I was considering it. "You would die in minutes."

He suddenly received a signal to scramble. Cooler waved good-bye and trotted out to fly after the Russians.

◇◇◇◇◇◇

In order to prepare for the Russian threat, Norway and its friends with polar real estate—Denmark, Canada, the United States, Finland, Sweden—need combat-ready forces for the coldest mountains. That means testing new ways to offset the climatic effects on bodies and equipment. Moving parts break, ice clogs optics, and batteries drain quickly. Moisture collects when going from cold to warm and back to cold, such as when entering and exiting a warm tent. Soldiers must be taught how to use parachute covers and stoves to warm medical fluids, engines, and satellite technology. And then there's procuring water in a place as cold as the North Pole, which is no easy feat: room-temperature water quickly freezes, while the snow contains too much air to melt for a sufficient quantity. Instead, you have to bring blocks of ice and melt them as necessary. To meet the water needs of sixty people, you'd need to fill the bed of a pickup truck with ice.

The best place to see soldiers in action was another 120 miles north in Åsegården, home to the Artic Allied Training Center. This is where

NATO trains its most hardened men for the high cold. Men learn to dig snow caves, slaughter reindeer, and ice fish. They claw their way out of glacial lakes and trek in deep snow with half their body weight on their backs.

To reach Åsegården, I took a coastal steamer through the blue fjords. Norway has historically used the rugged coast of inlets and snow-capped mountains to outwit bigger foes. During Viking times, villagers sent smoke signals from summits to warn of approaching raiders, and rolled logs down slopes to stop them. Later, the terrain helped stave off Sweden. Locals gloat about New Year's Eve, 1718, when 3,700 attacking Carolean soldiers froze to death. The Swedes were stuck in a blizzard in the rough Tydal mountain range, unable to resupply.

Shortly after dawn, the steamer docked at Harstad, a stolid port on an island in the Lofoten archipelago. Uniformed men ambled about the medieval architecture looking for beers and directions to the Adolf Gun, a behemoth with a sixty-six-foot barrel used by Hitler's occupying forces to defend the coast.

I was met by Lieutenant Colonel Lars Sundnes, the impish chief of Åsegården, whose wisecracks belied his serious mission: to make sure trainees survive. We drove a short distance to Åesegårten, where we saw crack troops slaloming down slopes. Sundnes explained that training here had decreased during NATO's adventures in Afghanistan. Now, though, interest in cold weather was back in vogue among Navy SEALs and special forces from other nations. This week five hundred marines and infantry were visiting from Britain and the Netherlands. They took over two barracks, bringing their own cooks and jokingly renaming the base SASegarden.

I was staying in the British quarters. Dropping off my backpack in my room, I noticed a bulletin in the hallway: "A general threat against Norwegian interests has increased." I wasn't sure if that meant Russians or the visiting troops.

◇◇◇◇◇◇◇

Back in the nineteenth century, Arctic explorers got their clothes from Inuit hunters, using the hides of whatever animals could be killed. Frederick Cook, who claimed to be the first white man to reach the North Pole, packed hare stockings, blue-fox coats, bear pants, and bird-skin shirts.

His rival, Robert Peary, favored seal. Technology has not advanced much since then. For men outfitting themselves to fight in the Arctic Circle, modern inventions such as Gore-Tex go only so far.

Before I left for Norway, the military press liaison e-mailed that I should bring "plenty of warm clothes." I spent many hours trawling outdoor sports stores in Manhattan; none carried gear warm enough for minus fifty-five degrees. But I cobbled together the next best thing—heavy boots that made me walk like Frankenstein and bulky layers of synthetic materials.

As soon as I checked into the barracks in Åsegården, I learned that I wasn't done contemplating apparel. Sundnes steered me to a conference room for what was billed as the most important briefing of all: the Clothing Lecture. "Everyone who comes here must take this lesson," he said. He switched on the PowerPoint. "For a 100 percent chance of survival, 20 percent is the proper clothing and 80 percent is knowing how to use it."

An assortment of brass from different military powers held forth on the proper garments to fight the cold. Animal fur did not guarantee sufficient protection. Dogs that helped rescue people from avalanches were relegated to kennels when the thermometer dipped below 28.4 degrees Fahrenheit. "There has never been a piece of research that shows you can acclimatize to extreme cold," cautioned Major Simon Guest, a medic with the British Royal Marines.

The next slide showed Hannibal on his Alpine campaign, in sandals. "He was not dressed right," Sundnes sniffed. He flipped to one showing Napoleon in a thin wool coat, which got a dismissive wave, then to an image of a musk ox: "Better."

Next we gathered around a young recruit who resembled a Ken doll, standing at attention in his skivvies. A colonel barked orders.

"Mesh!" On went a fishnet vest.

"Long shirt and pants!" The colonel fingered the material. "Seventy percent wool and 30 percent polyester. You have to get the right mix."

"Parka! Gore-Tex! Shell!" Three layers of pants and jacket followed. The colonel stuck his fingers inside Ken's waistband. "Note: Trousers should be a size too large to allow for air flow."

Then it was "Feet!" (Heavy rubber boots, covered by insulated sacks).

He threw in waterproof mittens thick as boxing gloves, and a balaclava like those worn by Chechen fighters, all covered with synthetic materials designed to trap body warmth.

Then the colonel inspected my gear, which had cost me $800. He pronounced it "adequate," and threw me a few extra layers. Only then was I allowed outside.

We took a tracked transport vehicle called a Bandvagn past ice that sparkled like crystals of beryl, the water like sapphire. The frozen landscape was pristine, except for men practicing survival skills. The temperature was a balmy minus 22 degrees Fahrenheit when we reached the top of a hillock, where British special forces new to skis balanced precariously. Despite all my gear, I was freezing. The soldiers unaccustomed to this clime and to slaloming didn't look happy, either. Nor did the Norwegian instructors, whose job it was to prepare these flatlanders to master the art of Arctic combat. One of the trainers looked disapprovingly at the tents the Brits had pitched in the snow. At twenty below, it's colder inside the tent than outside, he explained. Norwegian mountaineers knew to use stoves fueled by diesel mixed with kerosene to stay warm, but the Brits were resisting. "I say to them, 'When your marines train hard like hell during the day, you want them to have rest in a comfortable way. If you are shivering you won't have a productive debriefing discussion.'" He shook his head again at this lowland intransigence. "I am pretty sure in Afghanistan they wished they had those stoves."

The Brits were adjusting their skis. I went over and asked one soldier how he felt. He had fought in Afghanistan but said this was even harder. "When you start and it's rainy and cold, the word *fuck* comes up a lot. At the start I thought, why am I doing this? I can go to the captain and say, 'I quit,' and then go home and order a pizza."

Today's drill involved dragging two-hundred-pound "casualties" on sledges called *hjelpers.* Soldiers hook the stretchers to belts with ropes and pull them, like huskies on skis. The slippery surface was better suited to ice-skating and a lot of men struggled to stay vertical, their legs splaying like giraffes at a drinking hole.

Periodically the troops stopped and flapped their arms around and inspected each other for signs of frostbite. "You need to stay sharp in this environment. There's no room for error," explained one of the instructors. "We have a saying, 'Don't expect, inspect.' It's not good enough to ask a strong marine with tattoos and big muscles if he's okay. He will say, 'Yes, sir.' You have to check to see that his toes aren't frozen."

He went on to say that while their soldiers used skis for fast movement in the high mountains, even experienced skiers would have trouble in six-foot snow, and they'd be better off on snowshoes. If ambushed, soldiers leave on their skis, although turning around on them isn't easy. Shooting on skis was hard, too. The heartbeat influences how steadily you can hold a weapon; it's hard to shoot accurately while in motion. Most bring an insulated blanket or sleeping bag to lie on top of to shoot. Their knees and elbows are padded with insulation as well.

The Scandinavians have a long history of expertise in this terrain. There's a famous story from World War II of a David-versus-Goliath victory. The Finnish army was grossly outnumbered and outgunned when the Soviets invaded in 1939–40. No one thought they had a chance. Yet the Finns used the complicated topography to their advantage, zipping around the forest on their wooden skis. They shamed the mighty Red Army, and inspired the US military to train soldiers in those methods— and to create the Tenth Mountain Division. These novice British skiers were not quite there yet.

By then I had been outside for a few hours, and I was in agony. The human body creates heat as it moves, and I'd been standing still, watching the training. My lungs began to burn with each breath. Icicles formed inside my nose; my toes were numb and the snow glare hurt my eyes. Worse, I couldn't take notes. The gloves were so thick that I had to remove them to grip the ballpoint pen, which in any event didn't write because the ink had frozen. The tape recorder wasn't functioning either; the cold had drained the batteries. I managed to revive the equipment with hand-warmers in my pants pocket, but the instructors grew nervous every time I took off the gloves to write, checking for white spots on my skin.

All I could think about was food. I felt I was losing pounds just shivering. I fondly recalled breakfast, which consisted of a mound of salmon, herring, lamb, potatoes, hamburgers, liver, eggs, and sausages. They didn't allow seconds, because you feel colder when blood rushes from the skin to a heavy stomach.

◇◇◇◇◇◇◇

Like their Vermont counterparts, a lot of the mountaineers stationed here were so deeply attached to the lifestyle and landscape that they passed up promotions in other regions to remain above the Artic Circle. They felt more at home in the empty and untrammeled highlands than in more populated regions further south. As at the Mountain School, I noticed that the soldiers here would take any opportunity to commune with nature, even if it meant sleeping in a snow cave on a glacier. One night after training, a couple officers invited me on a camping excursion by the side of a frozen lake. Our tent came equipped with the customary stove and reindeer skins placed on birch twigs on the floor. They explained that the hollow hairs provided insulation unmatched by any synthetic gear. The wet fur stank, but so did the men's feet when they took off their boots. The men burned a candle near the entrance to ensure there was enough oxygen.

One of the campers lived in a cabin on a fjord, when he wasn't teaching mountain survival skills at the base. Everyone agreed that was paradise. Another shared his thoughts on mountain society. "Coastal people are always travelers, but in the northern mountains inland people are more isolated and the communities are tighter. In the north you just show up at someone's house. In the south you call six days in advance."

"In the northern parts people are more blunt," said another.

"Certainly," they all agreed.

The soldiers stuck a florescent green stick into the snow outside the tent to mark where to pee, so that we wouldn't get lost in the frigid dark. Overhead, the northern lights put on a spectacular show, white swirls of magic. One of the guys hacked at the ice and dropped a line to catch fish.

We spread out sleeping bags on the reindeer pelt. The hide provided wonderful cushioning, better than any foam mattress. The men told folk stories about the trolls who slumbered in mountains. The mythic giants surrounded us, but we would never see them because they turned to stone at first light.

The soldiers warmed cocoa on the stove. It smelled divine, and the major reminded everyone to stay hydrated because of all the sweating in heavy clothes. But then I thought about standing by the pee stick in the permafrost. Temperatures had dropped and the wind was picking up. I politely declined the drink, and contemplated the long night ahead.

◇◇◇◇◇◇◇

An avalanche moves like a thundering wall of snow, at a power greater than a speeding train. It is one of the most catastrophic forces of nature, yet can be triggered by a single gunshot, a skier gliding by, or vibrations from airplanes or vehicles. They are called the White Death, the most dreaded killer on mountain fronts, an enemy that lies in wait for unsuspecting victims. Their might hinges on the angle of the slope and how the snow is layered. Once unleashed, an avalanche can dump thousands of tons of snow, smothering victims in an icy grave. Most are suffocated instantly, their chests crushed under the weight of snow, trees, and rocks. The few who find air pockets have at most two hours to survive beneath the surface.

During World War I, Alpine avalanches killed an estimated fifty thousand men on the Italian-Austrian front—one-fifth of them over a mere twenty-four hours in December 1916. Some historical accounts speculate that the avalanches were triggered on purpose, a claim no one can prove conclusively. Yet Norway and its allies take seriously the possibility that an avalanche can be used as a weapon of war.

Wednesday, March 5, 1986, marked a turning point in how the Norwegian army prepared for avalanches. Shortly after 1 p.m., thirty-one men from the North Norway Brigade were slowly moving snowmobiles along a valley stream on the north side of the Storebalak, a mountain near the village of Vassalen, close to the Arctic port of Narvik. They were taking part in a routine NATO winter exercise, this one called Anchor Express. The brigade was supposed to advance northward along the highway, while engineers opened a snowmobile track through the valley. Suddenly an avalanche rumbled down on them, depositing a load forty-five feet deep, filling up the river at the foot of the mountain. All the men were swept up in it. Miraculously, fifteen of them kept their heads above the snow mass, or made air pockets right under the surface, and survived. The rest were entombed.

It was one of the worst avalanche tolls in military history since World War I. Major Geir Nordrum was on helicopter ambulance duty that afternoon and is still haunted by what he saw. We sat in the control room at the Bardufoss base, twenty-seven years later to the day, as he pulled out the flight log, now yellowed by age. It had been an exceptionally windy day. Ordinarily they wouldn't have embarked on a seven-hour flight in such gusts. He was shocked when he landed at the bottom of the avalanche: the snow was packed as hard as cement. The rescue medics and dogs went from spot to spot, poking poles and praying for voices. They flew in and out, all day and into the night, forgoing customary formations. The last victim was found twenty-one feet deep. "Can you imagine what it was like to die in such a grave?" Major Nordrum asked.

He and the other rescuers strapped corpses outside the helicopter for lack of room inside. For the shivering hypothermic survivors, he shut off the heaters inside the chopper; otherwise they could go into shock from the sudden transition from extreme cold to warmth. "That was the first avalanche, and hopefully the last, for me," he said, closing the logbook. "I don't want to talk about the memories."

The 1986 avalanche linked the survivors and rescuers not only to one another, but to all mountain soldiers past and present. The terror and tragedy of it, the awareness that another such disaster could happen at any moment, the years and expert know-how devoted to avoiding it—all informed the training today of those who must fight at altitude.

Ever since, Norway's military has used more precise mapping, developing a color-code system for danger zones. They send experts to scout geological conditions before military exercises. Every Norwegian officer gets training in how to evaluate the risks of wind, weather, temperatures, the consistency of snow, and the angle of slope. Yet all of that, I soon learned, could not guarantee safety.

One of the resident avalanche experts was Reconnaissance Platoon Commander Jacob Helgersen, whose bounding physique and lantern jaw would look at home in an L.L. Bean catalog. Except that clothing models don't generally seem as worried as he did; I noticed him frowning over a map of varying pinks indicating the greatest risks, depending on the shifting weather and quality of the snow. He had reason to believe conditions here today were risky, because a fresh layer of snow had fallen on top of hoar frost.

"A crystal surface is weak," he explained. "It creates thin unstable layers. If you slide on the slippery top layer you can trigger an avalanche." He cautioned me to tread carefully. "Often the only warning is a *voomp* noise, which signals cracks in the snow."

Helgersen went on to describe terrifying scenarios. An avalanche usually occurs on a slope at 33 to 55 degrees, which is what we were heading toward. There are three causes of death from avalanches: trauma, exposure, and the mouth and lungs getting packed with snow. The last is especially likely in loose snow, like we had that day. You could be crushed against a tree, or hurled over a cliff, out onto the fjords. Flattened terrain, like the bottom of a bowl, provides greater chances of being smothered. Slab avalanches are the most dangerous—large blocks of packed snow can put so much pressure on your chest that you are squeezed to death, even if your head is above the surface. The only way to survive burial is to make an air pocket with a Dracula-like motion, an arm crooked in front of your face, with some inches to spare. Then you're supposed to stick the other arm above the surface with a pole and hope someone spots you.

At that, Helgersen took off, scampering up the hill with ease. I, in contrast, sank knee-deep into the snow, pulled down by my heavy boots. My lungs burned. Twenty minutes later, I caught up with Helgersen at the top of a hill. He was standing in a freshly dug hole five feet deep, to reveal the layers of snow and ice.

Every soldier carries a probe, and a beacon that can send or search for signals. The beacon has an arrow to search distance and location, accurate down to ten to twenty centimeters. "You stick in the probe and hope you don't drive it through the victim's eye," Helgersen said, whacking at the sides of the snow. "But that's better than leaving him down there for a long time. Most people die in about fifteen to eighteen seconds. Some men panic from claustrophobia during training. I have to take care not to collapse snow into their air pockets. So we try to extract them horizontally. It's scary."

The snow was not as white as Helgersen desired. He whacked again. And again. The snow crumbled at the third blow. "Worse than I thought," he muttered, picking up his tools. Helgersen rushed off calling, "Follow me!"

This time I managed to keep a closer pace. As we hurtled downhill, Helgersen turned and made the air pocket gesture, his arm folded across his face.

◇◇◇◇◇◇

Since 2006, Norway has hosted giant war games called Cold Response. They attract about sixteen thousand soldiers from sixteen countries to practice amphibious landings, air support, evacuations, firing, and surveillance in high winter conditions. For the Norwegian military, it's an opportunity to road-test equipment and methods. Smaller exercises take place regularly, and a lanky major named Ivar Moen was assigned to shepherd me at one such simulation. With his shaven head and sunken cheeks, he evoked a monk from another age. An obsessive skier, Moen does one and a half hours of cross-country tracks every night, even in blizzards. I noticed he was wearing a Soviet belt buckle with a red star. "Need to be prepared," he joked.

As we drove to the exercise site, we made a detour to Narvik, a sleepy inlet where iced mountains rise thousands of feet from the fjords. The Nazis had their eye on the strategic port, with the aim of controlling the transit of iron ore from Sweden. In spring 1940, a ferocious battle erupted here. The harsh climate and terrain made it tough for both sides. Even the Norwegians struggled with the cold, but at least they had skis and knew how to use them, unlike the poorly-equipped-and-trained Poles, French, and Brits fighting alongside them. Ultimately, the Allies won the battle thanks to the glacial landscape's obstruction of land supply lines—and air supply lines, too, when nine feet of snow fell on Bardufoss airport. It was the first major Allied land victory of the war. Yet it illustrated Norway's vulnerability, and how it needed the help of bigger friends.

Further along, Moen pointed out an anvil shape in the distance. This was Stetind, Norway's national mountain. In 1904, it was called "the ugliest mountain" by a prominent British mountaineer. Norwegians, however, are fond of the 4,500-foot mound. "We have hundreds of peaks," Moen said with affection. "This one won the public vote on the radio station."

We reached the site of the exercises, a field right by the road. It was a perfect blue day and the air was crisp and fresh. An instructor described the scenario: recapturing an oil refinery from terrorists. The idea was to move fast into an area and neutralize enemy supply.

"Terrain is very hilly and dense forest will give short fields of fire," the instructor said. "Inside these valleys you'll have problems shooting. Narrow valleys and steep slopes restrict off-road mobility, and provide narrow mobility corridors. The enemy has thermal capability. They have better eyes and weapons than us."

Dozens of soldiers in puffy white camouflage readied their mortars and rifles. Observation teams in orange hovered about. The exercise would involve rifle practice, air mobility operation, indirect fire. "You'll see ground insertion of fire, a sniper team, a javelin squad, and a mortar squad," Moen said. "Helicopters pick up the assault force, and hover in a holding area."

The day was clear, and the snow packed. Winds here can reach forty knots, but today it was still. The pilots were in luck; otherwise they would have to worry about whiteouts, when billowing snow impairs perception so badly that the ground blurs into the clouds. You don't know if you're up or down, and in whiteouts you lose visual reference points like posts and trees. They did, however, have to make sure they avoided the clouds, where ice can start forming on the blades and windscreen within seconds.

Military drills take place near ordinary houses in the High North. Three civilians in red jackets skied by with their dogs, barely looking up at the snipers taking up positions by the trees. This proximity makes things easy for Russian spies, who often camp by the side of the road next to fields where the military drills.

"We keep an eye out for campers with antenna," Moen said. "They are interested in tactics, which unit was where or playing what role and any new equipment. If a rental car drives by more than one time you advise your superior. Guard your weapon."

The helicopter flew in. The shooting began.

If it had been real combat, the enemy would have easily spotted the troops in the vast whiteness of the open terrain. The men wore balaclavas to hide frost from their breath but we could still see their shadows. And the white camouflage uniforms didn't match the snow. Moen explained why. "Even if the snow looks white, it changes color all the time. Sun on snow throws a shadow."

That wasn't all. Extreme cold impairs sharpshooters' accuracy by influencing bullet speeds. Powder burns slower when cold, so artillery rounds can fall short of the desired impact area. Plus you don't have the same fragmentation effect when it hits snow, especially deep snow, which absorbs much of the blast. It's like firing into cotton.

"No one has perfected it yet," Moen said.

Suddenly, he began to jump up and down like a frenzied kangaroo.

"Frostbite," he said through gritted teeth. "Had it a dozen times in the toes. Hurts like anything."

I silently repeated the slogan, *If you can survive and fight in the extremes of the Arctic, you can fight anywhere in the world.*

◇◇◇◇◇◇◇

My visits to Vermont and Norway brought home to me the fact that nations need to better prepare themselves to wage war at elevations, frosty or otherwise. Without preparedness, superiority in equipment and numbers is illusionary, and victory is impossible. And seeing it firsthand, I finally fully grasped another, equally crucial point: in freezing mountain regions, conquering the environment is just as complex and difficult as conquering the enemy.

The Norwegians, who did freezing mountains better than anyone, were more handicapped by physical conditions than by Russian preparedness. No matter that they were evenly matched and well equipped. Neither side could defeat the frozen wasteland itself.

Vermont further illuminated what I'd observed in the chronic belligerence in Colombia, Chechnya, and Kashmir. Irregular mountain forces scuttling around caves and forested slopes have advantages over better-equipped interlopers. And tactics are just one of the many components of conquest. Psychology plays a powerful role, too, and generally favors the defenders in the steeps. No war chest can crush angry people living on the elevated margins of society.

Because the worn formula of military "solutions" has repeatedly failed, policy makers need to think beyond political domination and armed intervention. Too little thought is given to the psychology of the people in the mountains, to the unmovable physical barriers that shape their outlooks, and to their specific needs and aims. Flatland governments must comprehend what motivates the resistance in upland regions, and the futility of trying to dominate them. And then they need a whole new blueprint to address decades-long fights effectively.

It is precisely because mountains don't move, and the tactics deployed to conquer them almost invariably fail, that we need political solutions for their disenfranchised inhabitants. To explore this issue, I returned to Europe once more.

8

Cantonment (Contentment)

THE PYRENEES, 3,500 TO 11,168 FEET

THE SWISS ALPS, 4,239 TO 15,203 FEET

> Their country free and joyous
> She of the rugged sides
> She of the rough peaks arrogant
> Whereon the tempest rides:
> Mother of the unconquered thought
>
> —Victor Hugo, "The Swiss Mercenaries" (1859)

Jean Lassalle invited me to his village in the Pyrenees to see the shepherds' struggle against the alien Slovenian bears. The predators were being introduced into the region to replenish a local species that had died out, over local objections of sheep farmers who fear mauled flocks. Lassalle deplored the government's failure to consult locals, calling it a "dialogue of the deaf."

"This valley of freedom is in the process of being relegated to the rank of museum where time would be stopped and where everything would be perfectly controllable. But the mountain cannot be domesticated. We find ourselves now with shepherds whose flocks are attacked by bears that have never lived in these places before."

He added, "On every continent, mountain populations suffer from the same troubles. . . . [They] are the first victims in conflicts and their voices are inaudible in negotiations. Each situation is singular and occurs in a very particular historical context. If each of these conflicts touches mountain-dwelling populations fragmented between multiple states

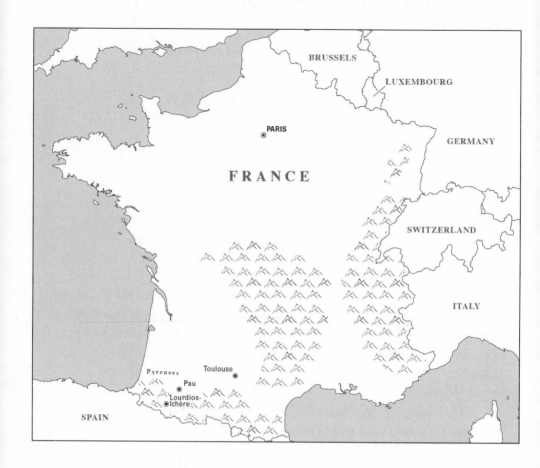

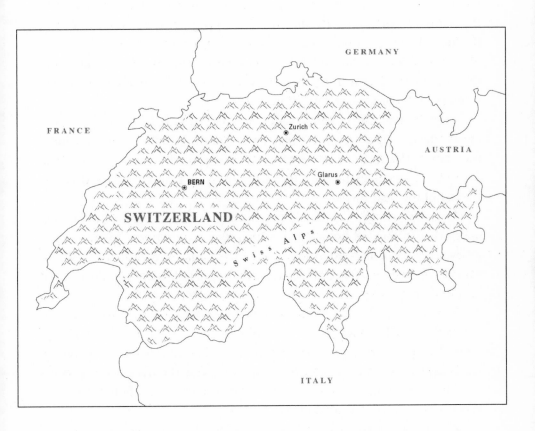

claiming sovereignty over the territory, each situation calls for a particular solution."

Of course, the interloping bears in the Pyrenees can't be compared to the daily trauma of life in Chechnya or Kashmir. But the Lassalle family's enduring trouble with the French government has given this son of the mountains not only empathy for highlanders who live amid violent conflict, but also an intimate understanding of the challenges they face: namely, they are invisible and inaudible, both literally and figuratively, to the national leadership. Because they are geographically removed from the locus of power in the lowland capital, they are actually, physically out of sight and mind. Thus powerless, their needs and concerns rarely enter the awareness of governments—or, worse, they are actively disregarded when political or financial profit is at stake.

Lassalle had parliamentary business in Paris, but his family would receive me in the hamlet where they had lived since 1600: Lourdios-Ichère, population 150, in the westernmost reaches of the Pyrenees in the Béarn district. The town lay on the edge of the sprawling national park that was the site of the bear dispute.

Lassalle's village had no auberge and his family felt shy about hosting me in their unheated homestead, which had acquired few modern amenities since its construction in 1825. In the name of comfort, the World Mountain People Association arranged pension accommodation ten minutes' drive away.

Silver-haired Pierre Gondard, a cartographer and general coordinator of the WMPA, met me in the lobby, accompanied by Didier Hervé, a middle-aged agronomist who headed the Institution Patrimoniale du Haut-Béarn, an organization that tries to better the lives of local peasants. He was trying to convince Paris that sheep farmers should take precedence over imported predators.

As we took seats in Hervé's white sedan, the men told me that local shepherds earn their keep from the Basco-béarnaise, a long-haired sheep with distinctive horns that curl under the ears. The ewes' milk produces a raw semisoft cheese with a nutty flavor called Ossau-Iraty. Hervé said it had been made for a millennium, since the Romans brought cheese making to the region. He estimated that eighty thousand of the animals grazed in communal upland pastures during the summer. Sheep farmers lived in crude huts policed by ferocious Great Pyrenees dogs that guard the flocks.

Yet even these feared canines, which have been known to attack hikers who stray too close, could not protect the livestock from wild predators. Hervé was worried about wolves and griffon vultures, which had developed an unusual taste for living lambs on top of the customary diet of carrion. But the bears were the bigger concern; about three hundred sheep were lost to them each year, from mauling or fear-induced miscarriages and falls.

By 1991, hunting had rendered the native Pyrenean brown bear extinct, but the shepherds' reprieve from these predators was cut short when the government later brought in others in order to restore the ursine population. The immigrants became the pet cause of celebrities, including actors Gérard Depardieu and Fanny Ardant, who served as "godparents" for one particularly large male named Balou after the character in Rudyard Kipling's *The Jungle Book*. Balou roamed the national park, whose popularity had increased among foreign tourists eager to spot the creatures in the wild. Peasants did not share their delight and blockaded roads with signs screaming *Non a'lous*, "No to the Bears." They destroyed bear-tracking equipment and dumped manure at a town hall. Balou was wounded in 2008 when a boar hunter shot him. The hunter's claim that it was an accident did not stem government suspicions of his, and the protestors', intent.

Gondard saw the controversy as emblematic of the mountain-center divide, "a problem we see the world over." We were driving to the top of a ridge for a view of the spectacular Aspe Valley, immortalized in Alexandre Dumas's *The Three Musketeers*. After snaking upward for a while, the car stopped and we got out to admire the unspoiled valley below, deep green sprinkled with shepherds' huts. Across the valley, magnificent and stark granite poked the sky. Eagles and peregrine falcons flew by, hunting for prey. The rock called to mind Albania, though I knew that tarred roads and Michelin-starred restaurants lay nearby. It was a relief not to worry about personal safety or lack of comfort as I had in the other places I'd visited.

This relatively tamer landscape, however, offered no reassurance for the shepherds, whom Gondard said were "always" at odds with Paris. "The state has never understood that the mountain area is sacred to us," he explained. "The central government imposes its will on the peasants. It doesn't take into account their wishes."

With a last look at the natural splendor, we got back into the car and headed down toward chez Lassalle. The stone farmhouse was situated on the banks of a rushing jade-colored river. A muddy guard dog rushed at the vehicle with fangs extended. A massively tall man bounded after the hound to prevent it from biting the tires. His height and craggy face made him easily recognizable as the brother of Jean Lassalle.

Julien Lassalle wore the farmers' uniform of rubber boots and blue coveralls stained with milk, the source of which baaed like old men around the plot. We slogged ankle deep onto a muddy path that led to the storage shed, where hundreds of rounds of cheese ripened for market. Julien Lassalle explained that the road leading to the house from the highway several miles away was only built in 1975, which made him ashamed to invite school friends home. Life was still simple. He pointed to a clearing amid the overgrown bush on the banks of the river, where he and his elderly mother still cut the high grass with hand scythes. It took them an entire month to clear that much.

Entering the homestead, we sat at a rough-hewn table and benches that could accommodate twenty. Sheep competition medals adorned the hearth. Madame Marie, the matriarch, arrived, looking like Gertrude Stein in a worn denim apron and fleece vest. She plunked down a plate of prune jam and chunks of home-cured bacon and cheese.

"There are some who talk and those who listen. I talk," she said, taking a knife out of her pocket and slicing chunks of cheese onto thick grainy bread. "The peasants are the true owners of the land. Those who come from the outside have salaries and they don't live off the land like we do. They only come to dictate laws that are not adjusted to our life here. For example, they change the hour in summer. How is that progress?"

Julien reached for short glasses and poured from a bottle of red wine. "We should all be like the Swiss. They take care of the small peasants. But the European Union and global society has another way of looking at things. It doesn't put emphasis on our priorities. The government wants to introduce bears here. This will promote biodiversity. But they have to think about shepherds as biodiversity, too. Cohabitation with the bear will make it hard for us to pursue our lifestyle."

What about reparation measures? I had heard that the government was installing electric fences and offered compensation for mauled sheep.

Julien Lassalle gave a shrug. "They don't pay for the collateral damage of fear. When the bear grabs one, the others panic. They run away.

They miscarry. They plunge off the edge." He cut more cheese, looking at the sliver as though contemplating its monetary worth. "Shepherds have an expression, 'If the bear robs one sheep to eat, we will pardon him.' The shepherds can't accept if it kills two or three. We have to live as well."

What next? They looked at each other and then back at me.

"There are plans," the matriarch said vaguely.

I helped her clear the table, and looked at my watch. The fast train was leaving soon for Paris and I didn't want to miss it. We shook hands good-bye and the WMPA men drove me to the train station in Oloron-Saint-Marie. Nestled comfortably in the plush seats as the Pyrenees receded into the plains, I again thought of what Lassalle's friend, Mario Conejo, had said to me earlier in the trip: "Don't mess with mountain people." I for one would not want to go up against the Lassalle family. Despite all the outside support for the bears, the outcome of this quarrel was difficult to predict. And even if the highlanders didn't prevail, they would remain a permanent irritant for the French government.

A few months later the central government announced it was freezing plans to introduce more bears. People speculated that the then prime minister, Nicolas Sarkozy, was worried about the farmers' vote. Then a bear died, the very same Balou, who earlier had been shot "by accident." According to officials, he died from a fall. But was that likely? Left to their own devices, bears don't just fall off cliffs.

The clash over the introduction of bears into the Pyrenees might seem quaint, from the lowlander point of view, but it is merely a less severe version of the conflicts this book has explored elsewhere. Lassalle and his comrades may have won this one battle, but new ones will invariably flare again soon. The question is, are there political solutions to the challenges faced by mountain people, and by the nations to which they nominally belong? How can we put an end to the deadly clashes mountains seem to naturally birth? In an attempt to find answers, I went to a country comprised nearly entirely of mountain people, which one might suppose might be the most violent of all.

◇◇◇◇◇◇◇

The 8:12 a.m. train from Zurich pulled into Glarus one hour and four minutes later, exactly on schedule. Normally it's easy to get a seat on Swiss trains on Sunday mornings—this is an observant Christian country, and most stores and services shut down on God's day. But this train was practically full and our group of five had to walk through various compartments to find seats together. Other passengers greeted each other with stiff handshakes and quiet talk. They wore formal black attire to mark the solemnity of the occasion, the men in felt Alpine fedoras and the women in pearls and heels. This was the first Sunday in May, when everyone sixteen and older in the canton, or local district, votes in the *Landesgemeinde*, an open-air assembly that has been held since 1387.

Our party included my Dutch brother-in-law, Carel, who headed the anthropology department at the University of Zurich. He was eager to witness this arcane mountain practice that had survived intact over the centuries. Carel normally could help translate German for me, but the dialects from small cantons baffled him. A Swiss colleague of his came to our rescue, and brought her two little girls along for a day out.

The train glided past the mountains, rivers, and lakes that fortify this landlocked nation at Europe's core. It had been a particularly rainy spring, and today was no exception, but it didn't obscure the stunning scenery; snow-tipped peaks watched over the meadows of yellow wildflowers and grazing brown cows. We didn't need to consult precision timepieces to know we had arrived: everyone got out at Glarus and walked briskly into the town center, a mass of umbrellas bobbing overhead. The street took us past market stalls selling plastic toy cars and specialties emblematic of Switzerland's three main language groups: panini, bratwurst sausages, and quiche. Medieval flags of the canton's villages festooned the narrow streets, banners of war from centuries past when Switzerland's main export was mercenaries.

It all felt a bit like a county fair, with rides and ice cream trucks for the children, but the festive atmosphere was tempered by gravitas; voting is taken seriously in the twenty-six cantons that form the Swiss Confederation, Switzerland's formal name. This is the world's most direct form of democracy, where an ordinary citizen with enough supporting signatures can challenge a law passed by parliament or call a referendum to change the constitution. The people of Glarus assert this right forcefully.

Strolling through the staid and prosperous crowd, I pondered how Switzerland was so markedly different from—much less dramatic than—other mountain regions I'd journeyed to: no arrests by corrupt authorities; no kidnapping attempts; no need to check for frostbite or avalanche risks at regular intervals; no scary helicopter trips under armed guard; no psych ward full of patients deeply traumatized by decades of violence; no guerrillas, or warlords, or jihadis; no war. Instead, democracy and reliable plumbing. Switzerland had held at bay poverty and war for a comfortable life of banking and political participation.

A raised map of Switzerland resembles the head of a particularly bumpy cauliflower: mountains cover nearly every acre. The profusion of valleys, piedmonts, and peaks has shaped the political destiny of the country's 7.1 million people. The soaring Alps posed a natural barrier to foreign invasion and isolated villages from each other. The diversity of ethnicities and languages discouraged political unity and the kind of hierarchical monarchy that took root in other parts of Europe. Logic would have it that these divisions and myriad dialects would have squashed any hope of harmony. Instead they have resulted in tranquil unity.

The ever-pragmatic Swiss devised a unique and ingenious formula for accommodating their geographic reality. Their political system, which gradually evolved over seven hundred years, binds diverse upland valleys together by devolving powers to each of them. A loose alliance of small self-governing towns that formed a confederacy in 1291 developed into today's system, in which each of the twenty-six cantons essentially runs its own affairs. Each has its own constitution, laws, government, and parliament, which operate alongside a national parliament and central government. They placidly decide on issues that prove fraught elsewhere, such as setting income tax rates.

Switzerland's internal harmony stems from what Jean Lassalle would call the "mountain mentality," or defensiveness against the outside world. Surrounded by Germany, Austria, France, and Italy, the Swiss eventually realized that they had to transcend the infighting among their religious and linguistic factions to avoid being swallowed up by the neighbors. In many other parts of the world, factionalism breeds divisiveness—and that has sometimes been the case in Switzerland, too. The country was shredded by peasant revolts and religious strife in the seventeenth and eighteenth centuries, and then was spooked by a short civil war in 1847 between Catholics and Protestants. That last confrontation birthed a constitution the following year that celebrated differences rather than forcing everyone to accept a singular national identity. Accordingly, Switzerland has four official languages—French, German, Italian, and Romansch. Unlike in so many places I'd visited, Chechnya or Kashmir among them, dissent is almost nonexistent, since citizens are allowed, expected even, to fully express their ethnicity and decide how they want to live. In the process, individual cantons serve as a check on national monopolies of any kind.

No other mountainous country I'd gone to integrated its highland communities so successfully, though there were regions within countries where heterogeneous groups cooperated. In Mexico and Colombia, for instance, various mountain communities have joined forces and won some measure of autonomy; and in the Caucasus, different clans have united under a strong leader at certain points in the past. But those efforts at unity were hard-won, and often short-lived. In many places, mountain communities' mentality does not make for peaceful coexistence with anyone else, whether highlander or lowlander. It's striking that the same topographic realities that promote division in most mountain regions serve to bind Swiss communities together. Perhaps that's because all of Switzerland is mountainous, not just peripheral pockets. The downside of the Swiss wariness of outsiders, routinely called the "hedgehog" mentality, is a doctrine of isolation and hostility to immigrants that runs counter to many of the ideals and laws of our increasingly globalized world. The rest of the planet feels distant, even abstract.

Glarus is among the smaller cantons, measuring a mere 254 square miles and comprised of only three municipal districts. It's situated along a break in the earth's crust that UNESCO declared a World Heritage Site for its "exceptional example of mountain building through continental collision." The highest mountain in the area measures nearly 12,000 feet, a looming, omnipresent giant. The population numbers approximately 39,500, evenly split between Protestants and Catholics. As in much of Switzerland, Glarus was a Reformation- and Counter-Reformation-era hotbed of religious fervor and violence, prompting a decision in 1623 to hold separate Landesgemeinde. In 1836, the two faiths in the town united politically as the country moved toward federated harmony.

Since the introduction of the constitution of 1848 Switzerland has seen 595 referenda, of which about half were approved, and 288 amendments to the constitution. Most citizens mail their ballots, an option meant to facilitate an electoral process that in some cantons occurs three to four times a year on anything from speed limits to taxes. Glarus is one of two cantons that cling to the archaic practice of balloting in public. (The other is Appenzell Innerrhoden, Switzerland's smallest and most traditional canton, where tourists go to see yodeling and alphorns. It only granted women the vote in 1991.)

Each canton still makes much of its coat of arms, which were once actually displayed on flags during medieval battle and beyond—when, for instance, Swiss soldiers earned repute as skilled and determined combatants as the nation expanded into Italy and repulsed the Austrian Habsburgs. Modern Switzerland is infamous for its military isolationism, but from the fifteenth to the seventeenth century, poorer cantons seeking income lent units of trained militias, or *Reisläufere* ("one who goes to war") to serve French kings and other European powers. The mercenaries' prowess with pikes and halberds earned them mentions in Shakespeare's *Hamlet* and Machiavelli's *The Prince*. Victor Hugo, however, bemoaned that these men from the free mountains were rented out:

> *When the regiment of Halberdiers*
> *Is proudly marching by,*
> *The eagle of the mountain screams*
> *From out his stormy sky*

Today, the last remnants of this era are the Vatican Swiss guards, who inspire nostalgia with their colorful medieval doublets and ceremonial halberds.

The banner of Glarus pays homage to its patron saint, Fridolin, who allegedly hailed from Ireland and converted the area to Christianity in the sixth century. The flag has a crimson background from which the holy man looks out with yellow halo and staff. The fighting men of Glarus carried this pennant when they drove the Habsburgs out in the Battle of Näfels of 1388. The day I visited, a large example of the flag fluttered in the main square where voting was to begin when perfectly aligned clocks struck 9:30 a.m.

Church bells rang, signaling the start of ceremonies. A marching band led the way with an *oom-pah-pah* as representatives of the three levels of government—first the canton, then parliament and federal—filed out of the solid city hall and through the main street, grave as a funeral procession. Soldiers flanked the rear. (With its armed neutrality and compulsory military training for men—even the sons of the industrial and banking elite generally serve—the country has a saying: Switzerland does not have an army but is an army.) Ordinary citizens clutching canary yellow ballots followed the officials. It was raining heavily and I fell into step with a suited man. This was Martin Duerst, the chief financial officer of the cantonal bank, who wore a red tie to match the cantonal flag. Did he mind the downpour? He looked determined. "The rain is not important. Voting is."

Townspeople went past the police barricades into the central square, holding ballots up to show they were registered, and took seats in a semi-circle of wooden benches. They faced an equally austere stand full of microphones and communal officials. The crowd numbered at most a couple thousand. The mayor of Glarus, Robert Marti, opened the event by reminding everyone of their responsibility to the greater good.

"It's important to keep traditions alive," he intoned. The black fedoras nodded. "Switzerland is the happiest country in the world and we have the opportunity to build our happiness today." Restrained applause. "In freedom and responsibility, let us have God's blessing: reconcile, reduce conflicts, and increase wealth."

Then he explained the rules, which included no smoking in the fresh outdoors. Also, voters should present their issues with dignity. Everyone stood up to take the oath, holding two fingers in the air. "I swear to the Constitution of Switzerland and the canton, independence and freedom of the people in the name of God."

This year's agenda had eleven issues, which would entail roughly three hours of voting. The first item proposed the cantonal tax rate for the following year. No one objected and it passed within minutes. The second issue proved more contentious: allowing homeowners to convert cellars and attics into living areas. Two communal leaders stood up to argue in favor. "It's better to use the space in your house rather than build more," one reasoned. Two other mayors, however, argued against the measure, one proposing an amendment that each commune should decide for itself. "We don't want our freedom taken away," he explained.

The people of Glarus closed umbrellas to vote. First the "against" camp. A block of yellow cards rose in the air. The officials on the platform didn't count each vote, taking a visual estimate instead. The throng looked evenly split. A second vote occurred. Same ambiguity. More officials got on the podium to count. "We're going to try one more time," one announced stoically. This time, the canton fathers discerned a slight advantage for the opposition camp. Freedom lovers would hold on to their right not to convert storage space into spare bedrooms.

Glarus moved on to the next point: amending the tax law.

By now the clock on the tower read 11 a.m., time for the pubs and pastry cafes to open. The crowd thinned by half to head for the dry indoors, and those who couldn't fit inside huddled in the gardens under dripping tarps, revitalized by drinks in plastic cups. We canvassed people as they left the voting square. Everyone was pleased with the voting; they simply wanted to fortify themselves for the remaining issues. These included amendments to health insurance, the use of forest roads, and supportive measures for child day care.

"I mainly came for the living space vote," confided a grandmother in a flowered headscarf and sporting a gold-rimmed front tooth. She was seventy-three-year-old Lilly Traschsler-Knöpfel, a retired printer, who joked that she had the highest education in the canton because she lived at an altitude of 2,916 feet. She was heading to a food truck where her son was selling grilled sausages and we walked together, past vendors selling chocolate and stuffed animals. She preferred the public nature of the Landesgemeinde to more private voting. "I like feeling part of a community and I am not scared to show my opinion."

Swiss citizenship is based first on citizenship of a municipality of origin, then of a canton, and finally of the nation as a whole. A municipality of origin is inherited from your father and is not determined by where you live or were born. (This makes it hard for foreigners to obtain Swiss nationality; a town must vote on whether it will accept you as one of its own.) When asked where they are from, Swiss generally cite the village of their ancestors, not the current place of residence.

Thus Frau Traschsler-Knöpfel said she came from Appenzell Innerrhoden rather than Glarus, where she now lived and voted. The fact that as a woman she was only granted the right to vote late in life led her to cherish the privilege all the more, and she made it a point to turn out for every election.

She had especially strong views about public transportation. That day she was collecting signatures for a referendum to make buses run more often.

Might she succeed? She turned to face me quizzically. "Why not? This is Switzerland."

◇◇◇◇◇◇◇

Over the years, I stayed in touch with Jean Lassalle, checking in periodically to share impressions of the fraught communities I traveled to. It was easy to lose hope for solutions to these intractable conflicts, something Lassalle expressed in one particularly frustrated e-mail.

"It is dramatic that some populations adopt such forms of radicalism in order to make themselves heard and to preserve their way of life," Lassalle wrote. "It is intolerable that these populations should see their way of life and their natural habitat destroyed, their resources thus exploited without their input, without a single bit of profit or attempt at re-distribution."

He concluded with sadness: "In-so-far as mountain dwelling populations do not have the ability to freely express themselves or the power to demand their rights, to think of autonomy is simply illusory. In order for a sincerely sympathetic dialogue among all the different actors to see the light of day conflict zones must be pacified and the different actors must meet and propose the basis for a really constructive approach."

It was Lassalle who recommended that I go to Switzerland, positing that it offered a deceptively simple solution for fraught mountain communities elsewhere. Switzerland's devolution of power to localities, he suggested, presented a formula policy makers around the globe should emulate when faced with mountain areas that chafe at central control. Such a political federation, of course, was easier to implement in almost fully mountainous nations like Switzerland where there was no disparity between cosmopolitan lowlanders and less developed folks higher up.

On the return train ride from Glarus to Zurich, I asked the Swiss anthropologist if she thought the political system worked. She answered that it was annoying to vote so often, and some of the issues seemed petty. But she appreciated that she had a voice in matters that concerned her, and for all its faults she couldn't imagine an alternative system. She had great faith in it, a refrain I had heard repeatedly in Glarus.

My brother-in-law was equally struck by the Swiss emphasis on consensus and repudiation of cults of personality. In Switzerland, the community is prized over the state and also over the individual. The president of the nation serves only one year; the executive councilors who constitute the federal government rotate into the position. This is how Switzerland avoids dominance by one or two parties. Decision making by compromise and committee reigns and conformity is stressed, even in large cities.

"This collectivity forges extraordinary stability, despite the many referenda and amendments to the constitution," Carel mused.

Much is made of the *rosti graben*, the supposed cultural and ideological line that divides the country between more liberal French-speaking voters and conservative German ones. (The Italian and Romansch speakers are too small to matter as a voting bloc, constituting just 8 and 0.5 percent of the population respectively.) Yet this line is not always stable. The most recent example was a vote in March 2012 to ban second homes in communes where they already exceeded 20 percent of total housing stock. Swiss voters, concerned that development would spoil the mountains' natural beauty, passed the initiative by a slim majority of 50.4 percent. The vote created a bombshell for cantons that rely on tourist wealth, most notably the Valais canton whose inhabitants were indignant that the rest of the country would dictate what they could and could not do with their property. The initiative also sowed an unusual rift between the French-speaking Alpine and urban areas, and among the Alpine cantons themselves.

◇◇◇◇◇◇◇

Mountain scenery, perfect as a picture on a chocolate box, flashed past the train window. I recalled the work of a Swiss economist who studies political satisfaction. In a 2000 study, Bruno Frey took a previously conducted survey of more than six thousand people from across Switzerland who rated their level of contentment on a scale of one to ten. Frey checked the results against the degree of political autonomy in their cantons. (This varies, with some districts enjoying greater ease in conducting referenda on taxes, schools, transportation, and social services.) The results? Those with a great degree of direct democracy registered the highest degree of happiness. For instance, the canton of Basel Land, which is near but does not include the city of Basel, had the highest autonomy rating: 5.69 out of 6. It was notably happier than the canton of Geneva, which has the lowest rating, of 1.75.

In other studies, on conflict and motivation, Frey noted that Switzerland's unique system prevented a separatist minority from following the path of violent separatist groups elsewhere. From the end of World War II through the early 1970s, secessionists in the French-speaking and marginalized district of Jura sought to break from the German-speaking canton of Berne. Young radicals known as *Béliers* ("rams") sabotaged trams, staged arson attacks, seized a police station, and stormed the Swiss Embassy in Brussels. The Swiss response? Hold referenda! The people voted, and in 1979 Jura became the twenty-sixth canton.

Imagine the bloodshed that could have been avoided if India allowed Kashmiris to vote on secession. Or if the Soviets hadn't disbanded the autonomous republics in the North Caucasus, and had then later allowed Chechnya to form its own state. Along similar lines, one could argue that Colombia would have prevented the rise and entrenchment of FARC if it had reached an accommodation with the Marquetalia Republic in 1964, instead of bombing it. Think, too, of what could have been if Mexican authorities had been flexible in Chiapas, or if the Rai of Nepal were granted compensation for the flooding of their lands. If only Albanian officialdom could provide a face-saving way to stop the Kanun killings—an amnesty program, perhaps. Instead frustration, and associated carnage, fester, unchecked and even ignored by those with the power to stop it.

Ever since my son Anton and I had played that game of Risk, he regularly returned to the globe to see what had changed. All but one conflict—of the Basque separatists—stubbornly persisted. And new ones had joined the list, or intensified their resistance. The Kurdish fighters had dug more deeply into their bases in Turkey. The territorial dispute of Nagorno-Karabakh in the Caucasus recently flickered again. At the time of writing, Colombian peace initiatives were laced with uncertainty. Even if a referendum approved the historic accord, nothing would guarantee that all the armed bands wouldn't leave their mountain havens, or that others smelling an opportunity would move into the territory. While negotiators were finalizing terms of their historic accord, the FARC rebel deserter Julio posted on Facebook that he had received death threats from armed aggressors clearly disinterested in peace. Other people I'd met during my travels—in Nepal, Mexico, Kashmir, Chechnya—remained similarly uneasy.

Today, since aggressive efforts to subdue mountain communities the world over have failed, concessions by central states are urgently necessary. Military occupation and the imposition of lowland ways will not make for peace with defensive and insular populations deeply rooted in customs going back centuries. Conflict resolution often depends not on cracking down, but on letting go. And when it comes to governing mountain people in particular, less is almost invariably more. Central states need to use a lighter touch, without leaving these communities totally alone.

Switzerland, after all, is not the only place where granting political autonomy to mountain communities has proved successful. Italy granted significant self-government to the northern province of South Tyrol—a happy resolution to an ethnic conflict. Elsewhere, too, potential rebels have been pacified after being given greater control over local affairs. The Iraqi government has calmed Kurdistan by assigning it virtual home rule and allowing it to keep its oil wealth. Spain cleverly sucked life from the Basque independence struggle by ceding substantial fiscal and political powers to the region while restoring the ethnic language, Euskera, to the public sphere. The ETA, or Basque Homeland and Freedom, separatists in the region, who at one point vied with the FARC for the title of longest-running guerrilla movement, lost momentum as the nationalist-minded locals got what they wanted: ad hoc autonomy. Consider, too, the GAM (Free Aceh Movement) rebels who sought a separate Islamic state in the Indonesian island of Sumatra. They stopped fighting following a peace agreement with the central government that allowed 70 percent of income from local resources to remain in the province.

Those governments that deny mountain regions at least some measure of autonomy witness ongoing conflict. Violence continues to flare in India's Tripura and Bangladesh's Chittagong Hills because land grievances and demands for greater local power have not been addressed. Abkhazia simmered down after achieving de facto independence from Georgia in the early 1990s, but tensions continue amid uncertainty over its status.

Policy makers talk endlessly about East versus West, North against South. Christian against Muslim. Communism or capitalism. Religion, ideology, income disparity, industrialization, race, nationality, oil, literacy, and education: these are the concepts we use to organize and explain the world. But what about high versus low? Politicians tend to assume that, with enough effort, any conflict can be resolved, eventually, by intervention or occupation. But what if mountains stand in the way? You can strafe a dune or napalm a jungle, but mountains won't budge. Acknowledging this natural fact is critical; even with the blurring of cultures that has accompanied digital technology, including widespread social media use, the world is not flat. While illiterate farmers in the remote, dusty plains of India manage their money through SMS on their cell phones, in many upland outposts, communication lines remain only face-to-face, because highland forests are dense, weather defeats wires and mail carriers, and the only phones that work are expensive satellite contraptions. Mountains remain as impervious to digital technology as to outside ideas.

Jean Lassalle and the WMPA emphasize again and again that the way to overcome the neglect and exploitation of highland regions by the plains—to make mountain people visible and audible—is dialogue. In order to determine the most effective and peaceable ways of governing such communities, national governments must spend a lot more time listening closely to what they need. Lassalle insisted that highlanders be recognized as the main actors in "every action" that concerns them. We privileged flatlanders need to check our mainstream, centralized, economic, and political privilege.

Human nature softens with concessions; any divorce lawyer will tell you that. Minority self-governance within a larger state won't work when secessionist demands are inflexible. Clearly a nonstate belligerent or criminal should not be rewarded for acts of terror; capitulation to a group like ISIS carries immense risks. On the other hand, when dealing with ethnic minorities with legitimate demands, the principle of greater devolution of power rarely fails. Guarantee a better standard of living, or rancor will deepen. In contrast to the possibility of secession, autonomy means maintaining the federal status quo. It's face-saving for all. Taxes are still collected, and the national unit survives intact.

Naturally, governments should proceed thoughtfully when granting certain areas greater autonomy, or less favored regions will become resentful, especially if the periphery thrives economically. Moscow has seen demonstrations by Slavic Russians, jealous of the money poured into Chechnya's reconstruction. The rest of Iraq envies Kurdistan's oil wealth.

Certainly no central state wants to forgo territorial control. Yet sometimes compromises are the only way to end conflict, which is not only dangerous and destabilizing but also, in the long run, expensive. Western democracies must accept that such homegrown compromises are the best path to peace and prosperity. Politicians can make progress in these areas only by listening, understanding, and reversing course so as to allow mountain people more autonomy over their own affairs and terrain.

That, at least, is the conclusion I arrived at after about 72,706 miles criss-crossing mountainous landscapes, leaving each site burdened by melancholy, and guilt. I collected wretched stories, took photos, and went home. "Don't forget us," a Kashmiri widow implored as I climbed into a jeep driving to the airport.

The world will see more mountain conflict in the near future. All the terrorist groups and outlaws that our government attempts to suppress with drones and guns and military advisers—Boko Haram, ISIS, Al Qaeda, the Taliban, the Colombian and Mexican narcotics smugglers— take to the hills when other sanctuaries fail. Pursued by Nigerian forces, Boko Haram is moving deeper through the forest with their captive girls, into the indomitable Mandara volcanic range. Balochistan grows thornier with the relocation of the Taliban's command. Iraq's northern mountains have housed ISIS's black banner on various occasions. Some of Yemen's worst fighting has pounded the highlands around Taiz.

Still, many of the bloodiest and most tenacious conflicts remain under the American public's radar, overlooked due to physical distance or the perceived lack of strategic importance. But that doesn't make them any less worthy of attention. Understanding why certain conflicts persist so obstinately—the answers lie in geography, in these cases—can help us identify similar trends and respond to them in the future.

We have a moral imperative to pay heed to these communities. We ignore them at our peril. Danger, like water, flows downhill.

ACKNOWLEDGMENTS

Mountaineering requires a team of experts, and an author attempting to scale literary heights needs Sherpas, benefactors, guides, and fellow travelers to get to the top. My squad was brilliant.

Helping from the first plan to the summit was my splendid agent Joy Harris. She seized upon the book idea during a casual dinner conversation seven years ago and ensured I didn't slip through any crevasses along the journey. I am equally indebted to the resplendent Alison Mackeen, who shepherded the proposal to Basic Books and continued to supply encouragement thereafter. One couldn't find better advocates.

Dan Gerstle at Basic steered me on track with his sharp edits and sharper deadlines. Climbing is all about overcoming limitations, and Dan pushed me to think bigger. Kudos, too, to the rest of the crew, particularly copy editor Bill Warhop whose keen eye kept errors at bay. I am further indebted to my researchers Naomi Cohen and Sulaf Elsalfiti, who somehow find information no one else can. Adam Reed helped me navigate oft-challenging technology.

Lucky is the author with bighearted friends. Mine were willing to plow through coarse drafts and suggest changes that profoundly improved the manuscript. A cornucopia of gratitude to my writing buddy Randi Epstein, and to Wylie O'Sullivan, Bridget O'Brian, Lieutenant Colonel Justin Davis, Louisa Campbell, Paul Gillingham, Mary D'Ambrosio, Paula Span, Alice Eve Cohen, Jon Reiner, and Annika Savill. The folks at the Invisible Institute—who prefer to remain invisible—supplied moral support.

Foreign research demands hefty budgets. I could not have traveled to Kashmir and Mexico without generous funding from the Fulbright Scholar Program, South Asian Journalists Association and the Dart Center for Journalism & Trauma. Some of the material was road tested in magazines before migrating to the book. Thanks to the following publications for commissioning stories and granting permission to reprint portions: *World Policy Journal*, *The World* (Chatham House), *Columbia Journalism Review*, *Christian Science Monitor*, Al Jazeera America, *L'actualité*, *The Forward*.

A seventy-thousand-mile trek would be unbearable without companions. I owe appreciation to the photographers barely mentioned but who provided entertaining conversation and contacts on the road. Robert Nickelsberg, Russ Finkelstein, Alicia Vera, Katie Orlinsky, Diana Markosian—I wouldn't have made it without you.

You can't roam far-flung places without the assistance and expertise of locals. Aside from the people quoted in the book, I benefited from meeting so many others, among them:

In Albania: Elsa and Elidona Ukcamaj, Tonin Vocaj, Zyhdi Dervishi, Agim Loci, Bardha Caushi, Marc Wiese, Orgent Niko. Manushage Haxhia, Gjin Marku, Astrit Villi, and Sokol Albaniet.

Mexico: Román Hernández Rivas, Nick Casey, Jorge Chabat, Raúl Mendoza, Miguel Ángel Paz, Jon Fox, John Burstein, Isaín Mandujano, Víctor Hugo López, Marina Page, Ross McDonnell, Raúl Vega, Ernesto Gallardo, and Severo Castro Godines.

Colombia: Ariel Ávila, Todd Howland, Jon Hairo, Jahel Quiroga Carrillo, Teófilo Vásquez, Carlos Humberto, Jairo Samboni, William Balaguera, Lieutenant Colonel Jason Velandia, Patricia Velez Romero, Yisela and Marina Goilondo, Marisa Horta Mogollan, Heriberto Baso, and Florinda Zúñiga.

Nepal: Anup Kaphle, Christopher Butler, Devi Rai, Temang Tahal Rai, Dambar Rai, Devrag Rai, and Deepak Adhikari.

The North Caucasus: Kathy Lally and Will Englund, Tanya Lokshina, Bela Khadzimouralova, and the human rights activists and dissidents who requested anonymity.

Kashmir: Basharat Peer, Deepak Puri, Yusuf Jameel, Imdad Saqi, Surinder Singh Oberoi, Muhammed Altaf Masoodi, Akke Dari Naheed, Farooq Ahmad Bhat, Ghulam Nabi Dar, Hameeda Nazir, Wasim Bhat, Takhliq Ali, Pervez Imroz, and more who wish to remain unnamed.

Vermont: Sergeant First Class Christopher Bushway, Master Sergeant Thomas Kontos, Captain Chad Dearborn, Major John Guyette, and Personnel Officer Therese Farrell.

The Arctic: Lieutenant Colonel John Espen Lien, Major Leif Bygdnes, Captain Sven-Kristian Lotveit, Major Helge Dale, Sergeant Bertie Bassett, Major Simon Guest, Captain Baz Colarusso, Private Olov Kris

Rorvik, Major Jason Milne, Colonel Geir Gillebo, Geir Nordrum, First Lieutenant Jack Parnell, Lieutenant Colonel Kurt Malme, Lieutenant Colonel Lars Roine, and Major Jan Helge Dale.

Switzerland and France: Carolus and Maria van Schaik, Judith Burkart, Marthe Clot, Matthieu Calame, and Denis Balmont.

My beloved son and husband could hardly have anticipated that a random board game would lead to long absences and the many sacrifices inflicted by writers on their families. Mountains and mountains of love to Anton and John. This book is dedicated to you.

BIBLIOGRAPHIC ESSAY

I found the opening translated epigraph by Ibsen on http://www.poetry -archive.com/i/mountain_life.html.

INTRODUCTION: A TOWERING PROBLEM

The poem by George Sterling appears in *Beyond the Breakers, and Other Poems* (Nabu Press, 2009).

I discussed the link between mountains and resistance with Yale anthropologist James C. Scott. His acclaimed *The Art of Not Being Governed* (Yale University Press, 2009) examines a territory transcending nine national borders whose diverse hill tribes shared an aversion to central authority. Scott attributes their distaste to central authority to a landscape that allowed people to run away and remain apart from the mainstream.

I turned to Roderick Peattie's *Mountain Geography: A Critique and Field Study* (Harvard University Press, 1936) for excellent background reading on mountain topography. Peattie was a prominent geographer interested in both the physical features of mountains and the humans living among them. Another book that helped orient me was Robert E. Rhodes's *Listening to the Mountains* (Kendall/Hunt Publishing Company, 2007). This short collection of essays is a cri de coeur about the damage wrought by lowland powers. The anthropologist dedicated his career to studying mountain societies, and coined the academic term *montology*.

I first became aware of the scale of conflict in mountains in a report, "Conflict and Insecurity in Mountain Regions: A Barrier to Sustainable Development," by the Food and Agriculture Organization of the United Nations in its journal (*Unasylva* 53, no. 208) released during the 2002 International Year of the Mountains; it's online at www.fao.org/docrep/fao/004 /y3549e/y3549e00.html. The report amply supports my son's observation that mountains can be violent places, for a variety of reasons.

The observations of Fernand Braudel about mountain people are found in *The Mediterranean and the Mediterranean World in the Age of Philip II*, vol. 1 (University of California Press, 1995). Braudel's descriptions of blood feuds and tribal councils in the region, first published in 1949, bear a strong resemblance to the current situation in Albania.

To get the full flavor of Ellen Churchill Semple's worldview, read her *Influences of Geographic Environment, on the Basis of Ratzel's System of Anthropo-Geography* (Henry Holt and Company, 1911). A trailblazer in the field of human geography, Semple was the first female president of the Association of American Geographers. Some of her assertions reflect the prejudices of white colonial thinking of the time, but other observations are worth consideration.

For background on Lassalle, I read the following articles:

"MP Ends Hunger Strike Over Factory Closure," *The Guardian,* April 15, 2006.

"Carla Bruni-Sarkozy Backs Bears in Pyrenees, Angering Locals," *The Telegraph,* August 19, 2008.

The Charter of the World Mountain People Association, in English, can be found at http://www.mountainpeople.org/en/histoire/charte.php.

Geographic determinism has returned to vogue in recent years. I found the writings of the Pulitzer Prize–winning geographer Jared Diamond especially provocative, most notably *Collapse: How Societies Choose to Fail or Succeed* (Penguin, 2006). He writes persuasively about the link between environment and society and specifically how competition for arable land in hilly Rwanda contributed to that country's genocide.

For a detailed account of Hannibal's trek across the Alps, I relied, like most historians, on Polybius's *The Histories* (Oxford University Press, 2010). Scholars have debated whether the ancient historian's account was fully accurate, as Polybius wrote about Hannibal seventy years after his death. But the historian said he interviewed men who were present at the events and even crossed the Alps himself to understand the circumstances. It's taken as a given that elephants joined the wintry march and thousands of poorly prepared men perished.

CHAPTER 1: ONE FOR ONE

The epigraph is from M. Edith Durham's *High Albania* (Echo Library, 2009). This entertaining read stands the test of time. Many of the landscapes and customs that she chronicled in the early 1900s survive today. All later references to her travels were from the same text.

For background on Albania, I read *The Albanians: A Modern History* (I.B. Tauris, 2011) by the political analyst Miranda Vickers.

To glean an understanding of the Kanun, I consulted a comprehensive summation of more than one thousand laws, found in *Kanuni i Lekë Dukagjinit—The Code of Lekë Dukagjini* (Gjonlekaj, 1989). Albanian scholar Shetjeten Gjecov began writing the codes down in the early twentieth century. The book was banned during most of the Communist regime. Gjecov did most of his research in Mirdita, not far from Sokol's hometown. Leonard Fox did the translation into English.

The reference to Iceland's common law came from *Bloodtaking and Peacemaking: Feud, Law, and Society in Saga Iceland* (University of Chicago Press, 1990). Law professor William Ian Miller examines the blood feud system of medieval Iceland from a legal perspective. The complex mechanisms of regulations to resolve conflicts that arose in the absence of centralized government bear resemblance to the Kanun and its honor codes.

For a vivid description of the Albanian north, I recommend Robin Hanburg-Tenison's *Land of the Eagles: Riding through Europe's Forgotten Country* (I.B Tauris, 2009.) The doyen of British explorers traveled in the Albanian highlands on horseback, often in great discomfort. He traversed much of the same territory covered by Durham a century earlier and found it little changed.

The line from Kemal Pashazade about the Rozafa siege can be found on http://albanianhistory.blogspot.it/2015/03/rozafa-castle.html. The residents' point of view is presented in *The Siege of Shkodra: Albania's Courageous Stand Against Ottoman Conquest,* 1478 (Onufri, 2012). This translation by David Hosaflook is of an eyewitness account by a Shkodran citizen, Marin Barleti, who fought in the battles and later became a priest in Italy.

The quote by Ismail Kadare is from *Broken April* (New Amsterdam Books, 1990).

I returned to Fernand Braudel's *The Mediterranean and the Mediterranean World in the Age of Philip II* for specific mentions of Albania.

CHAPTER 2: OUR LAND IS OUR LAND

The first quote appears in *The Memoirs of the Conquistador Bernal Díaz del Castillo, (Complete) Written by Himself Containing a True and Full Account of the Discovery and Conquest of Mexico and New Spain* (Project Gutenberg e-book, 2010), translated by John Ingram Lockhart at www.gutenberg.org /files/32474/32474-h/32474-h.html.

The letter by Diego Pardo was reproduced in *Guerrero: Textos de su Historia* (Instituto de Investigaciones Dr. Jose Maria Luis Morales, 1989), edited by Carlos Illades and Martha Ortega Soto.

I have been reporting on and off in Mexico since 1981. The interviews for this chapter took place in 2013 and 2014, while I was a Fulbright Scholar and then reporting stories for Al Jazeera America.

The quote by Graham Greene appears in *Lawless Roads* (Penguin Classics, 2006).

Evon Vogt, the late Harvard anthropologist, speculated that the Mayan pyramids were inspired by the mountains. Vogt wrote extensively about the society of the Tzotzil Mayas of Chiapas. Two of his best-known works are *Zinacantan: A Maya Community in the Highlands of Chiapas* (Belknap Press, 1969) and *Tortillas for the Gods: A Symbolic Analysis of Zinacanteco Rituals* (Harvard University Press, 1976).

The quotations of Conejo are from my interview with him in 2011.

The theories of political scientists James D. Fearon and David D. Laitin about resistance resonated with what I saw in Mexico. The men employ the phrase "sons of the soil" to refer to ethnic minorities living in peripheral regions who take up arms against the state when it exploits their land or other natural resources. They cite a litany of mountain mutineers who fit this category, most of them in Asia: the Chakma people in the Chittagong Hills of Bangladesh; Muslim Moros in Mindanao, the Philippines; many peripheral ethnic minorities in Burma; Bougainvilleans in Papua New Guinea; the Tuaregs of Mali; and Abkhazis in Georgia. See "Sons of the Soil, Migrants and Civil War," *World Development* 39, no. 2 (2010).

The quote by James C. Scott about marooned mountain societies in Asia appears in his aforementioned book, *The Art of Not Being Governed.*

The quote by Marcos has been widely circulated and appears, among other gems, on http://thinkexist.com/quotes/subcomandante_marcos/. Thinkexist.com is a useful source to find quotations by a variety of people.

For historical context on the relationship of Mexican rebellion and topography, I had the privilege of interviewing two eminent experts in 2014 and 2015, respectively John Coatsworth of Columbia University and Paul Gillingham of Northwestern University.

For background on rebellion in Mexico, I turned to *Popular Movements and Political Change in Mexico* (L. Riennar Publishers, 1990), which was edited by Joe Foweraker and Ann L. Craig. Foweraker refers to Mexicans as a *pueblo levantisco*, or prone to uprisings.

John Gibler, *Mexico Unconquered: Chronicles of Power and Revolt* (City Lights Publishers, 2009). Gibler has written authoritatively about Guerrero and presents a detailed list of the various indigenous uprisings in mountain zones.

The prominent Mexican anthropologist Gonzalo Aguirre Beltrán called these isolated and backward areas where indigenous people fled colonial rule "regions of refuge." See *Regiones de Refugio: El desarrollo de la comunidad y el proceso dominical en mestizo America* (Instituto Indigenista Interamericana, 1967).

For background on Marcos and the Zapatistas, I turned to Nick Henck's *Marcos, the Man and the Mask* (Duke University Press, 2007) and Nicholas P. Higgins's *Understanding the Chiapas Rebellion: Modernist Visions and the Invisible Indian* (University of Texas Press, 2004).

Yi-Fu Tuan wrote two seminal works exploring the impact of place on psychology: *Humanist Geography: An Individual's Search for Meaning* (George F. Thompson Publishing, 2012) and S*pace and Place: The Perspective of Experience* (University of Minnesota Press, 1977).

The Mexican journalist Daniela Rea has written insightfully and lyrically about the *auto defensas* in "El pueblo en rebeldía" (April 2013), an article in the cultural magazine *Gatopardo*; and also a chapter, "La justicia de todos," in *Entre las cenizas: historia de vida en tiempos de muerte* (sur+ ediciones, 2012), edited by Marcela Turati.

The translation of the lyrics of the *corrido* was my own. John Holmes McDowell supplies useful background about Guerrero's *corridos* in *Poetry and Violence: The Ballad Tradition of Mexico's Costa Chica* (University of Illinois Press, 2000).

The human rights group Tlachinollan has done much research on violence in Guerrero, including *Digna rebeldía: Guerrero, el epicentro de las luchas de resistencia,* Informe XIX, June 2012–May 2013 (Tlachinollan, 2013).

For informative reading on Guerrero and indigenous rebellion in general I turned to the following:

Aracely Burguete Cal y Mayor, ed., *Indigenous Autonomy in Mexico* (International Work Group for Indigenous Affairs, 2000);

Armando Bartra, *Guerrero Bronco: Campesino, cuidadano y guerrilleros en la Costa Grande* (Ediciones Sinfiltro, 1996) and *El México Barbaro: Plantaciones y Monterias del Sureste Durante el Porfiriato* (El Atajo Ediciones, 1996);

Vicent Casarrubias, *Rebeliones indígenas en Nueva España* (SEP, 1963);

Ian Jacobs, *Ranchero Revolt* (University of Texas Press, 1982);

Friedrich Katz, ed., *Riot, Rebellion and Revolution: Rural Social Conflict in Mexico* (Princeton University Press, 1988);

Lilian Scheffler, *Los Indígenas Mexicanos: Ubicación Geográfica, Organización Social y Política, Economía, Religión y Costumbres* (Panorama Editorial, 1992).

CHAPTER 3: HOLDING THE HIGH GROUND OF NOTHING

The opening quotes are from *The Art of War by* Sun Tzu (Barnes and Nobel Classics, 2003) and Gabriel García Márquez's *Love in the Time of Cholera* (Alfred A. Knopf, 1988).

I found Max Boot's database of insurgencies and their duration relevant to the case of Colombia. The list appears in his *Invisible Armies*: *An Epic History of Guerrilla Warfare from Ancient Times to the Present* (Norton, 2013).

Fearon and Laitin present their theory about conditions for civil war in "Ethnicity, Insurgency, and Civil War," *American Political Science Review* 97, no. 1 (Feb. 2003): 75–90. Also see Fearon's "Why Do Some Civil Wars Last So Much Longer than Others?" Department of Political Science, Stanford University, 2002.

For an official history of the FARC and their early days in Marquetalia, I read *Diario de la Resistencia de Marquetalia* by Jacobo Arenas, (http//www .cedema.org/uploads/Diario_Marquetalia.pdf). Arenas was the ideological leader of the guerrilla movement. His death in 1990, ostensibly of natural causes, dealt a big knock to the movement.

Another source I consulted is Arturo Alape's *Tirofijo: los sueños y las montanas 1964–1984* (Editorial Planeta Colombiana SA, 2007). This leftist journalist and author chronicled the FARC in great detail. Born Carlos Arturo Ruiz, he took his *nom de plume* from a Communist peasant leader from south Tolima who was active during la Violencia.

The role of helicopters in mountain warfare was emphasized in briefings at the US Army Mountain Warfare School in Jericho, Vermont, in August 2012. The specifics about Colombia arose in talks with political analysts in Bogotá later that year.

La Paz Frustrada en Tierra Firma: La historia de la Unión Patriótica en el Tolima, edited by Adriana Esquerra (Corporación Reiniciar, 2009), offers a leftist historical view of Tolima and its progressive movements. Anyone interested in military theory should read General Carl von Clausewitz's *On War*, which was originally published in 1832 (Penguin Books, 1982).

The quote by Ernest Hemingway is from *A Farewell to Arms* (Charles Scribner's Sons, 1929).

CHAPTER 4: THE DAMMED

The 1945 poem *Sankat* (The Crisis) in the epigraph appeared in Jayaraj Acharya's "Siddhicharan Shrestha (1913–1992) in Nepalese perspective," *Centre for Nepal and Asian Studies Journal* 29, no. 1 (Jan. 2002). Shrestha (1912–1992) opposed the repressive Rana regime and was sentenced to eighteen years in prison for his revolutionary writings.

For a general introduction to recent Nepali history and politics, I read *The Maoist Insurgency in Nepal: Revolution in the Twenty-first Century* (Routledge Contemporary South Asia Series, 2009), edited by Mahendra Lawoti and Anup Kumar Pahari.

John Whelpton's *A History of Nepal* (Cambridge University Press, 2005) offers a solid introduction on the tumultuous years since the overthrow of the Rana autocracy in 1950–51. He is also author of *Nationalism & Ethnicity in a Hindu Kingdom: The Politics and Culture of Contemporary Nepal* (Routledge, 1997).

The quotes of Gyali are from my interview with him in Katmandu in December 2015.

Most books in English about the Gurkhas are by Britons, which makes Colour-Sergeant Kailash Limbu's firsthand account as a Nepali a notable exception. *Gurkha: Better to Die than Live a Coward: My Life in the Gurkhas* (Little Brown, 2016) describes his training and rituals as well as his time fighting in Afghanistan.

There is useful information in *The Gurkhas: the Inside Story of the World's Most Feared Soldiers* (Headline, 1999). Author and journalist John Parker travels through Nepal to document the customs and mystique of the formidable fighters.

An interactive satellite map of hydroelectical projects planned across the Himalayas can be found at http://cla.auburn.edu/gangabrahma/damMap .cfm. The website, Ganga Brahmaputra, was put together by geographers, anthropologists, and geologists from Auburn University in Alabama as well as Himanshu Thakker, the coordinator of the South Asia Network on Dams, Rivers, and People and editor of the magazine *Dams, Rivers and People.*

Legends and songs of the Kosi are detailed in *Himal Magazine*, available online at http://old.himalmag.com/component/content/article/468-the -legends-of-kosi.html.

The Pacific Institute has a long list of water conflicts at http://worldwater .org/water-conflict/.

For background on the controversial Himalayan dams, read "Water Conflicts and Hydroelectricity in South Asia" by Dr. Nasrullah Khan Kalair (*Global Resarch*, March 21, 2002, http://www.globalresearch.ca/news).

Shripad Dharmadhikary analyzes the impact of the dam-building spree on the region's people, ecosystems, and economy in "Mountains of Concrete: Dam Building in the Himalayas" (*International Rivers*, December 2008).

CHAPTER 5: MOUNTAIN THISTLES

The title of the chapter is borrowed from Leo Tolstoy's *Hadji Murad* (Orchises, 1996). Based on true events, Tolstoy's antiwar novel involves a Chechen separatist who moves over to the Russian side in order to save his family, with tragic consequences. At the opening of the novel, he employs the hardy thistle as a metaphor for the Chechens: "Man has conquered everything, and destroyed millions of plants, yet this one won't submit. And I remembered a Caucasian episode of years ago. . . ." Later references to his writings are from this book as well.

The quote by Aleksandr Solzhenitsyn is from *The Gulag Archipelago* (Harper & Row, 1973). The anthem of the Chechen Republic was based on an old folk song. This English translation of the lyrics is from the nationalist website www.waynakh.com.

An excellent examination of the *teips'* society and use of the landscape for defense is by Aslan Souleimanov, "Chechen Society and Mentality," *Prague Watchdog*, May 25, 2003.

To get a sense of the prevailing attitudes toward Chechens during the tsarist expansion, I recommend Alexander Pushkin's *Prisoner of the Caucasus*, first published in the early 1820s; it was penned while he was exiled for six years to the mountains. It describes the romance between a Russian soldier and a Caucasian girl that blossoms while he is held captive on a summit. The poet helped perpetrate the view of Chechens as noble savages in need of Russia's civilizing touch.

Another literary lion who helped shape, and reflect, Russian public opinion about the Chechens was Mikhail Lermontov. The writer served in the imperial forces in the 1840 Battle of Valerik, which inspired his poem "Valerik." Official dispatches cited him for bravery, but the poet had misgivings about the brutality unleashed. In other writings, he wavered between romanticizing and fearing the tribesmen.

I enjoyed reading the entertaining accounts by Frenchman Alexandre Dumas of his journey through the region, entitled *Le Caucase: Impressions de voyage; suite de En Russie*. First published in 1859 (an English translation entitled *Adventures in the Caucasus* was published by Peter Owen in 1962), he was particularly taken with the kidnappings for ransom that he claimed took place nearly every night.

While in Chechnya, I heard the saying "Giving what you've got is hospitality. Hitting with what you've got is courage." I found James Hughes's *Chechnya: From Nationalism to Jihad* (University of Pennsylvania Press, 2007) vital to understanding the Chechen struggle. He dispels the mythologizing of the Chechen resistance.

I relied on the superb *Chechnya* (Pan Books, 1997) by Carlotta Gall and Thomas de Waal to better understand the first Chechen war.

To gain insights into the rise and consolidation of Kadyrov's power, I recommend *Warlords: Strong-Arm Brokers in Weak States* (Cornell University Press, 2012) by Columbia University professor Kimberly Marten.

CHAPTER 6: ON THE EXISTENTIAL BORDER

The opening poem is by Agha Shahid Ali, Kashmir's best-known bard. I found "The Season of the Plains" (1987) on http://www.bu.edu/agni/poetry/print/2002/56-ali.html.

A Kashmiri Muslim who moved to the United States, the poet was preoccupied with the themes of exile, loss, history, memory, and culture.

The human rights and government death tolls I cite are published widely, such as Human Rights Watch.

To get a sense of the enormity of Kashmir's mental health crisis, I interviewed Kaz de Jong in 2008. At the time he was a mental health adviser for Médecins Sans Frontières Holland, which had a mobile field clinic in Kashmir to dispense psychological treatment to remoter communities. He has done several comparative studies on the psychic cost of violence, including (with coauthors N. Ford, S. van de Kam, K. Lokuge, S. Fromm, R. van Galen, B. Reilley, and R. Kleber) "Conflict in the Indian Kashmir Valley," *Conflict and Health*; November 2008, published online October 14, 2008, http://europe pmc.org/articles/PMC2575189/#__secid652631title doi; and (with coauthors K. de Jong, I. H. Komproe, M. van Ommeren, M. El Masri, M. Araya, N. Khaled, W. van der Put, and D. Somasundram) "Lifetime Events and Post-traumatic Stress Disorder in Four Post-conflict Settings," *Journal of the American Medical Association* 286, no. 5 (Aug: 2001): 555–562.

Ashish Nandy's quote about Kashmir's pain appears in his essay "Negotiating Necrophilia," which serves as an afterword in Nyla Ali Khan's *Islam, Women, and Violence in Kashmir: Between India and Pakistan* (Palgrave Macmillan, 2010). Nandy is a social theorist who uses his clinical psychology training to examine politics, the legacy of colonialism, and societal dynamics.

For the discussion of buffer mountain states, I relied heavily on the observations in *Mountain Geography: Physical and Human Dimensions* (University of California Press, 2013), edited by Martin F. Price, Alton C. Byers, Donald A. Friend, Thomas Kohler, and Larry W. Price. The compilation is the most definitive book on mountains and their various aspects.

The Minorities at Risk project is based out of the University of Maryland. Researchers maintain data and analyze conflict by 284 politically active ethnic groups throughout the world from 1945 to the present. MAR focuses especially on nonstate communal groups that suffer from systematic discriminatory treatment, or whose identity serves as the basis for collective action in defense of the groups' interests. Not surprisingly, groups from mountainous areas figure throughout the data set. MAR data can be found at http://www.mar.umd.edu.

The lines quoted here are from Ko Un's poem "Names," in *The Himalaya Poems* (Green Integer, 2011). The poems were published after his forty-day pilgrimage into the peaks, a trip he took at age sixty-four; the physical rigors at more than 18,000 feet nearly killed him.

The quote by Lou Reed extolling Kashmir's serenity was in a letter in the guest book of the houseboat named *Buckingham Palace*. He said he would recommend it even if he "weren't too stoned to write to give this place due consideration."

One cannot find a more eloquent depiction of the wrenching life under Indian occupation than Basharat Peer's *Curfewed Night* (Scribner, 2010). Peer is Kashmir's best-known journalist and, incidentally, the brother of my translator Wajahat Ahmad.

The quote by Marco Polo is from *The Travels of Marco Polo* (Penguin Classics, 1958). The book was written by Rustichello da Pisa from stories told by Polo about his travels through Asia in the thirteenth century. Ronald Latham translated this English-language version.

CHAPTER 7: THE GODS OF THE VALLEYS ARE NOT THE GODS OF THE HILLS

Two excellent books about Operation Anaconda support Domey's personal account. They are *Operation Anaconda: America's First Major Battle in Afghanistan* (University Press of Kansas, 2011) by Lester W. Grau and Dodge Billingsley, and Sean Naylor's *Not a Good Day to Die: The Untold Story of Operation Anaconda* (Berkley Caliber Books, 2005).

I obtained a helpful orientation on Afghanistan and foreign meddlers in Tamim Ansary's *Games without Rules: The Often Interrupted History of Afghanistan* (Public Affairs, 2012). He shows how every foreign intervention has come to grief.

I am indebted to the history-loving Major (now Lieutenant Colonel) Justin Davis for walking me through mountain battles over the ages, as well as explaining the intricacies of American military approach. Davis especially urged me to read Erwin Rommel's *Infantry Attacks* (Zenith Press, 2003), the bible for mountain warriors. The book was first published in 1937.

Another book that Davis insisted I read was General Sir Andrew Skeen's *Passing It On: Fighting the Pushtun on Afghanistan's Frontier* (Foreign Military Studies Office, 2010), edited by Lester Grau and Robert H Barer. It provides great insight into the continued Afghan resistance to outsiders.

Everyone whom I spoke to in the US military said, "You must read Lester Grau" in order to understand mountain combat. A retired lieutenant colonel, Grau has published over one hundred articles and studies on tactics and geopolitics. Attached to the Foreign Military Studies Office at Fort Leavenworth, Kansas, his specialties are Russia and Afghanistan. Essential reading is *Mountain Warfare and Other Lofty Problems: Foreign Perspectives on High-Altitude Combat* (Foreign Military Studies Office, 2011), coedited by Charles K. Bartles.

In Norway, I mainly relied on firsthand reporting in March 2013. The history of the Finnish defeat of the Soviets arose in various briefings with Norwegian military officials.

The translated quote by Paolo Monelli appears in Richard Galli's "Avalanche!" on the historical website *La Grande Guerra, The Italian Front* 1915, http://www.worldwar1.com/itafront/avalan.html.

Monelli was a prominent Italian journalist who chronicled the Alpine brigade in his memoir *Toes Up: A Chronicle of Gay and Doleful Adventures of Alpini and Mules and Wine* (Harcourt, Brace and Company, 1930).

By far, the best primer to the Italian Alpine front is Mark Thompson's brilliant *The White War: Life and Death on the Italian Front 1915–1919* (Basic Books, 2010).

To obtain a vivid view of the David vs. Goliath battle between the outgunned Finns and the Soviets, I watched the BBC documentary, broadcast in 2015, *World War 2: The Winter War of Finland and Russia.* It includes news footage from the time. Watch it at https://www.youtube.comwatch?v=3aO3ErKT2CE.

The quote about Mount Stetind was by William Cecil Slingsby. It appears in his book *Norway, the Northern Playground: Sketches of Climbing and Mountain Exploration in Norway Between 1872 and 1903* (Rockbuy Limited, 2003). Many current climbers find his accounts of ascents still relevant today.

CHAPTER 8: CANTONMENT (CONTENTMENT)

The verse by Victor Hugo can be found on "Poems by Victor Hugo" (Project Gutenberg e-book, 2005), http://www.gutenberg.org/files/8775/8775-h/8775-h.html.

I relied on several books to grasp the evolution of Switzerland's unique political system:

Daniel J. Elazar, ed., *Commonwealth: The Other Road to Democracy. The Swiss Model of Democratic Self-Government* (Lexington Books, 2001);

Michael Butler, Malcolm Pender, and Joy Charnley, eds., *The Making of Modern Switzerland, 1848–1998* (St. Martin's Press, 2000);

Gregory A. Fossedal, *Direct Democracy in Switzerland* (Transaction Publications, 2009);

Clive H. Church and Randolph C. Head, *A Concise History of Switzerland* (Cambridge University Press, 2013);

E. Bonjour, H. S. Offler, G. R. Potter, *A Short History of Switzerland* (Oxford University Press, 1952);

Randolph Head, *Early Modern Democracy in the Grisons: Social Order and Political Language in a Swiss Mountain Canton 1470–1620* (Cambridge University Press, 1995).

I read about Bruno S. Frey's theories of Swiss happiness in several studies, among them Frey's *Dealing with Terrorism: Stick or Carrot?* (Edward Elgar Publishing, 2004) and, with Alois Stutzer, "Happiness Prospers in Democracy," *Journal of Happiness Studies* 1, no. 1 (Mar. 2000): 79–202.

Martin Schuler and Pierre Dessemontet explain the Valais vote in "The Swiss Vote on Limiting Second Homes," *Revue de géographie alpine*, 2013, online at http://rga.revues.org/1872.

Balou's untimely demise is documented in "Famous Pyrénées Bear Found Dead," *The Connexion*, June 11, 2014. The article can be read at http://www .connexionfrance.com/france-pyrenees-balou-brown-bear-slovenia-dead-fall -post-mortem-segolene-royal-replacement-wolf-15877-view-article.html.

The Swiss government website publishes statistics on referenda and amendments at https://www.admin.chu/ch/d/pore/va/vag_2_2_4_1.html.

The quotations of Lassalle are from my most recent e-mail exchanges with him, in early 2015.

The destructive impact of overlooked wars is outlined by political scientist Virgil Hawkins in *Stealth Conflicts: How the World's Worst Violence Is Ignored* (Burlington: Ashgate, 2008). He compellingly argues that the collateral damage from associated famine and mayhem is huge when wars fall under the international radar.

INDEX

Page numbers in italics refer to maps.

budget, 179
in High North of Norway, 190, 191
history of helicopter use, 77–78
lacking specialized mountain units, 8, 172, 176, 180
Operation Anaconda, 172, 173, 174, 175, 176, 179, 180, 186
specialized mountain training centers, 178
US Navy SEALS, 192

Vatican Swiss guards, 213
Vendetta culture, 15–16, 19, 122
  See also Blood feuds/honor killings
Venetian occupiers, 17
Vermont mountains, military school in. *See* Mountain Warfare School
Vermont National Guardsmen, 178
Vietnam, 71, 78
Violencehighest theater of war, 11
  prevalence of, 2, 6–7, 8, 9, 10
  promotion of, 6
  response of major powers, 7–8
Virgin of Guadalupe, 47

Wahhabis (Salafis), 124–125, 126, 137, 139, 140
Water supply, 7, 11, 97, 99, 102–103, 104, 118, 155, 164
Women
  cultural expectations of, in Albania, 13, 20, 22
  Islamic expectations of, in Chechnya, 126, 129–130
  psychological trauma affecting, in Kashmir, 162, 163, 164, 167–168

social position of, in rural Mexico, 46
treatment by Zapatistas, in Mexico, 46
World Heritage Site, 212
World Mountain People Association (WMPA), 1–4, 5, 6, 38, 40, 105, 206, 207, 209, 220
World War I, 173, 183, 188, 197
World War II, 17, 71, 176, 186, 188, 195, 200, 217
Worldviews, effect of geography on, 18–19

Yaqui Indians, 42
Yemen, 6, 221
Yope Indians, 42, 53, 55, 58

Zapata, Emiliano, 41, 47
Zapatista Army of National Liberation (EZLN)
  control centers, 44, 45, 47–51
  culture, 46
  foreign support, 38, 41, 44
  gateway to the territory of, 35
  government approach, 38, 39, 45
  health care and education, 46, 64
  intentions 40, 41
  Internet campaign, 40–41
  leadership, 40–41, 44, 45
  migration's effect on, 46–47
  other indigenous leaders meeting with, 62
  other rebellions inspired by, 52, 55, 64
  reality facing, 51–52
  uprising, 37–38, 39
  utopia, 51